# Scottish Surnames
# & Families

# Scottish Surnames & Families

## Donald Whyte

BARNES
&NOBLE
BOOKS
NEW YORK

This edition published Barnes & Noble, Inc.,
by arrangement with Birlinn Limited

1997 Barnes & Noble Books

ISBN 0-7607-0459-7

Printed and bound in the United States of America

97 98 99 00 01 M 9 8 7 6 5 4 3 2 1

QF

# CONTENTS

## ABBREVIATIONS

| | |
|---|---|
| AFC | Air Force Cross |
| Bt. | Baronet |
| COSLA | Convention of Scottish Local Authorities |
| Cr. | Created, creation |
| DBE | Dame Commander, Order of the British Empire |
| DFC | Distinguished Flying Cross |
| FRS | Fellow of the Royal Society |
| HEIC | Honourable East India Company |
| KCB | Knight Commander, Order of the Bath |
| MC | Military Cross |
| MP | Member of Parliament |
| NS | Nova Scotia (Order of Baronets) |
| OBE | Officer, Order of the British Empire |
| QC | Queen s Counsel |
| RA | Royal Artillery |
| RN | Royal Navy |
| RSA | Royal Scottish Academician |
| RSW | Member, Royal Scottish Society of Watercolourists |
| SSC | Solicitor before the Supreme Courts (Scotland) |
| UK | United Kingdom |
| WS | Writer to the Signet |

# INTRODUCTION

It was William Camden, the first serious student of British surnames who wrote: "Every person had in the beginning, only one proper name," and if we look at early record sources for Scotland we find that personal names predominate. In the charter of King Duncan to the monks of St. Cuthbert, granted in 1094, no surnames appear. The monarch and the witnesses made their rude crosses, over which the learned scribe Grento added their names – Acaerd, Hermer, Hemming, Ulf, Aelfric, Malcolu(m)b, Teobald, Duncan (the king), Eadger, Vinget and Earnulf.

'Sur' or additional names – not 'sire' names – are of comparatively late origin, and often appear in changed or corrupt form. They emerge slowly, and we can detect their evolution in early charters. That granted during the reign of David I, 1124-53, by Waldeve, son of Cospatrick, to Helias, son of Huchtred, of the lands of Dundas, has among the witnesses, Waldeve, son of Baldwin, William of Copeland and Adam the Steward. Baldwin may have become a surname through the dropping of 'son of,' but this is a written form and such a conclusion would be dubious. However, Copeland – a place-name – emerged as a surname, and Steward – or Stewart – did likewise. In small communities, personal names were sufficient and patronymics alone were all that custom required. The process grew with an increase in population and mobility in the 13th century. Surnames arrived late in the Scottish Highlands and Western Isles. In many parts of the world surnames are still a rarity. In Iceland the people are listed in directories under their given names, and the following is an example of how their system works. A man called Arnar might have a son named Gunnar Arnarson, who might marry a woman called Sigurlin Asgeirsdotter. If they had a son he would be called Arnar Gunnarson.

Surnames may be divided into five groups, with some overlapping. There are those derived from the personal name of the father, more correctly termed surnames of relationship. Patronymics come into this class, although these produced surnames under varying circumstances. Then come names stemming from places, and these form a large group. Next are hundreds of trade and office names, usually referred to as occupational surnames. Into a fourth class, which we choose to call divergent names, come surnames flowing from a number of sources. Lastly there are surnames derived from nicknames, personal traits and characteristics.

Easily recognised as emerging from personal names – themselves deriving from a variety of sources – are surnames such as Adam, Allan, Cecil, Henry and Thomas. Before the Christian era, personal names could claim numerical superiority; but since then, local, trade and divergent names have left these in the minority. Thousands might receive their name from a locality but not even two could be called Jacob or Moses except through a second-hand use by adoption or popular application. Patronymics commonly indicate whose son a man is, and they were borne in ancient times as we can see from the *ben* and *bar* of the Semitic languages. In the Homeric lists of heroes they can be identified by the suffixes *ades* and *ides*. The Romans too, had their patronymic forms, but with the fall of the Empire the system of nomenclature declined. In Latin documents men came to be linked simply with the name of the father, for example, Hugo *filius* Walterus, meaning Hugh, son of Walter. The Teutonic nations added sen or son to the personal name, while the Saxon style was the addition of *ing*, as in Atheling (Athel's son). In Welsh, a form of the Celtic *mac* emerged, which the Cambrians made *mab* or *map*, shortened to *ap*. The Irish, being Celts, also used mac, 'son of,' as a prefix, but often found greater charm in *ua*, originally for grandson, but by an extension of use came to mean any descendant. It is often written *hua* by Latin and English writers, but more often *O*, which is a common prefix in Irish surnames.

In Scotland the Gaels used the prefix *mac* to denote 'son of,' but there was no real surname until a late period, and often it was a remote ancestor of note whose personal name was commemorated by the clan chiefs. For the ordinary clansman, patronymics such as Dhomnuill mac Challum, vic Alastair, vic Iain Bháin (Donald, son of Malcolm, son of Alexander, son of fair John), sufficed, and were meaningful in small communities. Surnames eventually triumphed and stabilised. Examples are MacAlpine (son of Alpin), Diarmaid (son of Dermid), MacLaren (son of Laurin), and MacPhail (son of Paul). Many derive from trades or offices: Maceachern (son of the horse lord), Macgowan (son of the smith), Maclellan (son of the devotee of St. Fillan), Macintosh (son of the leader) and Macintyre (son of the carpenter). In ordinary English son is often added to the Christian name, like Thomson and Johnson. Some others require a little thought: names such as Dawson, an abbreviation of Davidson, and Watson, a shortening of Walterson. Another class is still less obvious, the suffix being curtailed in names like Andrews, Edwards and Richards.

Numerous surnames have their origin in place-names: sheriffdoms or counties, provinces, districts, lordships, baronies, towns, villages, hamlets, estates, farms, crofts and sheilings. Some are not easily recognisable as they now appear in archaic or distorted form. Some territorial names have been romanticised through the custom of styling landowners by the names of their estates, or 'of that Ilk,' which usually means their ancestors were the first private owners, and are always chiefs of the surname. Names such as Dundas of that Ilk, Moncrieffe of that Ilk, and Houston of that Ilk, run like a bright golden thread through the rich tapestry of Scottish history. Into the class of local names are a number derived from features of the landscape: names like Hill, Dale, Hope (in some cases), Moor or Muir, and Fields.

When we consider national names, we often find that a man had to move before these became applicable. A man from south of the border would be Englis, and modern forms are Inglis, English and Englander. There are more Scot(t)s in England than in Scotland. Wallace is thought to be very Scottish, but usually means origins in the old British kingdom of Strathclyde. Ireland is straightforward, and so is French. The lordly name of St Clair or Sinclair may indicate a place-name in Normandy, but can come from a sinkler in the old cloth-making trade (the person who steeped the flax), or from a tinker from Argyll. The non-resident principle can often be noted by record scholars. In Fife for example, names such as Berwick and Lothian appear frequently in old records. The surname Dutch, found in the Firth of Tay area, is said to derive from a survivor of a man-of-war from Holland, shipwrecked near Tayport during the reign of Queen Anne. People in the Orkneys called Mainland, probably originated on the largest island, called Pomona or Mainland.

Some of the great names in Scottish history have come from provinces or districts such as Buchan, Galloway, Lennox, Mar and Strathearn. Berwick, Roxburgh, Lanark and Stirling, are usually thought of as towns which had (or have) Norman style mottes or castles, around which sheriffdoms evolved, but they are also surnames of antiquity. A good number of names have hardly changed at all, and point unmistakably to the places which gave them life. Examples are Crawford, Cunningham, Dunbar, Home, Morton, Romanes and Traquair. It should be remembered that when a family had the same name as a place, the latter nearly always came first. There are a few exceptions, such as Hamilton, Livingston and Riddell.

Medieval townships are clearly responsible for another group of surnames originating in a central location and its four approximate compass points, followed by the suffix *tun*, *ton* or *toun*, denoting a dwelling-place, viz:

```
                   NORTON
                     |
WESTON — MIDDLETON — EASTON
                     |
                   SUTTON
```

Sometimes, although three or four geographical locations may exist, only one surname has evolved. In Mid Lothian, near Ingliston Showground, there are places called Easter Norton, Norton Mains, Middle Norton and Wester Norton, so a man named Norton may have come from any of these. Names like Northgate and Southgate generally come from gates of old walled towns, but are more common in England than in Scotland, where the access and egress points were known as 'ports.' The occupational name of Porter usually comes from a source like this, sometimes from a doorkeeper of a monastery or castle; but others may derive from a ferryman or 'phortair.'

Job-description is a much used (and occasionally abused) term today; but for many centuries the surnames of numerous officials and craftsmen proclaimed their calling. Frequently, as in the case of blacksmiths, son succeeded father, because the tools of the trade were inherited. Curiously, the ancients were reluctant to change a name which recalled brave deed or hallowed relationship. Moreover, they may have been influenced by the fact that occupational names are sometimes indefinite. One man in a community might be called Jacob, while dozens might be named Smith as the metal craft embraced a number of trades.

Many occupational names are easily understood: Gardener, Taylor, Baker or Baxter, Cook, Cooper, Glover, Dyer, Skinner, Wright and Weaver. Likewise numerous official names are recognisable: Usher, Marshall, Steward, Carver and Page, all derive from the multiplicity of functions in the great houses and establishments of the Middle Ages. Some others require thought. Barker is from the obsolete name for the man who prepared the bark of trees for the Tanner. Cordiner or Cordwainer comes from the man who made shoes of goatskin which was supposed to have come from Cordova, in Andalusia. With other shoemakers (soutar is from this source) and workers in leather they formed fraternities in the old Scottish burghs. Potinger comes from potage and indicates a maker of soups. Stoddart comes from *stot-herd*, a 'stot' being a general term for a young bull or bullock.

Surnames derived from nicknames form an interesting group, but many have disappeared because of their coarseness. Some can be taken literally, but others have contrary meanings, in the same way that Tiny is often used to denote a six-footer. Broadhead, Foot, Crookshank, Cudlipp, Longman and Hawkey all describe physical attributes or peculiarities, while Careless, Loveless (or Lovelace), Goodenough and Sharp particularise mental and moral character.

Flett, Old Norse, meaning an eager fellow, or a flayer or robber, is found in the Orkneys, as also Scollay, from the same source, *skalli* meaning bald-head. A few names which ended in 'head' have been reduced to leave the suffix *ett*, as in Blackett, Brockett, Duckett and Strickett (*stirk-head*).

Names of animals can be nicknames, but must be treated with caution. Lamb may denote weakness, and Bull great strength, but might come from a herd or keeper of these animals and be an occupational surname.

A large number of divergent surnames come from plants, flowers, animals and birds, examples being Mustard, Primrose, Goodlamb and Swan. Many are derived from mediaeval pageantry and religious festivals, as illustrated in Prophet, Priest, King, Marquess or Marquis, Duke, Bishop and Abbott. A few come from costumes or adjuncts of these, examples being Staff, Clubb, Bracegirdle and Broadbelt. Then there are names like Brand (sword) and sometimes Randal (shield). The Rendalls of the Orkneys, however, derive their name from a place in Westray. In England it is said to be a form of Randolph. Another group are mythological or biblical. Whatever their origin they all add colour to the study of surnames.

This book deals with surnames found in Scotland, and the choice for inclusion must to some extent be arbitrary. It covers a cross-section of the most prolific Highland and Lowland surnames, with some others regarding which little has been written. Introductory histories are given for each, and the meaning of the names explained according to the best evidence. A number of surnames, for long classed as Norman, have been shown by Mrs Beryl Platts, in her books, *Origins of Heraldry* (London: Procter, 1980), and *Scottish Hazard* (2 vols., London: Procter, 1985, 1990), to be Flemish, hence the families inherited a vastly different culture. It would be surprising if everybody agreed with her findings, but the writer is convinced that her highly original work is in the main correct. Books for further reading are suggested at the end of the volume, and some hints on commencing ancestry research are given.

*Donald Whyte*

# ALLAN

It is generally agreed that the surname Alan, Allan or Allen, is of two-fold origin. In old Gaelic it represents *Ailene* – the Ailenus of Adamnan, biographer of St Columba – or *Ailin*, from *Ail* 'rock', as seen in the old name of Dumbarton, 'Ail Cluade.' From this source comes *Alwyn*, the name of the first earls of Lennox, sometimes confused with the Old English *Aelwin*. A second origin is through the Norman French *Alan*, found at an early period as *Alamnvs* and *Alanus*. Alan, King of Brittany, is mentioned in 683. Alan or Alain Fergant was one of the leading Bretons who came to England with the conquerer in 1066. The form *Alamnvs* points to *Alemannus*, the Germanic tribal name meaning 'all men,' as the source of the personal name.

The name became popular in Scotland from its occurrence in the family of the stewards (Stewarts) to the Kings of the Scots, and ultimately kings. Alan, son of Waldeve, witnessed charters by David I, in 1139. Alanus, the brother of Galfridus Redberd, witnessed the sale of a tenement in Perth in 1219. Aleyn fitz Maucolum of Berwickshire, and John fiz Aleyn, burgess of Montrose, rendered homage to Edward I of England in 1296. Loughlan le fitz Aleyn, son-in-law of Alexander of Argyll, was received to the king of England's peace in 1301. Duncan Alowne was admitted burgess of Aberdeen, 1446, and Henry Alane was clerk of accounts in the royal household in 1498. The Allans of Bute appear on record as Callan, Callen, Macallan and Maccallan, and are properly MacAllans.

A few Allans became landowners, but many more distinguished themselves as individuals. David Allan, 1744-96, son of David Allan, shoremaster at Alloa, became a historical painter, having, at an early age, exhibited a talent for drawing humorous scenes. He studied at Glasgow and Rome, and his illustrations for collections of Scottish songs earned him the title of 'The Scottish Hogarth.' Another painter, William Allan, 1782-1850, born in Edinburgh was apprenticed to a coach-maker, but afterwards studied at the Trustees Academy and at the school of the Royal Scottish Academy in London. He went to Europe in 1805, and returned in 1812, resolved to become a historical painter. He became president of the Royal Scottish Academy in 1838, and in 1841 succeeded Wilkie as HM Limner for Scotland, being knighted at that time. Robert W. Allan, 1852-1942, born at Alloa, studied at Foulis's Academy of Art in Glasgow. He painted many watercolours and oils of harbours, landscapes and seascapes.

An interesting and able family of Allans sprang from John Allan, who was born about 1590 and lived at Gogar, near Edinburgh. His grandson John farmed at Monshill, Dalmeny, and married Helen Cunningham, and had eight children. Thomas, the second son, was tenant of Little Barnbougle, and moved to Newmains, Kirkliston, before 1763. He married Agnes Reid, and their fourth son, Robert, 1745-1818, settled in Edinburgh, where he became a notable citizen. Robert founded a bank with David Steuart in 1775, but the partnership was dissolved in 1780 when Steuart became Lord Provost. The firm was afterwards known as Robert Allan & Co. He was a member, and in 1795, captain of the Society of Golfers, later the Honourable Company of Golfers. He won a number of prizes as a player. In 1773, Robert married Ann Learmouth and had nine children, the eldest of whom was Thomas, 1777-1833, of Lauriston Castle. He was proprietor of the *Caledonian Mercury* and by his wife Christian Smith, left talented descendants. His daughter married John Harden, a landowner from Tipperary, who was a fine artist.

# ANDERSON/MacANDREW

The surname Anderson simply means 'son of Andrew,' hence MacAndrew, but as borne by Lowland families denotes 'servant' of St. Andrew, the patron saint of Scotland. The Lowland form influenced the Gaelic 'Gilleandrais,' Gillanders, or St. Andrew's *gillie* or servant. Donald MacGillandrish, from Moidart, was ancestor of a group who settled at Connage of Petty, and were considered to be a sept of Clan Chattan. A family in Islay named Macillandrais, adopted the Lowland form of Anderson. The name is prolific all over the Lowlands and the North-East. Curiously, an Anderson was recognised as "of that Ilk" in the 16th century, although there was no place-name. It seems that the Lord Lyon of the time wished to have someone who would be received in public ceremonial as representers of the race or clan of Anderson. However, nobody can now identify the 'representer' with certainty.

Andersons appear from the 13th century, and from different parts of Scotland. David le fitz Andreu, burgess of Peebles, and Duncan fitz Andreu, from Dumfriesshire, swore fealty in 1296. John Anderson was prior of Fyvie in 1424. Early landowners were John of Balmaddy in 1479; John of Pitfour in 1490; John of Struthers in 1576, and Herbert of Terraughty in 1577. Donald Makandro was one of the victims of the hership (plundering) of Petty in 1502. Mackallum MacAndro in Murthlac appears in 1550, and Dowgall McAndro Vuyear in Stuckvillage was fined for resetting MacGregors in 1613. Thomas MacAndrew vic William is recorded in 1618. Iain beag MacAndrea, a servant of William Mackintosh, tenant in Kilravock, was an expert archer who demonstrated his skills against a raiding party of Macdonnels in 1670.

The Andersons of Dovehill can be traced back to 1540.

John of Dovehill (1636-1710) was eight times Lord Provost of Glasgow, and in 1696 purchased stock to the value of £1,000 in the ill-fated Darien Scheme. Other estate owners were of Aucharnie, Bourtie, Candacraig, Bordland and Fingland, Montrave and Stobcross, and Tushielaw. Several Andersons appear in Stockholm, Sweden, towards the close of the 16th century, and Col. Anderson, whose mother was a Sinclair of Murtle, was enobled there in 1668.

Many Andersons have distinguished themselves. Alexander Anderson, an Aberdonian, went to Paris, and became a mathematician. He issued various treatises on geometrical science, 1612-19. Andrew Anderson, son of George Anderson, who introduced the art of printing to Glasgow in 1638, was invited to settle in Edinburgh, and became the King's printer for Scotland in 1671. James Anderson (1662-1728), achieved lasting fame as the compiler of *Selectus Diplomatum et Numismatum Scotiae* (1739), a work of learning never transcended in elegance. It was not however, published in his lifetime. John Anderson (1726-96), was a native of Roseneath, and became Professor of Oriental Languages at Glasgow in 1756, and of Natural Philosophy in 1760. He bequeathed money to found the Andersonian Institute. James Anderson (1739-1808), an eminent agriculturist and author was born at Hermiston. Dr Robert Anderson (1750-1830), born at Carnwath, was editor and biographer of British poets, and William Anderson (1805-66), was the industrious author of *The Scottish Nation*, first published in 1863. The MacAndrew baronets descend from Francis Glen MacAndrew, of Knock Castle, Largs, whose son Charles received the honour in 1959. An MP for several constituences, he also served with distinction in the Ayrshire Yoemanry. His grandson, Sir Cristopher, the 3rd Bt., resides at Archdeacon Newton, near Darlington.

# BAIRD

There can be little doubt that the Bairds (originally Baards), who first appear in Scotland as vassals of Robert, grandson of Baldwin de Biggar, were of Flemish extraction. Early in the 13th century, Richard de Baard gave the titles of his lands on the River Avon, to the monks of Lesmahagow. His son, also Richard, confirmed the gift. Robert Bard was a witness to the confirmation charter of the churches of Innyrwic and Liggerwood, to the monks of Paisley about 1275. Four individuals of the name rendered homage in 1296, and one of them, Fergus de Barde, of Lanarkshire, was probably ancestor of the Bairds of Kipp and Evandale. Robert Barde was made a prisoner of war in 1315, and is probably the man who had a charter of Cambusnaythen, and became sheriff of Lanark. John Barde is recorded in 1389, and Simone Bayard was town officer in Aberdeen in 1387. Bairds also appear at Aberchirder, Banff, around 1500, and in other parts of Scotland. The surname Bairdie, on record from the middle of the 16th century, may be a variant or pet form.

Bairds were prominent in Lanarkshire. Alexander Baird (1765-1833) of Lochwood, from whom descended the family of Elie and Muirkirk, was an ironmaster, and his son William founded the firm of William Baird & Co., Gartsherrie. Robert Baird of Gartsherrie, who died in 1856, was Dean of Guild of Glasgow. Hugh Baird (1770-1827), a Civil Engineer, constructed the Union Canal and was engineer for the Crinan Canal, and Robert Baird of Bellfield was a partner of the Canal Foundry in Glasgow. The Bairds of Craigton intermarried with the Hamiltons of Airdrie, the Dunlops of Househill and the Dennistouns of Colgrain.

The Bairds of Saughton Hall derive their descent from Andrew of Auchmeddan, in Aberdeenshire, which family came to be represented as heirs of line by the Frasers of Findrack. William Baird, created a baronet of Nova Scotia in 1680, was succeeded by his son, Sir John, on whose death in 1745 the baronetcy became extinct. Sir William's uncle, Robert Baird, was created 1st Bt. (NS) of Saughton Hall, Edinburgh, in 1695-96. The 2nd Bt., Sir James, continued that line, and from his brother William descended the baronets of Newbyth (cr. UK, 1809). The present and 5th Bt., is Sir David Baird, residing at Kirkcudbright. Sir James Baird, 10th Bt., of Saughton Hall lives at Guist, Norfolk.

The Rev. George Husband Baird (1761-1840), born at Bo'ness, after being minister at Dunkeld and New Greyfriars, Edinburgh, became Principal of the University of Edinburgh. Several Bairds have distinguished themselves in the army. Sir David Baird (1757-1829), descended from the Bairds of Pitmedden, entered the army in 1772 and rose to the rank of Lt. General, having served in India, South Africa, Denmark and Ireland. Edward Baird (1864-1956) served in the 10th Hussars and with the Imperial Yeomanry. He soldiered in War I (1914-18) and became a Brigadier-General in 1916. Sir Harry Baird (1877-1963), entered the army in 1897, and served with the 12th Bengal Cavalry. In World War I, he served in the Argyll & Sutherland Highlanders, after which he soldiered in the Afghan War. He rose to the rank of General and received many awards. The best-known Baird is John Logie (1888-1946), born in Helensburgh, who invented the televisor, the first practical television apparatus in 1926, and in 1928 showed that colour TV was possible.

# BEATON/BETHUNE

Two families named McBeth and Beaton practised medicine in the Hebrides. The MacBeths (*MacBheatha* – 'son of life') were hereditary physicians of the Clan Donald, and were endowed with Ballinabie and other lands in Islay as fee for their appointment. Fercos Macbetha appears in 1408, and Gilchrist McVeig, surgeon, is also on record. In 1609 another Fergus McBaithe appears as witness to a Gaelic charter, which he may have written. His son John succeeded him in 1628, but gave his lands to the Thane of Cawdor.

The Mull Beatons – possibly related – were hereditary physicians to the Macleans of Dowart or Duart. Hector Maclean granted a charter to Andrew MacDonil Vikinollif ('son of the doctor') and his heirs, of Peincross and Brolas in 1572. Another of the Mull family was Fergus McVeagh, whose medical manuscript is in the library of the University of Edinburgh. A branch of this family settled in the Fraser country and were at Glenconvinth before 1558, when James Betoun attended Lord Lovat. The family declined in the Aird before 1622.

Most authorities agree that the Skye Beatons were Bethunes from Fife, and that Dr David Bethune, a grandson of John, Vth Laird of Balfour, settled in Skye about the time of the Reformation. He left descendants who intermarried with the best families in the islands. The last of this medical family was Neil Beaton, who died in 1763. Rev. John Bethune (1751-1815), son of Angus in Brebost, Skye, emigrated to North Carolina in 1773 and became an army chaplain. In 1784 he went to Canada, and after organising a Presbyterian congregation in Quebec, became minister at Williamstown, in Glengarry County Ontario. Two of his sons, John and Alexander, were clergymen.

The Fife Bethunes are of Flemish extraction, deriving their name from a town in Flanders. Bethunes came to England with William the Conquerer in 1066, and to Scotland by 1165. Robert de Bethunia witnessed a charter registered at St. Andrews, probably about 1180. In old records the name appears frequently as Betun or Beton, and by the 16th century became confused with the Gaelic Beatons. The Fife Beatons owned land there and in Angus. Alexander de Bethune was slain at Dupplin in 1332. His son Robert married the heiress of Sir John Balfour of that Ilk, and received the estate of Balfour, from which sprang several branches. The family failed in the male line in 1760, and the estate was inherited by William Congleton, who assumed the name Bethune. Eventually it descended to Admiral Charles Ramsay Drinkwater-Bethune (1802-84), R.N. The Bethunes of Blebo descended from David, XIth laird of Balfour.

James Beaton (?1475-1539), was of the Balfour line, and became Provost of the Collegiate Church of Bothwell in 1503. After being Abbot of Dunfermline, Bishop of Galloway and Archbishop of Glasgow, he became Archbishop of St. Andrews in 1523. The celebrated Cardinal David Beaton (1494-1546) was his nephew, and one of the most influential men of his time. He was Lord Privy Seal in 1528, and Ambassador to France, 1533-1537. He was elected Cardinal in 1538, and became Archbishop of St. Andrews and Primate in 1539. His inglorious death at St. Andrews was a severe blow to the Roman Catholic church. Yet another Beaton, James (1517-1603), nephew of the Cardinal, became Archbishop of Glasgow in 1552. At the Reformation in 1560, he retired to France, where he became Ambassador for Mary, Queen of Scots.

# BELL

In Scotland the surname Bell may have three derivations. A local origin accounts for most. Someone who lived adjacent to a church might be called John at the Bell, or simply John Bell. Likewise a tavern-keeper called William, whose sign was a bell, would easily be called William Bell. A secondary origin seems likely from someone who was handsome, just *bel* (Old French). Probably a third derivation is from the forename Isabell or Bell.

The surname is prolific outwith the Highland line, and 'Tinker' Bells are almost as numerous as 'Nobby' Clarks. Dr Black says that in Islay and Kintyre, Bell is used as an Englishing of *Mac Illinamhaoil*. This is stated to have arisen from the marriage of a MacMillan with a Miss Bell, who held property, and took her name in English, but kept the old name in Gaelic.

A family named Bell seem to have been hereditarily associated with the church of Dunkeld. David Bell was a canon there in 1263. About 1330, William Bell was dean there, and a little later Thomas Bell appears as canon. William Bell, vicar of Lamberton, witnessed a charter of the priory of Coldingham, in 1271. Adam and Richard Bell, also from Berwickshire, swore fealty to Edward I, in 1296. That same monarch deprived Gilbert Fitz Bell of his lands. He was possibly the progenitor of the Bells of Annandale, who spread themselves throughout the West March. A common phrase in Dumfriesshire for anything plentiful drew a comparison with the Bells of Middlebie. Thomas Bell witnessed a charter to the abbey of Jedburgh about 1350. Numerous Bells appear in Angus, Fife and Perthshire in the 15th and 16th centuries. John Bell of Antermony (1691-1780), an Asiatic traveller, was born in Campsie parish, Stirlingshire, and went to Russia in

1714. He became physician to Russian embassies in Persia, Siberia and China, before returning to Scotland in 1746. His travel book was published in 1763.

In the Borders the Bells were as unruly as any of the larger clans under whom they lived. There does not appear to have been a unified clan, but David Bell, at the Water of Mylk, was called the Young King. The leading family appears to have been the Bells of Blackethouse. William Bell of Blackethouse, called 'Reidcloke,' had to find caution in the sum of 1,000 merks in 1607, for his good behaviour. Blackethouse passed to a collateral branch of the family and descended to Benjamin Bell (1749-1806), an eminent surgeon, who sold the estate in 1775 to John Carruthers of Brae, whose wife was Grisel Bell of the Auldhill branch of the family. Benjamin Bell was the father of George and Joseph Thomas Bell, both surgeons, and he was the grandfather of Benjamin Bell (1810-83), surgeon who in turn was the father of Joseph Bell (1837-1911), another medical man, who was the original of novelist Arthur Conan Doyle's character, Sherlock Holmes.

Several Bells were of an inventive turn of mind. Henry Bell (1767-1830), born near Torphichen, was the first man in Europe to apply steam to the purpose of navigation. He settled in Glasgow about 1790, and worked as a carpenter. In 1811 he induced John and Charles Wood in Port Glasgow to lay down the keel of his famous steamboat, the *Comet*, launched in 1812. Rev. Patrick Bell (1801-69), of Carmylie, in Angus, was the inventor of a reaping machine in 1827, improved in 1852. Alexander Graham Bell (1847-1922), born in Edinburgh, went to Canada with his father in 1870, and at Boston, Massachusetts, invented the articulating telephone, 1872-76.

# BOSWELL

The surname Boswell is probably best known in literary circles through James Boswell, 1740-95, the friend and biographer of Dr Samuel Johnson. He was the eldest son of Alexander Boswell of Auchinleck, who had a good law practice before becoming a Lord of Session in 1754. James studied law at Edinburgh, Glasgow and Utrecht, and passed advocate in 1766. He made the acquaintance of Johnson in 1763, and kept notes which were of prime importance later when he wrote the famous biography. The writings of James did much to influence the decision in the 'Douglas Cause,' 1767. In 1773 he accompanied Johnson on the epic tour to the Hebrides, and wrote his interesting *Journal*, published in 1785. Two of his sons, Sir Alexander, and James, were also literary men.

It is acknowledged that the family is of French origin, having come from the Seine Valley. They came to England before 1136 and had estates in Yorkshire. The first of the family to appear in Scotland was Robert de Boseville, who was given lands in Berwickshire. He may have come north in the train of Ada de Warenne, whose marriage with Prince Henry was solemnised in 1139. The family arms, Argent, on a fess Sable, three cinquefoils of the field, indicate the Hainaut-Ghent origins of the Seine Valley people.

The Boswells of Balgregie, Fife, no doubt migrated from Oxmuir, in Berwickshire, and Roger, the first of that family, appears to have married a daughter of Sir Michael Wemyss of Wemyss. James Boswell, 4th of Balgregie, acquired Balmuto. David, 2nd of Balmuto, by his first marriage with Grizel Wemyss, had two sons, David, who died before him, and Sir Alexander, who was killed at Flodden in 1513, but left issue who continued his line of the family. By his second marriage in 1480, with Lady Elizabeth Sinclair, he had four other sons, William of Lochgellie, Thomas; George of Craigside, and Robert a clergyman. Thomas had a charter of the Barony of Auchinleck, in Ayrshire, in 1504. He too, lost his life at Flodden, but left a son David, whose son John of Auchinleck, was ancestor of the Boswells of Duncansmuir, from whom descended the Craigston family, and of the Knockroon family, which ended in an heiress, Margaret, who married her cousin, John of the Knockroon line. James Boswell 4th of Auchinleck, was indicted for "abiding from the Raid of Dumfries," in 1600. With three sons who soldiered under Gustav Adolph of Sweden, he had a son David, who carried on the family of Auchinleck. His grandson, David, 6th Laird, had two sons, James, who succeeded him, and John, who purchased Balmuto from his kinsman, Andrew Boswell, WS, in 1722. Alexander, 7th of Auchinleck, was the father of Alexander, a Senator of the College of Justice, whose son James, 9th of Auchinleck was the above friend of Samuel Johnson.

Alexander, eldest son of James, was cr. a baronet in 1821. His son, Sir James, 2nd Bt. and 11th Laird, sold Auchinleck to his kinsman, John Douglas-Boswell of Garrallan, and died without male issue in 1857, when the baronecty became extinct. James Boswell's eldest son by a second marriage was Dr John Boswell, a distinguished physician in Edinburgh, whose eldest son Robert Boswell of St. Boswells, WS, was Lyon Depute and Keeper of the Records of Lyon Court, 1770-95, and interim Lord Lyon King of Arms, 1795-96. From him descended the 16th heir male of the Auchinleck family, David Rutherford Boswell, born 1927, educated at Epsom College and Guy's Hospital, who served in the Dental Branch of the RAF.

# BRODIE

The surname Brodie is said to be derived from the barony of that name, in Moray. However, the arms of the Brodies indicate Flemish origin, and they were probably descended from the Counts of Boulogne. They may have come to Scotland, *via* England, in the train of Freskin and Berowald. Brothie comes from the Flemish word for brother, cognate with the Dutch *broeder*. Information about the early lairds is scant, owing to the old muniments having been burnt by Lord Lewis Gordon in 1645. Malcolm, Thane of Brodie, appears about 1285. He is said to have had at least two sons, David, who succeeded him, and Alexander of East Grange, ancestor of the Brodies of Lethen. There is some haitus here, as Michael de Brothie had a charter of the lands in 1311, as heir to his father. It is possible he was an elder brother of David, who had several sons. Thomas de Brothy was a juror at Inverness in 1376-7. His son John appears in 1380. John Brodie of Brodie witnessed an agreement about the marches of Croy and Kildrummy in 1492, and Thomas Brodie of that Ilk was a juror at Inverness in 1546. He and his wife Agnes Shaw had a new charter of the Lordship of Brodie that same year.

A descendant, Alexander Brodie, was a Lord of Session 1657-61, and several other Brodies were in the legal profession in Edinburgh. Lord Brodie had a son John, who married Lady Mary Kerr. They had a large family of daughters, of whom Amelia married her cousin, James Brodie of Asleisk, and were the parents of Alexander Brodie of Brodie, Lord Lyon, 1727-54. His direct descendant, Montague Ninian Alexander Brodie of Brodie, married in 1939, Helena Budgeon, and their son is Alexander Ian Ninian Brodie. The imposing Castle Brodie, commenced about 1567, is now the property of the National Trust for Scotland. It contains many fine family portraits.

Among cadets of the Brodies of Brodie are those of Lethen and of Glasshaugh. The Lethen branch descend from a younger son of David of that Ilk, who purchased the estates of Pitgavenie, Eastgrange and Lethen in 1634. Of this line was Thomas, WS, who was Lyon Depute, 1769-70. The family is now represented by Ewen John Brodie of Lethen, who succeeded in 1966. Sir Benjamen Collins Brodie, of the Glasshaugh line, was surgeon to William IV and Queen Victoria, and was created a baronet in 1834. The 5th and present baronet is Sir Benjamen David Ross Brodie.

Brodies were prominent in Edinburgh from the close of the 16th century. The testament of Sir Alexander Brodie of that Ilk was confirmed at Edinburgh in 1583. One 'Mr' James Brodie, married Anna Forrett at Edinburgh in 1599. Alexander Brodie of that Ilk was admitted a burgess and guildbrother in 1648. Two students, Alexander Brodie and James Brodie, graduated at Edinburgh University in 1687. Ludovick Brodie, son of Francis Brodie of Milnton, in Moray, was admitted WS in 1706. A remarkable criminal confined in the Tolbooth of Edinburgh was Deacon William Brodie, a daring burglar, who was undetected until he raided the Excise Office. He fled to Holland, but was apprehended and brought back for trial. Brodie was hanged in 1788. Brodies also appear in Aberdeen. Elizabeth Brodie was the wife of Thomas Denman, a physician there in 1783, father of Lord Chief Justice Denman and of two daughters, who married Dr Mathew Baillie and Sir Richard Croft, another physician. Brodies were also prolific in the west. Sarah Brodie, wife of Rev. Archibald Sydserff of Dunbarton, died in 1730, and Robert Brodie, of Hazelhead, died in 1753.

# BROWN/BROUN

The surname Brown is derived from an adjective meaning in Old English, brown or dark red. There are a number of variants. Broun sometimes appearing in Scotland, and Browne in England. In Old High German the name was rendered *brun*, and was borrowed into French to give *Le Brun*. Brun appears in English charters from about 970, but is not recorded in Scotland until very early in the 12th century. Walterus le Brun was on an inquisition concerning the church of Glasgow in 1116, and Sir David le Brun witnessed the foundation charter of the Abbey of Holyroodhouse in 1128. He may have been the ancestor of the ancient family of Broun of Colstoun, East Lothian. Robert Brune witnessed a grant to the hospital of Soltre (Soutra), about 1260, and Richard Broun witnessed a charter of Donald, Earl of Mar, about 1285. Richard de Broun and others of the name signed the Ragman Roll, 1296.

It is remarkable that the Brouns of Colstoun may trace their ancestry for more than 850 years. Possibly they came originally from France, but it is uncertain if they descended from the knight shown as 'Braine,' who appears on the *Roll of Battle Abbey*. They were well established at 'Cummyrcollystoun' (Colstoun), by 1358, when David Broun had a charter of the lands of Westersegarystoun. He and his wife Agnes resigned the lands of Colstoun in 1361, in favour of their son David, reserving the life tenement. In the reign of James I, 1406-37, William Broun of Colstoun married Margaret de Annand, co-heiress of Sauchie, in Stirlingshire. Later in the 15th century Sir William Broun of Colstoun was Warden of the Middle Marches, and took part in a battle at Dornock, in Annandale, against the English led by Sir Marmaduke Langdale. Both commanders were slain. Patrick Broun of Colstoun was cr. a baronet (NS) in 1686.

Through their marriages subsequent baronets were related to the Hays of Yester, the Murrays of Stanhope and other influential families. The 12th and present Bt. is Sir Lionel John Law Broun, who resides at Mosman, NSW, Australia.

The family of Agnes, 1732-1820, mother of the poet Burns, also favoured the spelling Broun. She was the eldest daughter of Gilbert Broun, tenant of Craigentoun Farm, Kirkoswald, by his first wife, Agnes Rainie, and married William Burnes, a native of Kincardineshire, in 1756. Their son Robert, who was to become Scotland's greatest lyric poet, was born in 1759.

A number of Brown families have been small landowners. The Browns of Lochton, Perthshire, were descended from John Brown of Muirside, Forfar, who married Janet Walker. A descendant, James Brown of Lochton, was provost of Dundee, 1844-47. The family came to be represented by the Wemyss-Browns of Cononsyth. The Browns of Fordell, Perthshire, descended from Sir John Brune, High Sheriff of Aberdeenshire in 1368. James Brown, 1786-1864, of this family, a director of the Bank of Scotland, married Anne, daughter and eventual heiress of Lt. Col. William Mckerrell, VIIth of Hillhouse, and the McKerral-Browns of Peasenhall, Suffolk, came to represent them. The Browns of Newhall and Carlops, Peeblesshire, descended for Hugh Brown, a Glasgow merchant, whose son Robert, an advocate, purchased those estates in 1783. He published an edition of Allan Ramsay's *The Gentle Shepherd*, in 1808. His grandson, Hugh Horatio Brown, was an accomplished man of letters.

Today, George Mackay Brown, OBE, of Stromness, Orkney, is a noted author, poet and story teller: winner of the James Tait Black Prize in 1988. His novels include *Greenvoe, Magnus, Time in a Red Coat* and *The Golden Bird*.

# BRUCE

The story of the Bruces runs like a bright gold thread through the rich tapestry of Scottish history. They appear to have been of Flemish extraction, and settled at Brus (now Brix), hence the surname, near Cherbourg, in Normandy, about the time that Matilda of Flanders married William the Conqueror, an event which explains why so many Flemish noblemen took part in the Conquest in 1066. Their progenitor in Normandy was Adam, and it may have been his son Robert who fought at Hastings. His descendant, Robert de Brus, was probably a companion at the English court of Prince David, who, soon after succeeding to the throne in Scotland, granted him extensive lands in Annandale. They already possessed estates in England, and there may have been a distant relationship with Maud or Matilda, who became Queen of Scots in 1124. His great-grandson, Robert de Brus, brought the family closer to the royal line through his marriage to Isabel, daughter of David, Earl of Huntingdon, younger brother of King Malcolm IV and King William. Indeed this was how their son Robert, became a competitor for the crown in 1286. It was his grandson, Robert, Earl of Carrick, who was crowned King of Scots in 1306. His brilliant victory over King Edward II of England at Bannockburn in 1314, led to the famous Declaration of Arbroath in 1320, and to the independence of Scotland. His daughter Marjory married Walter Stewart, and they were the ancestors of the Stewart Kings.

The direct royal line died out, but branches of the family settled in Fife and Clackmannan. Edward Bruce of Easter Kennet, was given the Lordship of Kinloss in 1600/01. From him descended the Earls of Elgin and Kincardine. Of the Carnock line of this family was the Hon. Alexander Bruce, who was exiled in Holland with

Charles I. In 1662 he conducted experiments with Christian Huygens at The Hague and at sea, on short pendulum clocks, with a degree of success. The same year he succeeded as 3rd Earl of Kincardine. Charles, 9th Earl of Kincardine, succeeded to the Earldom of Elgin in 1747, after the death of his kinsman, Charles 4th Earl of Elgin and 2nd of Ailesbury. The present 11th Earl of Elgin and 15th Earl of Kincardine, Andrew Bruce, is clan chief. He served in World War II with the Scots Guards, and was Grand Master Mason of Scotland, 1961-65.

The Bruce family has many branches. One of the most important was that of Airth, in Stirlingshire, descended from the Bruces of Clackmannan. Sir Edward Bruce having married Agnes, heiress of Airth, Stirlingshire, before 1417, gained that estate. They also owned Stenhouse, in the same county. In 1628, Sir William Bruce of Stenhouse was cr. a baronet of Nova Scotia. His descendant, the present and 12th Bt. is Sir Michael Bruce, who served in the US Marines, 1943-46, and lives at Newport Beach, California. Another branch of the Airth family descended from Rev. Edward Bruce, who went to Ireland about 1609, and whose family obtained the estates of Kilroot, Co. Antrim, and Scoutbush, Carrickfergus. James Bruce, 1730-94, of Kinnaird, the explorer of the Nile, was also descended from the Airth line.

Sir William Bruce, ?1627-1710, of Balcaskie, cr. a baronet (NS) in 1668, purchased the barony of Kinross in 1671 became King's surveyor and Master of Works. He designed the fine mansion of Kinross, completed in 1690. Sir William restored part of Holyroodhouse, and was the architect of Moncrieffe House and the central part of Hopetoun House. To him belongs the credit for the radical change from baronial to classical architecture in Scotland.

# BUCHANAN

Clarinch, an island in Loch Lomond, opposite Balmaha, was granted in 1225 by the Earl of Lennnox, to Absolon or Anselan, son of Macbeth. He took his name from lands on the shore, and is recorded about 1224 as Sir Absolon of Bouchannane, supposed to mean in Gaelic, 'house of the canon.' It is suggested that he belonged to one of the old families of the Celtic church. 'Clarinch' became the war cry of the Buchanans. According to tradition the chief's surname was originally McAuselan, a name retained by a collateral line. Those of the 'stem' family adopted a territorial designation: *Mac-a-Chanonaich* in Gaelic.

In 1282, the Earl of Lennox granted a charter to Maurice de Bouchannane, confirming him in his lands and giving him the right to hold courts. The Buchanan chiefs held the lands for another 400 years. Maurice, son of Maurice, had a charter of the carucate of land called Bouchannane, with the land of Sallochy, by Donald, (6th) Earl of Lennox, confirmed under the Great Seal, in 1371. His descendant, Sir Alexander, went to France with the Earl of Buchan, to assist against the English, and was killed at Verneuil in 1421. Unmarried, he was succeeded by his brother, Walter of Buchanan. A younger brother, John, was ancestor of Henry Buchanan of Leny, from whose daughter descended the Buchanans of Leny and Bardowie. Walter married Isobel, daughter of Murdoch, Duke of Albany, and had two sons, Walter his heir, and Thomas, ancestor of the Buchanans of Drumakill, from whom descended George Buchanan, 1506-82, the greatest Latin scholar of his time. Walter's elder son, Patrick, was killed at Flodden in 1513, and before 1526, his eldest son George succeeded to Buchanan. From his younger son Walter descended the Buchanans of Spittal. George was sheriff of Dumbartonshire, and fought at Pinkie in 1547. His son John died before him and was succeeded by his son Sir George Buchanan, from whose half brother, William, the Auchmar family descended. Sir George's grandson, also Sir George, was involved in the Civil War, and died a prisoner in 1651. John Buchanan, the last laird, sold his ancestral estate in 1682 to the Marquess of Montrose.

From the Spittal and Lany lines of the family descended Dr Francis Hamilton-Hamilton, who established his claim to the chiefship in 1826, but his grandson John died in 1919, without issue. A branch of the Buchanans of Lany held the estates of Ardinconnal and Auchintorlie, in Dumbartonshire, and four brothers, George, merchant in Glasgow; Andrew of Drumpelier; Neil, of Hillington; and Archibald of Auchintorlie, were the promoters of the Buchanan Society in 1725, the oldest organisation of its kind. From Archibald descended Sir Andrew Buchanan, cr. a baronet (UK) in 1878. The 5th Bt. is Major Sir Charles James Buchanan of Dunburgh, Stirlingshire, residing in Nottinghamshire. The Leith (-Buchanan) baronets, cr. 1763, descend from Alexander Leith, of Aberdeen, who died in 1763. The additional surname of Buchanan was added by Sir Alexander Leith, 3rd Bt., who married in 1832, Jemima, daughter of Hector Macdonald Buchanan of Ross.

Dugald Buchanan, 1716-68, son of a Strathyre miller and farmer, became a teacher at Kinloch Rannoch, and wrote Gaelic poetry of high quality. James Buchanan, 1791-1868, 15th President of the USA, was son of James Buchanan, who emigrated from Donegal, Ireland, to Pennsylvania, and is said to have been a descendant of Thomas Buchanan, an Ulster-Scot.

# BUDGE

The surname Budge is found mainly in Caithness, Orkney and Skye. According to Hugh MacDonald, the Skye seannachie who wrote during the reign of Charles II, 1660-85, they were associated with Clan Donald. When Angus Og of Islay, a friend of Robert the Bruce, married Margaret, daughter of Guy O'Cathlan, an Ulster baron, he received as her dowry seven score of men, doubtless welcome as he had lost many followers harrying the English fleets. A later historian calls them 'Tochradh Nighean a Chathanaich' (The dowry of the daughter of O'Cathan). They received grants of land. Those who became known as *Butikes* or Budges, formed a clan, and one member who fled to Caithness when pursued for slaughter, founded a family there in the latter part of the 14th century. Walter, Earl of Caithness, granted the three-pennyland of Toftingall to Nicolas Budge in 1403. His son Magnus was infeft in the three-pennyland of Toftingall and in tenements in Wick, in 1415. Another son, Henry, born about 1404, supplicated for the treasurership of Ross in 1430, although he held a canonry and prebend of Caithness. This church office does not appear to have been too secure, and in 1432 there was a dispute about the office with Henry de Rynd. Budge died in 1444. The Budge family had feuds with the Baynes and other local families, who probably looked upon them as interlopers.

The Budges established themselves firmly at Toftingall, in Watten parish, and it has been said there were twelve generations from Nicolas in 1403, to Donald, who recorded arms in 1703, blazoned: Argent, a lion passant, Azure, armed and langued Gules. Crest, a hand holding a dagger, proper. Motto: *Stricita Parata Neci*. A Budge-Murray Thriepland of Fingask marriage resulted in a quartering of 1826, showing the arms of

Murray of Pennyland, and of Thriepland of Fingask. In the Orkneys the Budges were prominent in South Ronaldsy. Marion Budge, spouse of the deceased Robert Edmonson in Wydwall died about 1615. Katherine Cromertie, wife of Henrie Budge in Sandwick, died in March 1611, leaving children, Patrik, Adame, Andro, Christian and Marioun. The testament of Magnus Budge in South Ronaldsay was confirmed in August, 1663. A number of Budges from South Ronaldsay served in Canada with the Hudson's Bay Company between 1793 and 1850. One of those, William, a labourer in 1811, rose to be a clerk and trader. He cared for his accounts in a satisfactory manner, but a propensity to liquor kept him in a subordinate position. John Budge in Oxsetter, Northmavine, Shetland, died in 1613. Isabel Budge in Edinburgh, married Steven Hutcheson, a weaver, in 1662. In 1690, John, son of Daniel Budge in Fastingell, Caithness, was indentured apprentice to John Lowson, tailor-burgess of Edinburgh.

A branch of the family settled in Skye. According to tradition, William Budge, serving in a volunteer regiment, mended a damaged canon, and was invited by Col. MacDonald of Lyndale to become his estate blacksmith. Later, Lord MacDonald gave him lands at Balgown formerly held by the MacRuries. He married Christian MacDonald and had two sons. James, the elder, was also a blacksmith and farmer. By his wife Margaret MacDonald, he had a large family. His second son, Donald, followed the family trade, and his eldest son, Donald, became a hotelier at Dunvegan. The business was in the family from 1910-1946. Donald's eldest son, also Donald, graduated in arts at Glasgow and became a minister at Cumnock. During World War II he served as an army chaplain. In 1949 he was called to Jura. Rev. Donald married an American lady, Eleaner B Melchior, and died in 1978, without issue.

# BURNS

Whenever the surname Burns is considered, the name of Robert Burns, 1759-96, is remembered. He was undoubtedly Scotland's greatest lyric poet. It is fashionable today among intellectuals to compare him unfavourably with Hugh McDiarmid (Christopher M. Grieve), 1892-1978, but the work of the latter, with all its literary merit, will never be as popular as that of Burns. The Ayrshire bard wrote for the common man: McDiarmid did not.

The surname Burns or Burnes appears in English records as early as the 11th century, but not in Scotland until early in the 17th. Burn is however, a surname of great antiquity, and it seems probable that in many instances it became Burns. It certainly did with the Burn family who occupied the lands of Carntoun near Tillicoultry, for about 200 years. John Burn sold the lands about 1738 and became a schoolmaster in Glasgow, adopting the surname of Burns. He was the father of Rev. John Burns, 1744-1839, minister of Barony parish, father of a remarkable family. The surname of Burns is formed from the compound word. Burnhouse, a dwelling near a burn or stream. There are numerous Burnhouses in Scotland, and unrelated families of the name. Because most of the early ones were on the land as cottars and tenants, their appearance in records is late. James Burns, son of John Burns in Easter Gellat (?Dunfermline), was apprenticed in 1631 to John Quhippo, baker in Edinburgh. When he was admitted a burgess of the city in 1641, his name was recorded as Burne. John Burns, hammerman in Glasgow, was admitted burgess in 1641, for performing four days work for the commonweal every year, *gratis*. His son John was admitted burgess and guildbrother in his right in 1661. The testament of James Burns, maltman in

Dundee, and Elizabeth Bouman his wife, was registered in 1665.

In Kincardineshire, families who appear as Burnes, Burnas, Burnase, Burnace and Burness, are probably descended from a common ancestor. In 1637, John Burnes, servitor to Sir Alexander Strachan of Thornton, witnessed a bond granted to his master by the Earl of Traquair. In 1659, Patrick Burness, clerk to the Presbytery of Brechin, attested a bond in favour of the parish reader at Lochlea. Robert Burnace in Arbuthnott had a son Robert, baptised in 1633, who was placed by his father in a farm in the estate of Glenbervie. In 1655 he married Elspeth Wise. In leasing a farm in Glenbervie he was to neighbour persons of his name and kin who had farmed there for generations. John Stuart, 1813-77, advocate in Aberdeen, a historian and genealogist, whose ancestor, David Stuart of Inchbreck, fought at Pinkie in 1547, stated there were Burnes or Burness tenants on the estate at that time. When the parochial records begin, they are quite numerous. Walter Burness, in Glenbervie parish, had a son of the same name who leased the farm of Bogjorgan, on the estate of Inchbreck, and about them an alleged tradition has gained credence. Walter, senior, is supposed to have been an Argyll Campbell, and having given offence to his landlord, moved with his son to Stonehouse of Mergie, and adopted the surname Burness, from the name of his previous home. The story is at variance with recorded facts. Walter, junior, had by his first wife sons William and James, who farmed Bogjorgan. James, 1656-1743, married Margaret Falconer. Their son Robert married Isabel Keith, and he farmed at Clochnahill, Dunottar. They had with other issue a son William, 1721-84, who migrated to Ayrshire and married Agnes Broun, from Kirkoswald. Their famous son, the bard Robert, was born in the *auld clay biggin'* at Alloway.

# CAMERON

The Camerons, according to the late Sir Iain Moncreiffe, derive their name from *Cam-brun*, 'crooked hill,' an elevation in Cameron parish, Fife. A knightly family in the Tay valley in the Middle Ages, he suggested they were a branch of the Macduffs, the premier clan among the Gaels. Dr G. F. Black however, says the name is of two-fold origin, Highland and Lowland, pointing out that besides the Fife place-name, there is Cameron, now on the outskirts of Edinburgh, and Cameron, in the Lennox. He made the meaning *cam-shron* for 'wry' or 'hook nose.' Mrs Platts points out that Cambron, one of the earliest forms of the name, is a small place in Hainaut, less than five miles from Lens, where Count Lambert had his home, and that the arms of Cameron of Lochiel differ only in the tinctures to those of the great family of Oudenarde, nobles of Flanders.

Certainly, the surname is of great antiquity. Adam de Kamerun witnessed a charter by William de Haya to the monks of Cupar, 1214-49, and Hugh Cambrun was sheriff of Forfar in 1219. The Camerons of Lochaber became the most distinct group, and appear there by the beginning of the 15th century. The eponymous ancestor is given as Gillespick, son of Angus, who lived in the 11th century, but the hereditary patronymic of their Lochiel chief, *MacDhomnall Dubh*, derives from Donald *Dubh* (dark or swarthy), who lived in the first half of the 15th century. His son Allan was styled "Captain of the Clancamroun." Other smaller tribes attached themselves to the Camerons, particularly the MacMartins, MacGillonies and MacSorlies, while other small groups became auxiliaries to Lochiel, including Macphees, MacLachlans and Macintyres. The Camerons also settled cadets in Lochaber.

Allan Cameron, 12th chief and Constable of Strone

Castle, adopted the title of Lochiel in 1528 when his lands were erected into a barony. The succeeding chiefs came from his first marriage with a daughter of Celestine MacDonald of Lochalsh, while the Erracht line descended from his second wife, Marjory, daughter of Lachlan MacIntosh. The Camerons were a warlike race, and had fought at Harlow in 1411. Sir Ewen Cameron, 1629-1719, was the last Highland chief to hold out for Charles II against Cromwell. In old age he fought at Killiecrankie in 1689, but took the oath of allegiance to William and Mary. Donald Cameron, 'the gentle Lochiel,' is held to be the noblest of all Highland chiefs. He brought 700 clansmen to Glenfinnan to aid Prince Charles, and it was largely his support that took the Pretender so far, only to lose at Culloden in 1746. His brother, Dr Archibald Cameron, was also involved, and the family estates were forfeited. These were restored in 1784. The military tradition also emerged in the Erracht line, and in 1793 Allan Cameron raised the 79th Regiment, which became in 1881 the Queen's Own Cameron Highlanders (the Queen's Own Highlanders, 1960). Donald Walter, the 25th chief, served in the South African War and in World War I, when he led his own battalion at Loos. The present chief, Sir Donald Cameron, served with the Lovat Scouts in 1945, and as Colonel-in-Chief of the 4/5th Battalion, Queen's Own, 1958-69. The heir is his elder son, Donald Angus Cameron, yr. of Lochiel, a company director.

The Hon. Lord (Sir John) Cameron, son of an Edinburgh solicitor, was a Lord of Session, 1955-85, and his son, Kenneth John, was created Baron Cameron of Lochbroom (Life Peer) in 1984. He was Lord Advocate, 1984-89, and in 1989 became a Lord of Session.

# CAMPBELL OF ARGYLL

Norman, Celtic, British or Norse? The origin of the Campbells has been variously stated: even traced back to Arthur, of round table fame! Norman origin is not far-fetched when we now know that for ages historians have described all of William the Conqueror's followers as Normans, but his wife was Matilda of Flanders, and many armigerous Flemish nobles fought at Hastings, 1066. Not all were entered on the *Battle Abbey Roll*. The ancestors of those who were later named Campbell bore the Flemish name of Erkinbald, written in Scotland as Archibald (in Gaelic as *Gilleasbuig*), and his descendants bore arms blazoned gyronny of eight, Or and Sable: the bearings of the Baldwins, Counts of Flanders. Mrs Platts says pointedly that with a strong Flemish presence at the Scottish court, "there could be no possibility of any arms of Flanders . . . being borne by a man not of that blood." Erkinbald settled, as other Flemings did, in the old British kingdom of Strathclyde, and in the district of Lennox. He married Eva, daughter of Paul O'Duine, the native lord of Lochawe, descendant of Diarmid. Their son Duncan, is mentioned in 1369 in a charter to a descendant, and his son Colin appears to have been the father of Archibald, who held the lands of Menstrie in 1263. His son Colin 'Mor' or Big Colin, was knighted in 1280, and it is from him that the patronymic of the Campbell chiefs, *Macailein Mor*, is derived. The name Campbell evolved from a nickname *Cam-beul* meaning 'Crooked-Mouth.' There is no equivalent in Gaelic for 'Clan Campbell,' the term being always *Chlann O Duibhne*.

While the Campbells may have gained a footing in Lochawe before 1300, it was under Robert the Bruce that they became a power in Argyll. Sir Neil, son of Sir Colin 'Mor,' led his clan at Bannockburn in 1314, but was probably dead two years later. He had married the king's sister Mary, and had issue. His eldest son, by a previous wife, was Colin, who had a charter of the barony of Lochawe in 1315, and Archibald, son of Colin, received from the Countess of Menteith, a charter of her lands in Cowal, including Kilmun, which became the burial place of the chiefs. He had a further grant in 1369, of the lands of Melfort, Strachur and others, "with all rights enjoyed by his ancestor Duncan MacDuine." The star of the Campbells rose after the forfeiture of the MacDougals, enemies of Bruce. The family lived on an island in Loch Awe, but in the 15th century founded Inveraray, giving them easy access to the islands. Sir Duncan of Lochawe became Lord Campbell in 1445, and his grandson, Colin, was cr. Earl of Argyll in 1457.

The Campbells played a great part in national affairs. Archibald, 2nd Earl, led his clan at Flodden in 1513, and died there. Colin, 3rd Earl, held the border against the English, and Archibald, 4th Earl, fought at Pinkie in 1547. Above all, successive earls supported the Government and acted as its agents in the West Highlands. They also looked after their numerous cadets. Archibald, 8th Earl, cr. Marquess in 1641, and his son Archibald, 9th Earl, departed royalist traditions, becoming involved in the Civil War and the Covenants, and both died on the scaffold. The Revolution of 1688 altered matters, and Archibald, 10th Earl, was cr. Duke of Argyll in 1701. Successive dukes have distinguished themselves. John, 2nd Duke, became a Field-Marshall, as was John, 5th Duke. George, 8th Duke, was a Liberal Politician, and John George, 9th Duke, who married Princess Louise, Queen Victoria's daughter, was Governor-General of Canada, 1878-83. Ian, 12th and present Duke, is Keeper of the Great Seal of Scotland.

# CAMPBELL OF BREADALBANE

The leading branch of the Campbells of Argyll is that of Breadalbane, a district in Perthshire extending from Lochaber and Atholl on the north, to Strathearn and Menteith on the south. It is scored by deep glens and contains Loch Tay and numerous mountain torrents. The progenitor of this family was Sir Colin Campbell of Glenorchy, eldest son by his second wife, Margaret Stewart, of Sir Duncan Campbell of Lochawe. The patronymic of the House of Breadalbane is *Mac-Cailean-Mhic-Dhonnachaidh*, 'son of Colin, son of Duncan.' Glenorchy, from which the MacGregors were ousted, was given to Sir Colin by his father in 1432. Other lands, including Lawers, in Perthshire, were bestowed on him and his fourth wife, Margaret, daughter of Luke Stirling of Keir, by King James III, in recompense for his services in capturing Thomas Chalmers, one of the assassins of James I. He built Kilchurn Castle, at the north-east end of Loch Awe.

Sir Duncan Campbell, the eldest son, obtained a charter of the lands of the Port of Tay, 1492 and 1498, and of Finlarig in 1506. His lands of Finlarig, Shian, Balloch, Crannich and others, were incorporated in to the barony of Finlarig by charter, 1513. He was slain at Flodden the same year, and succeeded by his eldest son, Sir Colin, who built the chapel of Finlarig. He died in 1523. Sir John Campbell, Vth of Glenorchy, left no male issue and was succeeded by his brother Colin. He purchased certain lands in Glendochart. When he died in 1583, he was succeeded by Duncan, elder son by his second wife, Catherine, daughter of Lord Ruthven. He was known as 'Black Duncan with the cowl,' and made additions to his estate of certain lands in Menteith and in Strathgartney. He had the power of 'pit and gallows,' and amended statutes drawn up by his father for various courts held within the Lordship of Glenorchy, Discher and Toyer, Lochawe, and others. There were severe penalties for shooting deer and wild fowl: a fine of £20 Scots for the first offence, the loss of an arm for the second and hanging for the third. Persons found guilty were hung with a 'widdie,' a rope made of birch twigs. Duncan was cr. a baronet (NS) in 1625. He engaged the Scots artist, George Jamesone, to paint some family portraits, and a genealogical chart.

The 5th Bt., Sir John Campbell, was MP for Argyll, 1669-74, and in 1681 was cr. Earl of Breadalbane and Holland. By his first wife, Mary, daughter of Henry Rich, 1st Earl of Holland, he had two sons. Duncan the elder, was weak-minded and was passed over in the succession in favour of his brother Sir John, 2nd Earl. The line failed with John, 3rd Earl, whose two sons predeceased him. The nearest heir was his third cousin, John, eldest son of Colin Campbell of Carwhin, descended from Sir Robert Campbell of Glenorchy, 3rd Bt. He was a distinguished soldier and an agricultural improver, and in 1806 was cr. Baron Breadalbane. He was advanced to the dignity of Earl of Ormelie and Marquess of Breadalbane (UK) in 1831. His son John, 2nd Marquess, died without issue, when the UK titles became extinct. The earldom of Breadalbane devolved on John Alexander, his cousin, son of William Campbell of Glenfalloch. His son Gavin, was cr. Baron Breadalbane of Kenmore in 1873, and in 1885, Earl of Ormelie and Marquess of Breadalbane (UK). He too, died without issue, and the Scottish earldom devolved on his nephew, Ian Edward, 8th Earl, who died in 1923. He was succeeded by his kinsman, Charles, descended from the 6th Earl. John, his son, succeeded in 1959 as 10th Earl and 14th Bt. He has no children. Any future claims to the honours would be fraught with difficulties.

# CAMPBELL OF CAWDOR

Clan Campbell has numerous branches, some titled, and most of them armigerous. The Countess of Loudon (Barbara Huddleston Abney-Hastings), represents a very old branch, descended from Duncan, a grandson of Colin 'Mor' Campbell, knighted in 1280. Her heir is Lord Mauchline. Several branches possess baronetcies, including Auchinbreck, Aberuchil, Succoth, and Balcardine. Non-titled families still in existence include Glenduarel, Achallader, Airds Bay, Kilmartin, Strachur, Arduaine, Auchendarroch, Dunstaffnage, Jura, Kilberry and Skerrington. The Inverneill branch – 'Clan Tarlich,' produced the eminent folklorist, John Lorne Campbell, and Colin Campbell, family historian and armorist, who resides in New England.

No branch has shed more lustre on the clan than the Campbells of Calder, or Cawdor, in Nairnshire. Their story began with a flame-haired little girl, Muriel, daughter of John Calder of Calder and Isabella Rose. She became heiress in 1498, when an infant. The 2nd Earl of Argyll, having obtained a grant of the wardship and marriage of the heiress, sent sixty clansmen under Campbell of Inverliver, to bring her to Argyll. They were pursued by the girl's uncles Alexander and Hugh Calder, and their men, who killed seven of Inverliver's sons in Strathnairn. When asked if this was too high a price to pay, as the infant too, might die, Inverliver grimly replied that the heiress would "never die sae lang as there is a red-haired lassie on the shores of Loch Awe." In 1510, when she was barely thirteen years old, she was married to Sir John Campbell, 3rd son of the Earl of Argyll, who thus gained possession of Cawder and its old stronghold.

Muriel's grandson, John, IIIrd Thane of Cawdor, early in the 17th century, sold Croy, and disponed Ferintosh to

Lord Lovat, in order to purchase or conquer the island of Islay, which remained in the family, 1612-1726, when it was bought by Daniel Campbell of Shawfield. Sir Hugh Campbell, Vth Thane of Cawdor, made additions to Cawdor Castle, and built a carved fireplace to commemorate the Campbell/Calder marriage of 1510. Sir John Campbell, son of Sir Alexander, VIIth of Cawdor, married Mary, co-heiress of Lewis Pryse of Gogirthen, and died in 1777. In 1796, his grandson, John was elevated to the peerage (UK) as Baron Cawdor of Castlemartin, Pembrokeshire.

The first and second barons were Fellows of the Royal Society. In little more than a century, descendants have been awarded twelve mentions in despatches, three brevets, three French *Croix de Guerre* (one with Palm and Star), the Legion of Honour four times, one AFC, one DFC, the MC twice, the DSO fifteen times, and three Victoria Crosses: an amazing record, which does not include ordinary scholastic honours. John Frederick Campbell, 2nd Baron, was cr. Earl of Cawdor in 1827 and died in 1860. His grandson, Frederick Archibald, was First Lord of the Admiralty, 1905, and a member of the Council of the Prince of Wales, 1908-11. His grandson, John, 5th Earl, served in the Royal Navy in World War I, and in World War II as Lt. Col. of the 4th Batt. of the Queens Own Cameron Highlanders. He was Chairman of the Historic Buildings Council of Scotland, and a Trustee of the National Museum of Antiquities. High John, 6th Earl, was High Sheriff of Carmarthenshire, 1964, and an underwriting member of Lloyd's. The family is proud of their feudal Castle of Cawdor, which is the only privately inhabited castle in Scotland with its old drawbridge.

# CLAN CHATTAN

The Clan Chattan is a confederation of clans in Lochaber, Strathnairn and Badenoch, under the leadership of the Mackintosh chief, whose ancestor, Angus, 6th chief of that clan, married in 1291, Eva, daughter of Dugal Doul. The latter was the 6th chief of the old Clan Chattan, whose ancestry stretched back to the kings of Dalriada. Their 1st chief, Kellehathon or Gillichattan Mor, was the son of Bethoc, daughter of Malcolm, Earl of Atholl, by Hextilda, the heiress of King Donald Ban, who reigned 1093, and 1094-97. Her mother was Donald's daughter, also Bethoc, who married Uchred of Tynedale. Gillichatton means 'St, Cattans servant,' and he would be baptised under the special protection of the Saint. St. Cattan was venerated by the chiefs of the Cinel Lorne, and they built a shrine for him at Ardchattan. The name means 'little cat,' and the wildcat features prominently in the heraldry of the clan.

Gillichattan Mor had a son Dugal or Diarmid, who left two sons Gillichattan, the 3rd chief, and David *Down*, of Inverhaven, ancestor of *Clan Dhia*, or the Davidsons. The 3rd chief had two sons, Kenneth, who appears not to have succeeded him, and Muriach, Prior of Kingussie, who left the church when the succession opened to him, and became 4th chief. He married a daughter of the Thane of Cawdor, and had four sons: Gillichattan-Patrick, 5th chief; Ewan Ban, ancestor of the Macphersons (from 'son of the parson'); Neil, from whom some Smiths are descended; and Ferquhard, the eponymous ancestor of the MacGillivrays. Gillichattan-Patrick left a son, Dugal *Doul*, who left only a daughter, Eva. On her marriage to Angus Mackintosh, he became the 7th chief of Clan Chattan.

Eventually clans claiming to be of the blood of the old Clan Chattan, formed a confederacy under Mackintosh hegemony. Conspicuous among these were the Macphersons of Cluny (who at one period disputed the chiefship of the Clan Chattan). They were powerful enough to be noticed separately from the Mackintoshes in 1587, and they had many branches. The Davidsons, or *Clann Da'idh*, were recognised, and other claimants were the MacBeans, *Clan Vean*; the Cattanachs of Lochaber, and the Macphails or *Clan Phail* of Invernairnie. Other clans who joined were the Macleans of the north, including those of Dochfour; the Smiths or Gows in the clan territory; the Rosses or *Clan Andrish*; the Andrews or MacAndrews, possibly an offshoot of the Rosses; the Clarks or *Clan Clerich*; the Shaws of Rothiemurchus and others; the *Farquharsons* of the north-east, and the McCombies, or *Clan Thomas*. There are numerous sept names of the principal groups.

Much has been written by Sir Walter Scott and others about a conflict involving Clan Chattan, staged on the North Inch at Perth in 1396, at the instance of the Earl of Moray and the Lindsay chief, ostensibly to prevent an all out clan war. This was the battle between the 'Clan Qwhevil' and the 'Clan Yha,' with 30 men on each side (including Hal o' the Wynd, the Perth smith, for 'Clan Qwhevill'). The clans might be identified as the Shaws of Rothiemurchus and the Davidsons of *Clan Dhia*, but nobody has done so with certainty. The late Sir Iain Moncreiffe, suggested the combatants were the Cummins and Mackintoshes, and pointed to their dispute about the lands of Meikle Geddes and Castle Rait, in Strathnairn. A clan MacMillan historian and Gaelic scholar however, claimed that 'Clan Qwhevil' were Lochaber MacMillans known as *Clann 'ic 'illemhaoil*.

# CHISHOLM

The earliest reference to the surname Chisholm in Scotland is in 1248-9, when Alexander de Chesholme witnessed a charter. The name is derived from the barony of Chisolme, in Roxburghshire, said to mean 'waterside meadow good for producing cheese.' The lands are on the right bank of the Borthwick Water. It is interesting to note that the Chisholm arms: Gules, a boar's head couped Or, langued Azure, indicate that the family were connected at the dawn of heraldry with the interesting group of Border families who also bore boar's heads – the Gordons, Elphinstones, Nisbets, Rollos, Trotters. Hoggs and Swintons (perhaps the leading branch), who appear to have represented the male line of the Anglo-Saxon rulers of Bernicia.

In the reign of David II, 1329-32, Sir Robert Chisholm went north to become governor of Urquhart Castle. By his wife Margaret he had sons: John, who left an only daughter; Alexander; and another son who continued the Border line. Alexander married in 1368, Margaret an heiress of Godfrey del Ard de Ercles, and Isabel Fentoun. Their agreement about lands caused a long dispute with William Fentoun of Baky. Their son Thomas married Margaret, daughter of Lachlan Mackintosh of Mackintosh, and had two sons, Alexander who died without issue, and Wyland (from which name Valentine evolved) of Comar, in Strathglass. Wyland, son of Wyland flourished at the beginning of the 16th century, and was called *An t-Siosal*, 'The Chisholm.' The title of Chisholm of that Ilk was frequently assumed by the Border family, one branch of which owned the estate of Cromlix, and provided three pre-Reformation bishops of Dunblane: James, son of Edmund, his half-brother William, and their nephew William, who was loyal to Mary, Queen of Scots. By the marriage of Jane, daughter of Sir James Chisholm of Cromlix, to James, second son of David, 2nd Lord Drummond, before 1600, their lands passed to that family. Another branch held Stirches, near Hawick, and had marriage alliances with the Rutherfords, Andersons and Scotts. Robert Scott of Montpelier Park Edinburgh, who married Isabella Chalmers at Edinburgh in 1818, had a family in Roberton parish, and assumed before 1834 the style of Chisholm of Chisholm.

The barony of Comarmore, Strathglass, was erected by King James V, and held almost continuously in the Chisholm family from 1538 to 1937. The lands held by the Highland clan embraced the glens of the rivers Glass Affric and Cannich: fairly productive land. Their main cadets were Kinneries and Lietry, Knockfin and Muckerach. The fighting strength of the clan was around 200. Roderick, The Chisholm in 1715, brought the clan under his cousin John of Knockfin to Sheriffmuir and was forfeited, but pardoned in 1727. The clan were 'out' again in 1745. The various factors affecting the economy after the '45 caused families to leave Strathglass, but Alexander Chisholm, urged by his daughter Mary (from whom the present chief is descended) resisted evictions. However, his half-brother William did evict tenants in 1801, and they sailed with others to Canada. Jemima, daughter of this chief, married in 1845, Edmund Chisholm Batten of Thornfalcon, and it was to that family the estates went in 1935 when the Chisholm (female) line failed, and Erchless Castle and other Chisholm properties were sold. The chiefship however, went to James Chisholm Gooden-Chisholm, heir of line, whose mother Mary, was daughter of Alexander Chisholm of Chisholm, the chief who died in 1793. In 1943, Alastair Hamish Wiland André Fraser Chisholm, succeeded his grandfather Roderick as chief.

# CLARK(E)/CLERK

The style *clericus* was given in Latin charters to scholars and minor clergymen who wrote documents. Roger clericus held land between 1174-78, and Thomas clericus was one of those appointed in 1246 to determine the marches of Wester Fedale. A charter by Richard de Bancori, of land in Dumfriesshire in 1249, was witnessed by James the clerk. Johanne le Clerke de Rokesburghe, burgess of Berwick, is mentioned in a safe conduct to John le Brun de Hollesleigh, in 1291. Nine persons styled clerics swore fealty to Edward I, including Petrus le Clerke de Norton, in the shire of Edinburgh, who had his lands restored to him, 3rd September, 1296.

Clerk appears to have stabilised as a surname around 1400, and it was spread throughout Scotland. It is also common in England, often in the form Clarke. John Clerc possessed a tenement in Edinburgh in 1400. Adam Clark was a burgess of Dundee in 1406. Hugh and Alan Clerk were burgesses of Irvine in 1418. In 1446, John Clerk of Leith, shipmaster, had a safe conduct into England. John Clerk was prior of Scone in 1524. Alan Clerk, a smith, was admitted burgess and freeman of Glasgow in 1588, and John Clerk, a cordiner, was admitted likewise in 1594. The name was prolific in the north-east and in the west country. Alexander Clark, from Garioch, graduated at King's College, Aberdeen, in 1675, and became schoolmaster at Raine. Clarks are numerous around Kilwinning early in the 18th century.

Three Clerks or Clarks have been Lord Provosts of Edinburgh. Alexander Clerk of Balbirnie held the office, 1579-84, and his second son, later Sir Alexander Clerk of Stenton, was Lord Provost in 1619. The Clarks, styled" of Edinburgh," descend from Sir Thomas Clark, Lord Provost, 1885-88, who became a partner in the printing and publishing firm of T. & T. Clark. He was created baronet in 1886. His son, Sir John (1859-1924), the 2nd Baronet, was Colonel of the Royal Scots, and the 3rd Baronet, Sir Thomas, also served in that regiment. The 4th and present baronet, Sir John Douglas Clark, resides in Edinburgh.

The Clerks of Penicuik descend from John Clerk of Kilhuntley, in Badenoch, whose grandson John (1611-74), purchased the lands and barony of Penicuik, in Mid Lothian from Dr Alexander Pennicuick. His son John was created a Baronet in 1679, and was M.P. for Edinburghshire, 1690-1702. The 3rd baronet, Sir John (1676-1755), was one of the Barons of Exchequer and a noted antiquary. His seventh son, John Clerk of Eldin was a geologist and studied naval tactics. The 10th and present baronet is Sir John Dutton Clerk.

Clarks in Paisley, descended from the family Dunlambert, Belfast, have been associated with thread-making in Paisley. John Clark of Gateside, Paisley, died in 1864, and his son Stewart purchased the estate of Dundas, in West Lothian. in 1898. His son, John Stewart-Clark, was created a baronet in 1918. He had a pedigree dairy herd at Dundas Home Farm. The 4th and present baronet is Sir John Stewart-Clark, a Member of the European Parliament.

The surname Clerk passed into Gaelic and gave the name *Mac a chleirich*. Malcolm McCleriche is recorded in 1461. The most common form today is McCleary. Clarkson is derived from son of the clerk or scholar, and occurs in Aberdeen as early as 1402. Professor Joseph Andrew Clarke, B. Sc., Ph. D., educated at Whitehall and at Strathclyde University, is now Director of the Energy Simulation Research Unit at Strathclyde University. A senior research fellow, he was the recipient of a Royal Society Esso Energy Award in 1989.

# COCHRANE

Cochran or Cochrane is a territorial surname, derived from the lands of Coveran or Cochrane, near Paisley. The first to appear on record is Waldeve de Coueran, possibly of Bernician extraction, who witnessed a charter granted in 1262 by Dugal, son of Syfyn (MacSwein) to Walter Stewart, Earl of Menteith, of lands in Kintyre. William de Coughran, Lanarkshire (Renfrew not then a sheriffdom) appears on the Ragman Roll in 1296, and Cosmus de Cochrane appears in records between 1367 and 1371. His son William had a grant of the 10-merk land of Langnewton, in Roxburghshire, in 1360. By his wife Mary he had a son Robert, and possibly another, John de Cochrane, who served abroad for Edward I. A contempory was William Cochrane.

The first of the family to be styled 'of that Ilk', was James, son of Allan, so described in a sasine of 1486. His son James obtained a license under the Privy Seal to sell or mortgage his lands of Nether Cochrane, in Renfrewshire, and lands of Pitfour, in the sheriffdom of Perth, in 1509. The male succession failed on the death of his grandson, William, who made additions to Cochrane Castle. He had three daughters, two of whom must have died young. The third daughter, Elizabeth, married Alexander, a younger son of Alexander Blair of that Ilk, who assumed the name and arms of Cochrane. Their eldest son, Sir John, soldiered in Ireland, where he married Grace Butler, apparently without issue, as his brother William, 1605-85, succeeded. A royalist, he was cr. Lord Dundonald in 1647. During Cromwell's Protectorate he kept a low profile, and at the Restoration was appointed a Privy Councillor. In 1669 he was advanced to be Earl of Dundonald, Lord Cochrane of Paisley and Ochiltree.

It was Thomas Cochrane, a descendent of the 1st Earl who became the 8th Earl when the senior line failed in 1758. His grandson, Thomas, 10th Earl, had a remarkable career. He served in the Navy, and in 1807 was returned to Parliament as MP for Westminster. Making charges of abuse against the Admiralty, he was falsely accused of swindling and struck off the Navy list. In 1817 he accepted an invitation from Chile to organise and command their navy, which played an important part in both Chile and Brazil securing independence from Portugal. In 1832, a more liberal government at home restored his naval rank, and in 1854 he was Rear Admiral. Lord Dundonald promoted the use of steam and screw propellors, and urged the Admiralty to study the problems of naval architecture.

Douglas Mackinnon Baillie-Hamilton Cochrane, 12th Earl, had a notable military career. Entering the army in 1870, he went to the Soudan in command of a detachment of the Camel Corps in the expedition for the relief of Khartoum. He was decorated and breveted Lt. Colonel. In 1889 he was a full Colonel and in 1895 commanded the 2nd Life Guards. In the South African War of 1899 he had command of a mounted brigade. In 1902 he commanded the Canadian Militia, and brought out a scheme for re-organisation. The 15th and present Earl is Iain Alexander Douglas Blair Cochrane, who resides at Lochnell Castle, Ledaig, Argyll.

Some MacEacherns who removed to the Lowlands from Moidart and Ardnamurchan adopted the surname of Cochrane, apparently to conceal their origin. This has misled some persons into thinking there is a link between the names, or that Cochrane is derived from an old spelling, MacKauchern.

# COCKBURN

Not many families can rival the Cockburns for producing famous men. The family derive their name from a place in the eastern borders known in the reign of William the Lion, 1165-1214, as Cukoueburn, 'Gowk's Burn,' which lay in the lands of Clifton, Roxburghshire, belonging to the Abbey of Melrose. Their origin is obscure, but they may have been natives of the old Anglic kingdom of Bernicia. There are no early references to the surname further south. Peter de Cockburne witnessed a grant to the hospital of Soltre before 1220. The marriage of a daughter of Sir Robert de Cockburne is mentioned in 1266. Peter de Kokeburne, who witnessed a resignation of lands in 1285, is probably Peeres de Cokeburne, who swore fealty to Edward I. in 1296. Another who signed was Thomas de Cokeburn, Roxburghshire. One of those men was possibly the father of Alexander Cockburn, who lived in the reign of Robert the Bruce. He was twice married, and his sons were Sir Alexander, styled 'of that Ilk,' who was Usher of the White Rod in 1373, and Keeper of the Great Seal, 1390-91; John, ancestor of the Cockburns of Ormiston; and Edward, ancestor of the extinct branch of Skirling.

Sir William Cockburn of that Ilk, descended from Sir Alexander, was slain at Flodden in 1513. By his wife, Anna Home, he had several sons: William of that Ilk; Alexander, also killed at Flodden; Andrew, Robert, and probably also Christopher, progenitor of the extinct Choicelee line. From William descended John of that Ilk, who married Elspeth Oliphant, and had at least two sons, William, who died without issue in 1663, having sold the Cockburn estates in 1657 to his brother James, who was cr. a baronet (NS) in 1671. Sir James married Grizel Hay, and had two sons, Sir William, 2nd Bt., and John, of Kilkenny. His son and heir, Sir James, 3rd Bt., fought at Quebec, and was served heir to his father in Langton, and the office of Usher, in 1754. In 1757 he purchased Langton from his kinsman, Sir Alexander Cockburn, 5th Bt. Lt Col. Sir William Cockburn of that Ilk, 11th Bt., served in the South African War and in World War I. His son, the 12th Bt., and chief of the surname, Sir John Elliot Cockburn, lives in London.

John Cockburn, a Lord of Session who was knighted in 1591, was descended from John Cockburn. His son John, was MP for Haddington, and father of Adam, a Lord of Session, who married Susan Hamilton. Their son John, 1679-1758, was MP for Haddington, but is better known as an agricultural improver. His *Letters to his Gardener*, printed by the Scottish History Society in 1904, show that he was more interested in turnips, onions and trees! Although deeply in debt, he built a new mansion at Ormiston, but had to sell his estates to the Earl of Hopetoun and reside with his son George, Comptroller of the Navy in London. A baronetcy (NS) was conferred in 1627 on William, son of Sir William Cockburn of Langton. This baronety descended to Sir Alexander, 5th Bt., who sold the estate in 1757. His sons James, George and William, all succeeded to the title, which passed to Sir James Edmund, son of another brother, Alexander. He was the 10th Bt., and the title became extinct when he died in 1880.

Alicia Rutherford, 1712-94, wife of Patrick Cockburn, advocate, and a son of Adam Cockburn of Ormiston, wrote a version of 'Flowers of the Forest'. Lord Henry Cockburn, 1779-1854, of the Cockpen branch of the family, and a Senator of the College of Justice, was author of the fascinating *Memorials* of his time (Edinburgh, 1856).

# CRAUFURD

Reginald, youngest son of Alan, 4th Earl of Richmond, descended from Galfride, Duke of Brittany, who had Flemish connections, had grants of land including Ardoch, in the Barony of Craufurd, Lanarkshire, from which his descendants took the surname Craufurd. He died a young man and his widow (name unknown) married Baldwin of Biggar, Sheriff of Lanark. John, son of Reginald, was probably brother of Sir Gregan Craufurd. John was the father of Sir Reginald, sheriff of Ayr, and of Galfride. Sir Reginald married Margaret, heiress of Loudon, and had five sons, William; Adam; John, from whom descended the Crawfords of Craufurdland, near Kilmarnock; Hugh of Crosbie; and Reginald, parson of Strathavon. Hugh had a son Hugh, of Loudon, who died in 1288, whose 'carnal brother,' Reginald of Crosbie was progenitor of the Craufurds of Kerse. By his wife Alicia, Hugh, younger, had a son Reginald of Loudon, Sheriff of Ayr, murdered in 1297, and a daughter Margaret, mother of the patriot, Sir William Wallace. Reginald of Loudon had three sons, Reginald, whose heiress Susan married Sir Duncan Campbell, ancestor of the Earls of Loudon; Hugh of Crosby, from whom came the Craufurds of Auchinames; and another son, ancestor of the Craufurds of Baidland, afterwards of Ardmillan.

John Craufurd of Craufurdland's son James, was an adherent of his kinsman, Sir William Wallace, and assisted in the appointment of the latter as a guardian of Scotland, in 1297. His grandson, John, had a charter of confirmation of the lands of Ardock in 1391. He had two sons, William of Craufurdland, who was knighted by James I, and John of Giffordland, from whom came the Birkhead line. From Archibald Craufurd, who lived in the reign of James III, descended the families of

Auchenairn, Beanscroft and Powmill. His son John was slain at Flodden in 1513, but left a son John, from whom several other branches of the family descended. A later John Craufurd was twice married, first to Robina, heiress of John Walkinshaw of that Ilk, and secondly to Eleanora Nicolson. John assumed the additional surname of Walkinshaw, and was succeeded by his son Lt. Col. John Walkinshaw-Craufurd, who left his estate to Thomas Coutts, the banker. This was contested by his aunt Elizabeth, and the deed was reduced. By her second husband, John Houison of Braehead, she had a daughter Elizabeth, who married Rev. James Moodie, who assumed the additional names of Houison and Craufurd, and was succeeded by his son William Houison-Craufurd. This old family still occupy Craufurdland Castle.

The Craufurds of Auchinames had many branches. Thomas, alive 1401, married Margaret, heiress of Malcolm Galbraith, had two sons, Archibald of Auchinames, and Malcolm of Easter Greenock, from whom descended the Craufurds of Jordanhill. Archibald, who died in 1467, had also two sons, Robert of Auchinames, killed at Flodden in 1513, and Archibald of Previck and Thirdpart, ancestor of the baronets of Kilbirney, Stirling (cr. 1781), represented by Sir Robert James Craufurd, 9th Bt., who lives in London. Robert Craufurd, killed in 1513, was succeeded by his eldest son James, who lost his life at Pinkie in 1547. He was succeeded by his brother William, who died in 1582. His grand-daughter, Jane of Crosbie, married her second cousin, Patrick Craufurd of Drumsoy. Intermarriage of descendants with other cadets kept the Auchinames representation going into the present century, when Hugh Ronald George Craufurd, born 1873, sold his estates and emigrated to Canada, where he died without male issue.

# CUMMING

Of Flemish stock, and descended from a Count of Pol, the Comyns, or Cummings as they became, appear in Scotland during the reign of David I. (1124-53). It has been suggested that the surname derives from a humble herb called cummin. William Comyn was Bishop of Durham and Chancellor to King David. His nephew, Richard, married Hexilda, daughter of Uhtred, son of Waltheof, and was confirmed in lands in Tynedale and Roxburghshire. Later, the family received lands in Buchan and Speyside, and became the most powerful barons in Scotland. This provided Nigel Tranter with material for some of the incidents portrayed in the first of his Bruce novels, *The Steps to the Empty Throne*. Richard Comyn's wife was grand-daughter and heiress of King Donald 'Ban,' deposed in 1079, and after Richard's death she married the Earl of Atholl, by whom she was maternal ancestor of Gillechattan, progenitor of Clan Chattan.

William, son of Richard, married Marjory, heiress of Fergus, the last Celtic Earl of Buchan, and obtained that title. Their son Alexander, was Constable of Scotland. Another Comyn became Earl of Menteith and yet another was Earl of Angus. John Comyn, Earl of Buchan, became one of the guardians of the realm in 1286, and his son, John, the 'Black' Comyn, was a competitor for the throne in 1291, claiming as a descendant of Donald 'Ban.' This greatly enhanced the claims of his son, the 'Red' Comyn, who was slain by Robert the Bruce in a Dumfries church in 1306. Bruce afterwards carried out a raid on the Buchan lands, greatly weakening the positioning of the Comyns. He gave the castle of Slains, together with the hereditary office of Constable, to Lord Hay of Errol. The office remains with a descendant today.

On the borders of Badenoch, a branch of the family became a clan. Their chiefs, the Cummings of Altyre, claim descent from Sir Robert, an uncle of the 'Red' Comyn. They received grants of land and became powerful in Moray. They had a long feud with Clan Mackintosh, mainly over disputed ownership of Rait Castle, in Strathnairn. A descendant, Alexander Cumming, became heir to Sir William Gordon of Gordonstoun, and assumed the name. He was created a baronet in 1804. The present representative is Sir William Gordon Cumming, 6th Bt., who resides at Altyre.

About the middle of the 15th century, some Cummings, for an unknown reason denied their family burial-place, changed their names to Farquharson, and the families of Balthog and Haughton were among their descendants. In the time of Gilbert Cummin of Glenchearnach, it is said that oppressed people from a neighbouring glen were baptised as his clansmen at a hen-trough, and afterwards known as 'Cummins of the hen-trough,' to distinguish them from those of the true blood. Other branches of the old family were the Cummings of Inverallochy, Logie, Auchry, Culter (Baronets, 1672), Dumphail, and Relugas. Sir William Cumming of Inverallochy was Lord Lyon, 1512-19. One James Cummyng was a herald painter, 1770, and became Lyon Clerk Depute. Of the Relugas family, Rev. Patrick Cumming (1695-1776), distinguished himself as Professor of Divinity at Edinburgh.

James William Hunter Cumming, RSA, RSW, who resides at Lennel, near Coldstream, is a distinguished modern artist. Formerly a lecturer in art at Edinburgh, but now retired, he has been the recipient of many awards. Ronald Patrick Cumming, who resides in Aberdeen, had a notable career in medicine, and was an Honorary President of the Shetland Fiddlers Society, 1975-85.

# DAVIDSON

Occasionally a non-Gaelic form of patronymic was adopted in the Highlands. Davidson ('son of David') is a good example. They came to form the *Clann Da'idh*, associated with the Clan Chattan, but their early history is obscure. According to tradition, the Davidsons of Invernahaven, in Badenoch, were originally a branch of the Comyns, but in a troublous period (perhaps in 1308 when Robert the Bruce defeated the Comyns at Inverness) attached themselves to Clan Chattan. Donald Dhu, the eponymous ancestor, is said to have married a daughter of Angus Mackintosh, 6th chief, and to have become a leading member of the confederation. The Davidsons were once powerful, but were involved in clan feuds which did nothing for their prosperity. Some historians believe they were involved in the famous clan battle on the North Inch at Perth in 1396, but this is uncertain. At any rate, their influence in the north diminished, and they are afterwards found in small scattered groups.

The Davidsons, who owned Tulloch, in Ross-shire, from 1762 to early in the present century, were considered to be of ancient stock. Their ancestor was Donald Davidson of Davidson, in Cromarty, whose son was Alexander, father of William, who married in 1719, Jean, daughter of Kenneth Bayne, nephew and heir of Duncan Bayne of Tulloch. Their son Henry Davidson, purchased Tulloch in 1762. Henry's brother and successor was Duncan Davidson, 1733-99, who was MP for Cromarty, 1790-96. His son Henry was succeeded in 1827 by his son, Duncan. As 'younger of Tulloch' he had been MP for Cromarty, 1826-30, and served again, 1831-32. He was married five times, and left eighteen children. Duncan was succeeded by his eldest son, Duncan Henry, 1836- 1889, whose son Duncan, 1865-1917, matriculated arms in 1906.

The Davidsons of Cantray, Inverness, descended from Sir David Davidson, born about 1788, only son of David Davidson and his wife Marie Cuthbert. This family appears to have ended with an heiress, Edith Mary Davidson of Cantray, born 1892. Another northern group, the Davidsons of Inchmarlo, Deeside, descended from John Davidson of Tillychetly, who died in 1802. His son Duncan, an advocate in Aberdeen, succeeded to Tillychetly, and purchased Inchmarlo. He was succeeded by his son Patrick, also an advocate in Aberdeen, father of Duncan, whose second son, Leslie, served in the Royal Field Artillery in World War I. The association of Davidson with Aberdeen was of long standing, and Robert filius David, or Davidson, Provost of Aberdeen, was killed at the Battle of Harlaw in 1411. There were Davidsons at Auchinhamper, Aberdeenshire, in the 15th century, and at Newton, Tillymorgan and Carnbogie. Alexander Davidson of Newton assumed the name and arms of Gordon of Gight, and this line ended in an heiress, the mother of Lord Byron.

Clearly there are other Davidson families in no way connected with those of the north. In Ayrshire, there were Davidsons in Drumley, Greenan and Pennyglen. Davidsons in Roxburghshire seem to have formed a small independent clan in the 16th and 17th centuries. The chief family was seated at Samieston, and became extinct on the death of James Davidson of that place, whose four nieces were his co-heirs in 1670. There was an influential Davidson family at Currie, Midlothian. From another family, many of whom were clergymen, and once owned the estate of Murieston, Edinburgh, descended the Most Rev. Randall Thomas Davidson, 1848-1930, Archbishop of Canterbury.

# DEWAR

In mediaeval times the person who had custody of the relic of a saint was called *deoradh*, a word whose original meaning was pilgrim or stranger, from the fact that such relics were taken to distant places to obtain divine intervention. In time the word became a surname, and is found in various forms: Dear, Dior, Deoir and finally Dewar. The Macindeors derive their name from a man who escorted the daughter of Walter Buchanan to Argyll to marry a Campbell of Ardkinglas. There being no others of his own surname there, he was called Deoir, meaning 'stranger,' and his offspring became Macindeors.

The Perthshire Dewars are of great interest, as five families, originally all in Glendochart, had custody of the relics of St. Fillan, who died 703. The five sacred relics were the pastoral staff, for which a bronze protective head was made in the Dark Ages, and during the Middle Ages the head was encased in silver and decorated; the bell, called the *Bearnan*; the arm bone; the *fearg*, probably a missal; and the *meser*, possibly a small font. Robert the Bruce, while a fugitive, prayed at the priory of Strathfillan, and attributed his revived fortunes to St. Fillan. Accordingly, on the eve of the great Battle of Bannockburn in 1314, the Abbot of Inchaffray brought the saint's armbone to the King's tent. Perhaps St. Fillan had a hand in the victory! The bell and the quigrich both have chequered histoires. In 1798, when the bell hung in the churchyard, it was stolen by an English tourist. It was found in Hertfordshire in 1869, and given to the Society of Antiquaries of Scotland. The quigrich was taken to Canada in 1818, when the custodian, Archibald Dewar, emigrated. It was inherited by his son Alexander, who was persuaded to deposit the relic with the Society of Antiquaries of Scotland. With the consent of his son

Archibald, the quigrich was returned to Scotland. Both relics are in the Royal Museum of Scotland.

Patrick Dewar in Cambuskenneth, whose descendant Peter, tacksman of the King's Park, Stirling, purchased the farm of Craigniven in 1834, was probably of Perthshire extraction. Peter married in 1827, Jean Chrystal, and had a large family, now represented by David Dewar of Broomhill, Kiambu, in Africa. Of this family is also Peter de Vere Beauclerk-Dewar, genealogist. Another Perthshire family is that associated with John Dewar & Sons, whisky distillers in Perth. John Dewar, born 1806, who married Jane Gow, had sons James, John Alexander, Charles Arthur and Thomas Robert. Thomas Robert was cr. Baron Dewar in 1917, but died unmarried in 1930, when the title became extinct. His brother John Alexander was cr. Baron Forteviot in 1917. John James Evelyn Dewar, is the 4th present baron.

The Lowland Dewars derive their name from a farm in Heriot parish, Mid Lothian. In 1296, Peres de Dewere and Thomas de Dewere, swore fealty to Edward I. Taking their name from the place, the family styled themselves 'of that Ilk.' The testament of James Dewar of that Ilk, parish of Heriot, is recorded in 1600, and in 1618, William Deware 'de eadem,' occupied part of Harper-rig, Mid Lothian. The Dewars of Vogrie descended from James Dewar, ?1672-1740, possibly son of James Dewar, farmer in Kippielaw. The direct line failed in 1975, and in 1989, Lt. Col. Malcolm Dewar, residing in Sussex, was recognised not only as Dewar of Vogrie, but as chief of the surname, or 'of that Ilk.' It is thought that the Dewars, formerly of Doles, Andover, Hampshire, descend from the same stock.

# THE BLACK DOUGLAS'S

The surname Douglas is writ large upon the pages of Scottish history. The first of whom any certain record has been found was William Douglas, who witnessed charters between 1174 and 1200. He held lands at Douglas (said to mean 'black water'), from which he took his surname. William was surely related to Freskin the Fleming, who came to Scotland before the end of the reign of David I, and was given lands at Strathbrock (West Lothian) and at Duffus (Moray). He may have been his brother in law, and the family may also have come from Flanders: perhaps connected with the house of Boulogne. His eldest son, Archibald, was given lands at Hermiston, in Lothian. He had two sons, William, his successor, who also had lands in England, and Sir Andrew, progenitor of the Earls of Morton. William was succeeded in turn by William *le Hardy*, Lord of Douglas, an adherant of Sir William Wallace. The next Lord of Douglas, was called the 'good Sir James,' and next to Robert Bruce was the greatest patriot of his time. He attended Bruce at his death, and promised to take his heart to the Holy Land, but was killed fighting at Theba, in Spain in 1330. His son William was killed in 1333, and he left a natural son, Archibald. Hugh Douglas, his uncle succeeded, and although a clergyman held estates in Douglasdale and in the Borders. His successor was a nephew, William, son of Archibald, and he became Earl of Douglas about 1358. The lord's son, William 2nd Earl, was killed at Otterburn in 1388, and the lands of 'the Black Douglases' passed to Sir Archibald 'The Grim,' natural son of 'The Good' Sir James. He was captured by the English at Poitiers in 1356, but escaped and survived until about 1400.

It was not only in Scotland and England that the Earls were renowned as warriors. Archibald's son, also

Archibald, 4th Earl, fought against the English in France for Charles VII, and was rewarded with the Duchy of Touraine. He died in battle and his grandsons were seized in Edinburgh and executed. The house of Douglas was becoming too powerful! After the death of the 5th and 6th Earls of Douglas, James, second son of Archibald 'The Grim' succeeded as 7th Earl. Misfortune struck in the time of his sons. William, 8th Earl, displeased King James II, who had a hand in his death at Stirling in 1452. The same monarch obtained the submission of his brother James, the 9th Earl, then spitefully raised a charge of treason against his family. He was taken prisoner, and died in virtual retirement at Lindores. The Douglas estates were forfeited about 1455 and the earldom extinguished.

The Earls of Morton descend from Andrew Douglas of Hermiston, son of Sir Archibald, Lord of Douglas. He was the ancestor of Sir William Douglas, the 'Knight of Liddesdale,' killed in 1353 by a kinsman. His brother John, who succeeded, was ancestor of the Douglases of Dalkeith, from whom descended James, 1st Earl of Morton (cr. 1458), and Henry, from whom came the Douglas family of Lochleven, ancestors of the later Earls. Of the Lochleven line was the heroine known as 'Kate-Bar-Lass' (actually she was Elizabeth), who in an attempt to prevent the murder of King James in 1436/37, barred a door with her arm. Sir William, of the same family, was the custodian of Mary, Queen of Scots, at Lochleven, and became the 5th Earl of Morton, in 1588. The 14th Earl obtained from George III the money to finance Capt. Cook's voyage of discovery, but died just before the *Endeavour* set sail in 1768. This historic family is still very much in existence, and is represented by John, 21st Earl, a director of Dalmahoy Farms.

# THE RED DOUGLAS'S

When the star of the Black Douglas's was waning, that of the Red Douglas's was waxing. George, a natural son of William, 1st Earl of Douglas, by his sister-in-law, Margaret, Countess of Mar and Angus, having succeeded to the estates of his mother, became Earl of Angus. He was taken prisoner by the English at Homildon Hill in 1402, and later died of the plague.

The 5th Earl, Archibald, occupies an interesting place in history as 'Bell-the-Cat.' Both nobles and commons had grievances against King James III, and an impasse having been reached, Archibald 'Belled the Cat' by seizing some of the king's favourites and putting them to death. Not surprisingly his relationship with the monarchy deteriorated. His castle of Tantallon was beseiged in 1491, and he was forced to give up Liddesdale and Hermitage. He retained Ewesdale and Eskdale, and later obtained the lordship of Crawford. Even at Flodden in 1513, he had a quarrel with James IV, and left the field, where two of his sons were killed. Another son, Gavin who became Bishop of Dunkeld in 1516, was a renowned Latin scholar and translated Vigil's *Aeneid*.

Archibald, 6th Earl, had care of the young King James V, and fought at Melrose and Linlithgow Bridge in 1525 to retain custody. He died about 1590, and was succeeded by his nephew, David, son of Sir George Douglas, who had married Elizabeth Douglas, heiress of Pittendreich. David was succeeded by his son Archibald, 1555-88, a peace-loving noble, who left no male issue and the title passed to William Douglas, a great-grand-son of the 1st Earl, by a decision of the Court of Session. His eldest son William became 11th Earl and his second son, James, became Lord Mordington (title dormant since 1791). William, 11th Earl, was cr. Marquess of

Douglas in 1633. He was twice married and left six sons, of whom Archibald succeeded as 2nd Marquess; James, became colonel of the Scots Guard in France; William, by marriage became Duke of Hamilton; George was cr. Earl of Dumbarton (extinct since 1749), and James, also in French service. The eldest son had been cr. Earl of Angus and Ormond, 1651, and his son James became the 2nd Marquess.

Archibald, 3rd Marquis, was a child when he succeeded his father, and at the age of nine Queen Anne conferred on him the titles of Duke of Douglas, Marquis of Angus, Earl of Angus and Abernethy, Viscount Jedburgh and Lord Douglas of Boncle. In 1707 he received a charter which erected the Douglas and Angus estates into a dukedom and regality, and confirmed the ancient honours. After his death in 1761, Archibald James, eldest son of Lady Jane Douglas, his sister, and Col. John Steuart of Grandtully, succeeded, but his right was contested, he and his twin brother Sholto Thomas, having been born in France when the mother was 50 years old. There were three separate actions; one on behalf of the young Duke of Hamilton as heir-male, another by Lord Douglas Hamilton on the basis of an entail; and the third by Sir Hew Dalrymple of North Berwick, as an heir of line. This was the celebrated *Douglas Cause*. The three actions were conjoined by the Court of Session and ended adversely for Archibald James Steuart. An appeal was made to the house of Lords, who finally found in his favour in 1779. Three of his sons became successively 2nd, 3rd and 4th Lords Douglas, but all died without issue, and the representation passed through a daughter to Cospatrick, 11th Earl of Home, cr. Baron Douglas (UK) in 1873.

Alexander Douglas-Home, 13th Earl, disclaimed his peerage in 1963 to become Prime Minister of Great Britain.

# DOUGLAS OF DRUMLANRIG

The Douglas's of Drumlanrig, Dumfriesshire, later Earls, Marquesses and Dukes, descend from William, 2nd Earl of Douglas, who was killed at Otterburn in 1388. He left a natural son, William, upon whom he had conferred the Barony of Drumlanrig and other lands. In 1412, he was deputed ambassador to England to negotiate the release of King James I, and the same year had a charter confirming to him the baronies of Drumlanrig, Hawick and Selkirk. He married Elizabeth, daughter of Sir Robert Stewart of Durrisdeer, and died fighting in France in 1427.

William Douglas, 3rd of Drumlanrig, was present at the seige of Roxburgh in 1640, when King James II was killed by the bursting of a cannon. He was killed in a conflict at Lochmaben in 1484, and succeeded by his son James, grandfather of Sir William Douglas, who was fatally injured at Flodden in 1513. His son, Sir James, 1498-1578, survived his eldest son, Sir William, and was succeeded by his grandson, Sir James, who added considerably to his estates. In 1602 he was aquitted of killing two men, when it was proved they were stealing sheep. They were actually hanged later! Sir William, Douglas, the eldest son, was cr. Viscount of Drumlanrig, 1628, and in 1633 promoted to Earl of Queensberry. His second son was Sir William of Kelhead. The eldest son, James, who succeeded, had four sons, of whom William succeeded, and James, was colonel of the Guards and became a Lt. General. He adhered to the Covenants. His brother William was promoted to Marquess of Queensberry, 1682, and in 1684 to Duke of Queensberry, with subsidiary titles. The eldest son, James, succeeded, and is known as the 'Union Duke,' having played a conspicuous part in bringing about the Union of the Parliaments in 1707. His services were rewarded by a pension of £3000 per year, and in 1708 he was cr. Duke of Dover. Doubtless he was in the mind of the poet Burns when he wrote *Such a parcel of rogues in a nation*. His third son, Charles, was the 3rd Duke, and was also cr. Earl of Solway in 1796. He outlived his sons, one of whom had been cr. Earl of March, and was succeeded by his great-grandson, William, Earl of March, and in right of his mother, Earl of Ruglen, by which titles he was known until he became 4th Duke of Queensberry. He was made Baron Douglas of Amesbury, Wiltshire, in 1786. When he died unmarried in 1810, the title Earl of Ruglen became extinct; the title of Duke of Queensberry and other honours passed by charter (1706) to the heir male of Jean, Duchess of Buccleuch; the title of Earl of March passed to the Earl of Wemyss, while the marquessate and earldom of Queensberry devolved on Sir William Douglas of Kelhead.

Sir James Douglas, Younger of Kelhead, 1639-1708, was cr. a baronet of Nova Scotia in 1668. It was his great-grandson, Sir Charles, 5th Bt., who continued the senior line of the family when he became 4th Duke of Queensberry, in 1810. In 1821 he was made a Knight of the Thistle and in 1833, cr. a peer of the UK by the title of Baron Solway of Kinmount. The 9th Marquess and 8th Bt., John Sholto Douglas, a representative peer, is remembered as the originator of the famous 'Queensberry Rules,' which govern pugilistic contests. The present representative is Sir David Harrington Angus Douglas, who is 12th Marquess of Douglas, Earl of Queensberry, Viscount Drumlanrig, Lord Douglas of Hawick and Tibbers, and the 11th Bt. He is Professor of Ceramics at the Royal College of Arts. The heir is his elder son by his second marriage, Sholto Douglas.

# DRUMMOND

According to ancient family tradition, Maurice, ancestor of the Drummonds who became earls of Perth, came to Scotland from Hungary in 1057 with the Anglo-Saxon exiles, who included Princess Margaret, who married Malcolm, King of Scots. Traditions must be treated with some reserve, but considering that the Leslies and Livingstons have the same tradition, the essential part of the story can scarcely be doubted, and all of them received lands. However, since Hungary is landlocked, the party probably sailed from northern Europe. Probably they resided for a time in Flanders, and married into Flemish families. The Drummond arms, Or, three bars wavy Gules, indicate some link with the great Flemish family Oudenarde, cadets of Petegem and peers in their own right. The descendants of Maurice took their name from the lands of Dromyn or Drymen, in Stirlingshire. Maurice had a son, Malcolm Beg, who left two sons, Malcolm, who succeeded, and John, who left no male issue. Malcolm had two sons, Gilbert, probably killed at Dupplin in 1332, and Malcolm who succeeded. He appears on record as 'Malcomo de Drummond,' and had two sons, John, who succeeded, and Maurice, coroner of the earldom of Lennox. He had also a daughter Margaret, who, as widow of John Logie, became the mistress, then consort of David II, King of Scots. After this alliance the Drummonds had further grants of land. John, the heir, is styled 'of Concraig,' and he had two sons, Malcolm, who had a licence from his brother-in-law, the king, to build a fortalice on the lands of Kyndrocht or Braemar; and Sir John, who succeeded his brother. John also had a daughter, Annabella, who married John Stewart of Kyle, who became King of Scots, assuming the forename of Robert.

Sir John Drummond's great-grandson, Sir John, of Cargill and Stobhall, was cr. a Lord of Parliament about 1488. He was forfeited and imprisoned for striking the Lord Lyon of the time, but was later pardoned and restored to his lands. James, 4th Lord Drummond, was cr. Earl of Perth about 1605. The 4th Earl, also James, was one of the twenty-four proprietors of New Jersey, and encouraged emigration to that colony. He followed the fortunes of James VII, who cr. him Duke of Perth. He died in 1716. James his son, 2nd titular Duke, married Lady Jane Gordon. His elder son, James, 3rd titular Duke, commanded the right wing of the Jacobite army at Culloden in 1746, and was wounded. On the death of the 6th titular Duke, the direct line expired, and the representation of the earldom passed to his kinsman James 10th Earl, whose son James, 11th Earl, was succeeded by his cousin, James Lewis, 4th Duc de Melfort. This line expired in 1902, when the succession opened to William, 11th Viscount Strathallan descended from James Drummond, cr. Lord Maderty in 1610, second son of the 4th Lord Drummond. The 4th Lord Maderty was cr. Viscount Strathallan in 1686. His brother Eric succeeded as 16th Earl of Perth. He was the first secretary of the League of Nations. His son John David, is 17th Earl, and has his seat at Stobhill, Perth. The heir is his eldest son, John Eric, Viscount Strathallan.

Among the principal branches are Drummond of Hawthornden, Mid Lothian, and Drummond of Blair Drummond, represented by the Home-Drummonds. The Hawthornden line is descended from the Drummonds of Carnock, and produced the distinguished historian, poet and inventor, William Drummond, 1585-1649. He lamented the death of Prince Henry in *Tears on the death of Meliades*, in 1613, and wrote a *History of Scotland* (1423-1524). The family representation devolved on Sir James Williams-Drummond, who died in 1980.

# DUNLOP

The well-known Ayrshire surname of Dunlop derives from the lands of that name in the district of Cunningham. The property of Dunlop Place was possessed by the de Morvilles, but it is not known when it passed to the ancestors of the Dunlop family. In 1260, Willelmus de Dunlop is recorded as a witness to an indenture between Godfrey de Ross – possibly the previous heritor – and the burgesses of Irvine. Neel fiz Robert de Dullop, Ayrshire, appears on the Ragman Roll in 1296, and he appears in an inquest held at Berwick on the lands of Lady Elena la Zouch in Conyngham. The property of Dunlop seems to have been alienated from them around 1300, probably on account of their support for John Baliol, but by the middle of the 14th century they had been restored to the estate, and James de Dunlop appears on record. Alexander, probably his grandson, was the first to use the style of that Ilk.' Constantyn Dunlop of that Ilk, probably son of John is mentioned in 1483 and 1496. He died in 1505, leaving a daughter Janet, who married James Stewart, Sheriff of Bute, grandson of Robert II. Constantine was succeeded by his brother Alexander, whose nephew, John Dunlop, had sasine of the lands in 1507. He married Marion Douglas, and died in 1509.

Alexander Dunlop, XIIth of that Ilk, was in 1558 accused of killing his son Alexander. In happier times, James Dunlop of Dunlop was a supporter of the Presbyterian cause, and to secure his estate from forfeiture he executed a deed of resignation in favour of his next brother, John of Garnkirk. John took possession of the estate, but resigned it in favour of his nephew James, son of his brother. James, who married Elizabeth Cunningham, also supported the Presbyterian cause, and about 1667 made over part of his estate to the Earl of Dundonald. He was imprisoned from 1645 to 1667, when he signed a bond to keep the peace. His son Alexander, XVIth laird, also suffered in the Presbyterian cause, and did not recover the lands made over to the Earl of Dundonald. He married Antonia, daugher of John Brown of Fordell, and emigrated to South Carolina in 1684, having made over his estate to his son John, who died unmarried. His brother, Lt.Col. Francis Dunlop succeeded, and when he died in 1748, was succeeded by his son John, whose wife, Frances Ann Wallace, was a friend and correspondent of the poet Burns. Their second son, Thomas, succeeded his maternal grandfather as 6th Bt. of Craigie (cr. 1669). His younger brothers, Andrew and James, succeeded in turn to Dunlop, and another brother, John, succeeded his nephew James as XXIVth laird in 1858. His nephew, John, XXIInd laird, was cr. a baronet (UK) in 1838, but the dignity was lost when his son James died unmarried in 1858. The estate was sold by the Trustees to Thomas Dunlop (Douglas), a merchant in Glasgow, whose son Thomas was cr. a baronet (UK) in 1916. The 3rd Bt. is Sir Thomas Dunlop, who resided at The Corrie, Kilmacolm, Renfrewshire. Robert Wallace Dunlop, grandson of John, XXIVth of Dunlop, married Elizabeth Sandwith, and their eldest surviving son, Keith Wallace Dunlop, born 1862, emigrated to the USA, and became a naturalised citizen.

The Dunlops, formerly of Lockerbie House, claim descent from Constantine, third son of John Dunlop, IXth of the Ilk. The Dunlops of Garnkirk are well documented. Those of Househill descended from Thomas, a younger son of James, XIIth laird. The Doonside family descend from Magdalen, daughter of Francis, XVIIIth Laird, who married Robert Dunlop, RN. Their son David married the MacGregor heiress of Clober, in Stirlingshire.

# ERSKINE, EARLS OF MAR AND BARONS GARIOCH

The ancient mormaers of Mar appear to have been of Pictish origin, and they became the premier earls of Scotland. By 1014, the dignity passed to a scion of the Norse race of Ivar, and it descended to Thomas, 9th Earl of Mar and Lord of Garioch. His eventual heiress, Isabella, Countess of Mar, married as her second husband, Alexander Stewart, a natural son of the 'Wolf of Badenoch.' In 1404 she gave him the Earldom in liferent, and after her death in 1408, he resigned the earldom to the Crown. He fought against the Lord of the Isles at Harlaw in 1411, and although possessing only a liferent, received in 1426 a re-grant of the earldom. The Earl died in 1435, and was succeeded by the heir of his late Countess, Robert, 1st Lord Erskine. His surname of Erskine was territorial, and derived from the barony of Erskine, in Renfrewhsire. The family may have originated in Flanders: descended from a younger son of Gilbert de Ghent. Mrs Platts has commented on the similarity of their arms.

Robert's right to the honours was recognised in 1395, and he was served heir to half of the earldom. He was later divested on the grounds that the earldom had passed to the Crown as *ultimus haeres* of the Countess Isabella, and the title was borne by various members of the Royal Family between 1459 and 1562. Parts of the lands were alienated. The Court of Session, in 1626, described the grant of 1426 as a pretended provision of tailzie, and ruled that the Crown had no right to the earldom. By his first wife, Janet Keith, Robert left two sons, Thomas, his heir, and Nicol (some say Malcolm) of Kinnoul.

John Erskine, *de jure* 18th Earl of Mar and 11th Lord Garioch, was high in favour with Mary, Queen of Scots, who entrusted him with the care of her son Prince James. In 1565, he received a charter restoring him *per modum justitae*, as Earl of Mar, with destination to heirs-general. His captaincy of Stirling Castle was destined to heirs-male. The charter was ratified by Parliament in 1567. John, 23rd Earl and 16th Lord Garioch was forfeited in 1716 for his part in the Jacobite Rising, but his grandson, John Francis Erskine was restored by Parliament, in 1824 as 24th Earl and 17th Baron Garrioch. John Francis Miller Erskine, 1795-1866, 26th Earl and 19th Baron Garioch, proved his claim to the Earldom of Kellie in 1835, on failure of the male line of the 1st Earl, Alexander, second son of John, 4th Lord Erskine, descended from Sir Robert Erskine, 13th Earl of Mar. When he died without issue in 1866, the earldom of Kellie passed to his cousin and heir male, Walter Coningsby Erskine, and the earldom of Mar devolved on his nephew and heir-general, John Francis Goodeve Erskine. Walter Coningsby, an army officer, claimed the Earldom of Mar, as cr. in 1565, but died before the Lords decided the case. His son, Walter Henry was allowed the honours in 1875, and thus became the 11th Earl of Mar and 13th of Kellie. The ancient earldom was carried on by his nephew, John Francis Goodeve Erskine, and his son, John Francis Hamilton Erskine has been numbered as 28th of Mar and 21st Baron Garioch. The 30th Earl and 23rd Baron was James Clifton, of Mar, whose son David died unmarried in 1967. His sister Margaret became Countess of Mar and Lady Garioch in her own right. She married in 1959, Edwin Noel of Mar (recognised in the surname by warrant of the Lord Lyon), son of Edwin Artiss, but they were divorced in 1976. There is one daughter of the marriage, Lady Susan Helen, Mistress of Mar. The Countess maintains a private officer of arms, called Garioch Pursuivant.

# ERSKINE, EARLS OF MAR AND KELLIE

The Erskine succession to the Earldom of Mar and lordship of Garioch is best understood by grasping details relating to Gratney, 7th Earl. He married Christian, sister of King Robert the Bruce, and besides Donald, his heir, had a daughter Christian. She married as her second husband, Sir Robert Erskine of that Ilk, by whom she had a daughter Janet, who married Sir David Barclay of Brechin, who died about 1368. Janet married secondly, Sir Thomas Erskine, son of the above Sir Robert, by his first wife, Beatrix Lindsay. They had two sons, Robert, who succeeded Alexander Stewart as the 13th Earl, and John ancestor of the Erskines of Dun and Pittodrie. The barony of Dun descended through the male line to John Erskine, who married in 1770 Mary Baird of Newbyth. Their co-heiress, Margaret, married Archibald Kennedy, 12th Earl of Cassilis, and from them came the Kennedy-Erskines.

Robert Erskine became a Lord of Parliament. The Erskines stoutly asserted their claim to the Earldom of Mar, but the succeeding 14th, 15th , 16th and 17th Earls can only be described as *de jure*. John, 5th Lord Erskine *de jure* 17th Earl, married Margaret, daughter of Archibald, 2nd Earl of Argyll, and had, with other issue, John, the heir, and Alexander, father of the 1st Earl of Kellie. John, who would be *de jure* 18th Earl, was high in favour with the Queen of Scots, and Mary entrusted him with the care of her son James. In 1565, she granted him the earldom of Mar, with its seat at Alloa. His heir, John, 2nd Earl (numbering from 1565) and 7th Lord Erskine, had by his first a son John, 3rd Earl, and by a second had issue, of whom James was ancestor of the Earls of Buchan; Henry was progenitor of the Lords of Cardross, and Charles was the ancestor of the Erskines of Alva, now St. Clair-Erskines, Earls of Rosslyn. Alexander Erskine, son of John, 4th Lord Erskine, was the father of Thomas, cr. Earl of Kellie in 1619. Alexander, 5th Earl of Kellie was involved in the Jacobite Rising of 1745. On the death of Methven, 10th Earl, he was succeeded by his distant kinsman, John Francis Miller Erskine, 9th Earl of Mar, who thus became also 11th Earl of Kellie. He was succeeded in the earldom of Kellie by his cousin, Walter Coningsby Erskine, who claimed the earldom of Mar (cr. 1665), allowed to his son Walter Henry in 1875. John Francis Erskine, 13th Earl of Mar and 15th of Kellie, is the present holder of the titles, and Hereditary Keeper of Stirling Castle.

James Erskine, son of the 7th Earl of Mar by his second wife, married Mary, only child of James Douglas, 6th Earl of Buchan, and had a son James who succeeded as 8th Earl of Buchan. His son William, 9th Earl, never married. Henry, another son of the 7th Earl of Mar, had a son who succeeded to the Lordship of Cardrose, conferred on his grandfather in 1610. His son Henry, 3rd Lord Cardross, was half-brother of John of Carnock, father of the jurist, Professor John Erskine, author of standard text books. Henry was succeeded in turn by his son David, 4th Lord Cardross, who succeeded to the Earldom of Buchan on the death of William, his father's second cousin. David Stewart Erskine, 11th Earl of Buchan, founded the Society of Antiquaries of Scotland in 1780. His brother, Henry of Almondell, was the famous legal wit who coined the phrase for the snuff-maker's carriage: 'Wha wad hae thocht it, that noses had bocht it.' He was the father of the 12th Earl. From him also descend the Barons Erskine of Restormel Castle, Cornwall. The 16th Earl of Buchan, Donald Cardross Flowers Erskine, is also Lord Auchterhouse, Lord Cardross, and 7th Baron Erskine (cr. 1806).

# FALCONER

The surname Falconer derives from the office of falconer: one who breeds or trains falcons and hawks for sport. Falconers appear in Kincardineshire during the reign of William the Lyon, 1165-1214. Matheus the Falconer, witnessed a charter about 1202, and about the same time, William the Falconer granted land to the Abbey of Arbroath. In the vernacular he may have been called 'the hawker.' While his descendants took Falconer as a surname, the family home was Halkerton. About 1211, Ranulf the Falconer, son of Walter of Loutrop, had a grant of lands in the Mearns (Kincardineshire), including Balemacoy (?Balmekellie) and Lacherachgeich Kennie (which may have become Halkerton). Gervase the Falconer was taken prisoner at Dunbar in 1296 and was still in an English prison in 1207. A contemporary Robert le Fauconer de Kyncardyn, rendered homage to Edward I. at Aberdeen in 1296. His seal shows a falcon striking a small bird. The arms of the Falconers and their cadets have undergone many changes, but the falcon has always been the dominant charge. Subsequent Falconers were styled of Lethens, then of Halkerton. David of Halkerton was one of a jury in an inquisition in 1448, and his grandson, Sir Alexander, was ancestor of the Falconers of Innerlochtie, Kincorth, Dinduff and Phesdo.

In 1646, Sir Alexander Falconer, 1594-1671, was cr. Lord Falconer of Halkerton. His brother, Sir David of Glenfarquhar, had a son Alexander, cr. a baronet, and his son, Sir Alexander, 2nd Bt., succeeded as 4th Lord Falconer in 1724, but died without issue in 1727, when the baronetcy became extinct. His cousin David, a Lord of Session, succeeded as 5th Lord Falconer. Another brother of the 1st Lord was Sir John of Balmakellie, Master of the Minthouse. By his first wife, Sybil Ogilvy, he had a son David, an Edinburgh merchant and

Quaker, whose son Gilbert, 1686-1736, emigrated to Maryland. By a second wife, Esther Briot, he had further issue, including Sir John, 1636-86, Warden of the Mint. Sir David of Halkerton married in 1703, Catherine, daughter of William (Keith), 2nd Earl of Kintore, and their grandson, Anthony Adrian Falconer, 8th Lord Falconer, inherited the Kintore Peerage in 1778.

The two peerages continued in the family until the death in 1966, without issue, of Arthur George, 10th Earl of Kintore and 13th Lord Falconer of Halkerton. The Scottish title of Lord Falconer of Halkerton then became dormant, and the earldom passed to his sister, Ethel Sydney. She married John Lawrence Baird, cr. Viscount Stonehaven, 1925. He was a son of Sir Alexander Baird, cr. 1st Baronet of Urie in 1897. Their son, James Ian, succeeded as 12th Earl in 1974. He married in 1935, Delia, daughter of William Loyd and the Hon. Bettine Knatchbull-Hugessen. She is the present Countess of Kintore, and her son, Sir Michael, is the 13th Earl of Kintore. He assumed the surname Keith in lieu of Baird, and succeeded to the Viscountcy of Stonehaven and also through his maternal grandfather, the baronetcy of Urie (cr. 1897).

There are Falconers in many parts of the world who are of Scottish descent, and a few of them may have a claim to the dormant Scots title of Falconer of Halkerton. The matter would not be easily resolved. An English architect, Peter Serrel Falconer, has long styled himself the heir presumptive, claiming descent from Patrick of Newton, a younger son of Alexander Falconer of Halkerton, who died in 1595.

# FARQUHARSON

Clan Farquharson derives from Farquhar, fourth son of Alexander *Ciar* Shaw of Rothiemurchus, a branch of Clan Chattan. The family took up residence in Aberdeenshire, and eventually assumed the surname of Farquharson. A descendant, Donald, married Isobel Stewart, heiress of Invercault. Their son was the famous Findla Mor, 1st of Invercauld, who was killed at Pinkie in 1547, bearing the royal standard. After him the Farquharsons are known as *Clann Fhionnlaidh*. He was succeeded by Robert, son of his first marriage with Beatrix Garden. From them also descend the Farquharsons of Whitehouse, represented by Capt. Colin Farquharson, Lord Lieutenant of Aberdeenshire. Robert's grandson, Alexander, married Isabella, daughter of William Mackintosh of that Ilk, and died in 1681. His second son, John of Invercauld, joined the Clan Chattan regiment in 1715, and was taken prisoner at Preston, where he remained for ten months. John was married four times, and by his third wife, Margaret Murray, of the Atholl family, had with other issue, James of Invercauld, and Anne, who married William Mackintosh, XXIst of that Ilk, who held a commission under King George. Lady Anne, only 20 years old, raised the Clan Chattan regiment in 1745 for the Young Pretender.

James Farquharson died in 1750, and was succeeded by his son James, a captain in the Hanovarian army in 1745. The clan had fought under the Clan Chattan banner in 1715, but in 1745, James of Inverauld and his son, Capt. James, were on the side of the Government. At Culloden, the Farquharsons were led by Francis Farquharson of Monaltrie, who mustered 300 men. Capt. James Farquharson died in 1806, and was succeeded by his surviving daughter Catherine, who married in 1798, Capt. James Ross, RN (second son of John Lockhart

Ross of Balnagown), who assumed the surname of Farquharson, and died in 1810. Their grandson, James Ross Farquharson, XIIIth laird, died in 1888, and his son Alexander Haldane Farquharson, became chief of the clan. On his death, the crest, arms and supporters were, by decree of Lyon Court, 1936, confirmed to his daughter Myrtle. Her nephew, Capt. Alwyn Farquharson, was recognised as chief in 1949.

The 'stem family' produced many branches, among them Monaltrie, Whitehouse, Haughton, Allargue, Breda and Finzean. The Farquharsons of Inverey were a celebrated Jacobite branch, of whom, the 'Black Colonel,' John, of Inverey, lives on in Deeside legends and ballads. His eldest son by his first wife, Margaret Gordon, was Peter or Patrick, was appointed in 1715 by Lord Mar, to raise Farquharson vassals, and was made Colonel of Mar's Regiment. He narrowly escaped forfeiture, and died in 1737. Charles Farquharson, his full brother, also took part in the '15, as did James, their half brother, and Charles of Balmoral, their uncle. The Whitehouse branch and others were also Jacobites. Many Farquharsons rose also for Prince Charles in 1745, including Donald of Auchriachan; Francis of Monaltrie (who afterwards became a model landlord); Gregor of Tombae and his son Cosmo; James of Balmoral; John of Allargue; Lewis, farmer in Tarland; Robert in Tullich, Glenmuick, and William, of the Auchindryne family.

The Finzean branch of the clan produced the celebrated artist, Joseph Farquharson, 1845-1935, RA, born at Edinburgh. He was taught by Peter Graham and painted many Highland landscapes. This family is now represented by Angus Durie Miller Farquharson, of Finzean House, Finzean, Aberdeenshire.

# FERGUSON/FERGUSSON

It is very unlikely that all Fergusons or Fergussons descend from a common ancestor. The name appears in various parts of Scotland from the 12th century onwards. The Gaelic form was MacFhearghuis, which became Englished as Fergus-son, but corrupt forms such as Mackerras and MacHerries appear. Fergushill was an old variant. Sometimes the suffix 'son' was dropped, to give Fergus, Fergie, Ferrie and Ferries. According to tradition the West Highland Fergusons descend from Fergus MacErc, King of Dalriada in 1503. Possibly some in the south-west take their name from Fergus, Lord of Galloway, who died in 1161.

The Fergusons of Craigdarroch, Dumfriesshire, appear on record during the reign of David II, 1329- 71. Several members of this family were MPs before and after the Union of 1707. Two 18th-Century members have achieved fame in verse. Anna, died 1764, daughter of Sir Robert Laurie of Maxwellton, and wife of Alexander Ferguson of Craigdarroch, is the heroine of Lady John Scott's famous song, '*Annie Laurie.*' Her grandson, another Alexander Ferguson, a Dumfries lawyer, was the winner of the contest which gave rise to Robert Burns's racy ballad, '*The Whistle.*' The line ended with an heiress, Ella Ferguson, who married in 1918, Col. Wallace Smith Cuninghame of Caprington. Cadets of the Craigdarroch line probably include the Fergussons of Spittalhaugh, Peeblesshire. Sir William Fergusson, 1808-77, 1st Bt., cr. 1866 (UK), was son of James Fergusson, Lochmaben, and Elizabeth Hodge.

From the banks of the Tummel to Strathardle and Glenshee, the Fergussons of Dunfallandy, with their numerous cadets, were influential. They first appear in the late 15th century, styled 'of Derculich,' but must have obtained Dunfallandy, Logierait, by 1620. Various lairds were styled barons, but unofficially. The cadet branch of Baledmund, descends from Finlay Fergusson, on record about 1602, and Grizel Bruce. A later Finlay of this line was tried for treason after the '15 Jacobite rising, and acquitted. He seems also to have been involved in the '45.

In Strathyre and Balquhidder, the Fergusons were numerous, but not landed proprietors. Like their neighbours the MacGregors, they were frequently in trouble with the authorities. Duncan Ferguson and several others in Strathyre, were accused in 1612 of killing deer in the Forest of Glenfinglas, and put to the horn. On Lochearnside, there was a dynasty of Ferguson masons. In the Cowal and Kintyre districts of Argyll, the name Fergusson is ancient and often recorded as McKerras. At Glenshellish, near the head of Loch Eck, a family of Fergussons held lands for over 200 years. The last of the family to possess the lands was Daniel, who sold the farm in 1803. In Fife and Angus, Fergusons have had a long association. From one family long resident in Inverkeithing, descends the Munro-Fergusons of Raith, who have produced soldiers and statesmen. The Fergussons of Kilkerran, in Ayrshire, appear as a landed family in 1464, and may be descended from John, son of Fergus who witnessed a charter about 1315. John Ferguson of Kilkerran was cr. a baronet (UK) in 1703, and his successors came to be recognised as chiefs of the surname. Sir Adam, 3rd Bt., is referred to as 'aith-detesting' by the poet Burns in *The Author's Earnest Cry and Prayer.*' The 7th Bt., Sir Charles, was a high ranked soldier for nearly 40 years, and was Governor of New Zealand, 1924-30. His son, Sir James, 1904-73, 8th Bt., was Keeper of the Records of Scotland, 1940-44.

# FLEMING

Countless lives have been saved by 'a triumph of accident and shrewd observation' by a Scottish physician and bacteriologist named Alexander Fleming, 1881-1955. The son of an Ayrshire farmer, he studied at the medical school of St. Mary's Hospital, London, and at London University. After a brilliant student career, he worked under Sir Anwoth Wright, pioneer in vaccine therapy. During World War I he served as a captain in RAMC, and was mentioned in despatches. As professor in the Royal College of Surgeons he continued research on anti-bacterial substances and his first reward was the discovery of the anti-biotic lysozyme. The 'accident' was some mould having been allowed to develop on a plate where bacteria were being cultured. The 'observation' was that the mould was so destructive of the bacteria that even when diluted hundreds of times, it still destroyed them. Fleming's epoch-making discovery of the mould from which penicillin is made brought him numerous honours. He was knighted in 1944 and was awarded the Nobel Prize for medicine jointly with Sir Howard (later Lord) Florey and (Sir) E.B. Chain in 1945.

The surname Fleming sufficiently denotes the nationality of the people who bore it in Scotland in the 12th century. The earliest Fleming of note was Baldwin of Biggar, Sheriff of Lanark, who had grant of land and was a powerful baron around 1160 x 1170. He seems to have come from Bratton, in Devonshire, and his forebear was Stephen Flandrensis, a Latinised form of the name. Several others who came to Scotland may have been related. A family of Flemings lived in Boghall Castle, Biggar. Theobald the Fleming held land on Douglas Water, and Jordan Fleming was taken prisoner at Alnwick in 1174, along with King William the Lion.

Robert Fleming, ancestor of the Earls of Wigtown, rendered fealty in 1296, and his son, Malcolm of Fulwood and Cumbernauld, was granted lands in Wigtownshire, with the title of Earl of Wigtown, in 1341. His grandson, Thomas, 2nd Earl, sold his whole rights to Archibald Douglas, Earl of Galloway, in 1372, and certain of his lands were granted to Sir James Lyndsay. The title was also lost. His lands at Lenzie devolved on his cousin, Sir Malcolm Fleming, sheriff of Dumbarton. A descendant, Sir Robert of Cumbernauld and Biggar, was created a Lord of Parliament about 1452. Malcolm, 3rd Lord Fleming, who fell at Pinkie in 1547, was father of Mary, one of 'the four Maries,' who tended Mary, Queen of Scots. John, the 6th Lord, was advanced to the dignity of Earl of Wigtown, Lord Fleming and Cumbernauld, in 1606. His eldest son, was granted lands in Peeblesshire. John, 6th Earl, died without male issue. His estates of Cumbernauld and Biggar were inherited by his daughter Clementina, and the title devolved on his brother Charles, who died in 1747, since when the honour has been dormant. Clementina married Charles, Lord Elphinstone. Her grandson, Charles, heir to her lands, became an Admiral and assumed the surname Fleming. He was the father of John, 14th Lord Elphinstone.

Another link with the Elphinstone family is found in the marriage of Marjory, only daughter of Sir Gilbert Fleming of Ferme, who married James, Master of Elphinstone, and died without issue in 1784. Archibald Fleming of Ferme, was cr. a baronet of Nova Scotia in 1661. Another old Fleming family was seated at Auchintoul, in Banffshire. Patrick, of this family is credited with having been the finest swordsman in the Jacobite army of 1745.

# FLETT

An Orcadian of the 12th century appears in the *Orkneyinga Saga* as Thorkel *flettir*. The nickname may be connected with Old norse fletta, 'to fla' or 'to rob,' and with Nyorsk *fletta*, 'an active, eager fellow.' There was a Dane of the same period called Haraldr Flettir in 'Heimskringla,' and one or two Norwegians had the same name. Throkell *Flettir* was a farmer on the island of Westray, Orkney, and the saga tells us he was "quarrelsome and overbearing."

The Fletts were among the chief landed families in Orkney in the later Norse period, and the surname had clearly become stabilised by the 15th century. Kolbein Flett was one of those who laid charges against David Meyner of Weem in 1427. The name of Ioni Blatto, one of the prominent men of that time, is thought to be a mispelling of Flett. Mawnus Flett is recorded at Kirkwall in 1480, and Jhone Fleytt of Hare was a member of an assize there in 1509. William Flett of Howbister is mentioned in 1516, and George Flett, husbandman in the parish of Orphir, was retoured heir of Robert Flett, merchant in the town of Kirkwall in 1665.

A number of Fletts appear in the *Orkney Register of Testaments*. John Sklaitter in Arquyle, parish of Rendall, died in December, 1592, and Mareoun Flett his widow is mentioned along with his son Johnne, executor. Margaret Flett, widow of Nicoll Lesk, who died in 1605 in Grindwater, in Orphir parish, acted for their children, Andro, Alexander, Katherin and Barbara. William Flet in Clouk in Costa, parish of Evie, died in 1609, survived by his widow, Elizabeth Houstoun and daughters Mareoun and Christiane. Jasper Flett in Howbister is mentioned in 1607 and 1612. Hutcheon Flett is recorded in 1613, also Alexander Flett. Another Alexander, in Sabay, St. Andrews parish is mentioned as a debtor in 1614.

There is a place-name Flett in Shetland, from *flotr*, a strip of land, and the surname itself appears in the Shetlands. It is one of the most prolific in the Orkney Islands today, and has been especially associated with the tunship of Netherbrough, in Harray parish. It appears in New Zealand and in the USA, where the spelling Flatt is recorded. Numerous Orcadians were employed in Canada with the Hudson's Bay Company. Among them was William Flett, who went out in 1782 and became a canoe builder and buffalo hunter. George Flett (1775-1850), from Firth parish, arrived at York factory in 1796, and was a labourer-boatmen. He retired to the Red River settlement in 1823, and married Peggy, half-breed daughter of James Peter Whitford. Another Flett, Thomas, from Harray, was an interpreter and post master at Fort Colville, 1838-53. James Flett (1824-99), from Rousay, was a fisherman and canoeman in the Mackenzie River district. After a spell as a clerk in the Athabasca district he retired on a pension to Edmonton.

Sir John Smith Flett (1869-1947), Director of the Geological Survey of Great Britain and of the Museum of Practical Geology, was a distinguished Orcadian who received much recognition. Ian Stark Flett, an Aberdonian, now retired and residing in Kirkcaldy, after serving in the Signals and Intelligence Branch of the RAF, became a leading figure in the field of education in various parts of Britain. Iain Flett, of the Dundee District Archives, is one of Scotland's best-known record-keepers, lecturing and writing on associated matters.

The Rev. William Nugent Flett, a clergyman in New Zealand is undoubtedly of Scottish ancestry. His talented wife, Ethel Snelson Flett, is the author of a number of books, including *New Zealand Inheritance* (1957) and *The Essie Summers Story* (1974). She has contributed to several newspapers and periodicals, including *The Scots Magazine*.

# FORBES

The surname Forbes is derived from the lands of Forbes, Donside, Aberdeenshire, and comes from the Gaelic *forba*, a field or tract of ground, with the place-name suffix *ais*, probably Pictish. Duncan de Forboys, who rendered homage in 1296, was probably a Forbes. Another John appears in an English roll of 1306, and a third was *dominus ejusden* in 1358. Sir John de Forbes, justiciary of Aberdeenshire, 1394, was father of Sir Alexander, 1st Lord Forbes (1445), and of Sir William, progenitor of the Pitsligo branch of the family. Over the next three centuries the Forbes family had disputes with the Gordons. James, 2nd Lord Forbes, was permitted to fortify the tower of Drymynour, commonly called Forbes, and in 1467, the 3rd Lord, 'Grey Willie,' entered into a mutual bond with the heads of the cadet houses of Pitsligo, Tolquhoun and Brux, and Duncan Macintosh, Captain of Clan Chattan, for defence and protection against all but the king and their respective superiors.

William, 7th Lord Forbes, was faithful to Mary, Queen of Scots, and in 1573 had a charter of the lands of Corsindae. He married Elizabeth, the daughter of Margaret, Countess of Marischal, and Sir William Keith of Inverugie. One of their daughters, Christian, married George Johnston of Caskieben, and was mother of Arthur Johnston, 1587-1641, the famous physician and Latin poet. William Forbes, 1570-1606, would have been 9th Lord, but entered the Capuchin monastery at Ghent in 1589 as 'Brother Archangel.' His brother John was also partial to the monastic life, and when he died in 1606, was succeeded by his half-brother, Arthur, 10th Lord. His son, Alexander, soldiered under Gustav Adolph of Sweden, becoming a Lt. General. The 13th Lord was a supporter of the Treaty of Union, 1707. James Ochoncar, 17th Lord, had a distinguished military career, and for some years commanded the forces in Ireland. One of his daughters, Charlotte, married Sir John Forbes of Craigievar, father of William, Lord Semple. Walter, his eldest surviving son, was also a soldier, and at Waterloo commanded a company of the Coldstream Guards in the defence of Hougoumont. Atholl Laurence Cunyngham, 21st Baron, served as a major in the Grenadier Guards during World War I. His son, the 22nd Lord Forbes, Sir Nigel Ivan, was a major in the same regiment World War II. He was Minister of State at the Scottish Office, 1958-59, and is chief of the clan.

During the Jacobite Risings several Forbes men distinguished themselves. Robert Forbes, 1708-1775, Rector of the Episcopal Chapel at Leith, recorded the main events of the '45, and his collection of material was printed by the Scottish History Society, in 3 volumes, 1895-96, under the title of *The Lyon in the Mourning*. Alexander, 4th Lord Pitsligo, escaped attainder for taking part in the '15 Rising, and in 1745 became a hunted rebel for raising a troop of horses for Prince Charles. His estates were forfeited, and the title has remained under attainder. The male heirs are probably the Forbes family of Newe, Aberdeenshire, baronets. Sir John Stewart Forbes, 6th Bt., died in 1984. The most distinguished Forbes of the Jacobite period was Duncan of Culloden, President of the Court of Session. The 1st Bt., (NS, 1630) of Craigievar, Sir William, built the outstanding castle there, now in the care of the National Trust for Scotland. The baronetcy of Monymusk (cr. NS, 1626), was conferred on Sir William Forbes. This family is now represented by Sir William Stuart-Forbes, 13th Bt., who resides in New Zealand.

# FRASER

Volumes have been written about the Frasers, and more could be added, along with notes on their interesting heraldry and the numerous titles held. They may have come from France into England after the Norman Conquest, and from the Seigneurie of Freseliere, in Anjou. The Seigneurs were called Fresel, and variants of the surname found their way to Scotland. Cinquefoils, which have prominence in the Fraser arms, derive from those found in 12th century noble families of St. Omer, in Flanders. The first on record in Scotland was Simon, who gave the church of Keith to the Abbey of Kelso. He is probably the man styled 'son of Malbet' and Sheriff of Traquair in 1184. His son, Sir Gilbert, also Sheriff, appears to have been brother of Udard, who married a daughter of Oliver, son of Kylbert, and obtained Oliver Castle. Udard was succeeded by a nephew, Adam, from whom descended Sir Simon Fraser, an adherant of Sir William Wallace. He was barbarously executed at London in 1306. Sir Gilbert had a son John, father of Alexander of Cornhill, Stirling, and of Richard of Touch-Fraser, progenitor of the Frasers of Philorth, in Buchan.

Richard's grandson, Sir Alexander, married Lady Mary, sister of King Robert the Bruce, and their grandson, Alexander of Durris, by his marriage to Joanna, daughter of William, Earl of Ross, obtained Philorth, with a home at Cairnbulg. Sir Alexander Fraser, 8th of Philorth, founded the town of Fraserburgh, and the 9th laird, Alexander, married Margaret Abernethy, the daughter of the 7th Lord Saltoun. On the expiry of the Abernethy line in 1668, their son Alexander was confirmed as heir. The title has descended to Flora Margaret, daughter of the 19th Lord Saltoun. Alexander of Cornhill was ancestor of the Frasers of Muchal, in

Mar, of whom Andrew built the imposing Castle Fraser in 1617. He was created Lord Fraser in 1633, which caused a dispute about the chiefship, but the title was confirmed by statute in 1622, and in 1672, Lord Fraser was awarded the arms of the chief of the family. Charles, the 5th Lord, took part in the '15 Jacobite Rising, and died in 1716, when the peerage expired and the chiefship fell to the Philorth or Saltoun line.

The Lovat chiefs descend from Hugh Fraser, about whose ancestry genealogists disagree, some deducing his line from the Frasers of Oliver Castle, and others from the Touch-Frasers, making them collaterals of the Philorth family. William Fraser, 4th laird, is found as Lord of Lovat prior to 1464. The line continued to Hugh, 9th Lord, on whose death his daughter Amelia was adjudged Baroness Lovat, to the chagrin of Simon Fraser of Beaufort, the heir male, who obtained the dignity in 1730. This Simon, 11th Lord Lovat, notorious in Jacobite intrigue, was created a Duke by the Chevalier, but was captured and executed after Culloden. The representation passed to Thomas Fraser of Strichen, who was recognised as chief of the Lovat Frasers and created a Baron (UK) in 1837. The forfeited Scottish title was restored to him in 1857. His grandson, Simon, 14th Lord, raised the Lovat Scouts, and his son, Simon Christopher, the 15th Lord *(de facto)*, served in the Scouts as well as the Scots Guards. The veteran soldier is best remembered as an outstanding Commando leader of World War II. His brother, Sir Hugh Fraser, married in 1956, Lady Antonia, daughter of the 7th Earl of Longford, and a distinguished biographical writer. There are children, but they were divorced in 1977. In 1980 she married Harold Pinter, the eminent playright and theatre director.

# GIBSON

Gibson simply means 'son of Gib,' a diminutive form of Gilbert, and is cognate with Gibbieson. Thomas Gibbieson was charged with breaking parole in 1358, and in 1390, Sir James Douglas of Dalkeith bequeathed £10 to John Gibson. Thomas Gibson held land in Dumfries, 1425, and in 1473, John Gibson, merchant, had a safe conduct into England. The surname was prolific in Edinburgh, and those of Caithness and Orkney mainly originated there. The most distinguished family were the knightly Gibsons of Pentland, in Mid Lothian, and Durie, in Fife.

Alexander Gibson of Pentland became a clerk of Session in 1594. In the early part of the 17th century he had charters of various lands, including the Barony of Durie, in Fife. He was made a Lord of Session in 1621, and is wrongly stated to have been made a baronet of Nova Scotia in 1628. In 1633 he was knighted and had his arms confirmed as Gules, three keys barways Argent. He died in 1644, and was succeeded by his eldest son, Alexander, who was knighted in 1641, and made a Senator of the College of Justice in 1646. He was deprived in 1649 and died in 1656. Another Alexander, a Privy Councillor who was knighted, died without male issue in 1661, and was succeeded by his brother, John of Durie, who matriculated arms, 1672-78. His son Alexander died without issue in 1699. The first Lord Durie had a second son, Sir John, an ardent Royalist, who had three sons: Sir Alexander of Pentland; Sir John Governor of Portsmouth; and Thomas of Keirhill, created a baronet in 1702. This baronetcy was eventually twinned with another created in 1831.

Sir Alexander Gibson of Pentland was one of the clerks of Session and died in 1706, having married Helen, daughter of Sir James Fleming of Ratho Byres, with issue: Sir John of Pentland; Sir Alexander, a clerk of Session, who succeeded to Durie in 1699; Thomas, who married Anna Wright, heiress of Cliftonhall; and Lt. Gen. James Gibson, in Hungarian service. Sir John Gibson, married Helen Carmichael, and died in 1767, leaving issue: Alexander of Durie; William, merchant in Edinburgh, and father of Sir James Gibson (1765-1850), created a baronet in 1831, who assumed the additonal name of Craig on succeeding to Riccarton as heir of entail; Lt. Col. Thomas; and Margaret, who married Alexander Gibson Wright of Cliftonhall, from whom descended the Ramsay-Gibson-Maitlands. John, son of Alexander, sold Durie in 1786, and succeeded to the estate of Skirling on the death of his grand-uncle, John, 4th Lord Hyndford, in 1787. Sir James Gibson-Craig of Riccarton was succeeded by his elder son, Sir William, Lord Clerk Register in 1862. The 1702 baronetcy came to his descendants, now represented by Sir David Peter William Gibson-Craig-Carmichael, 15th Bt., (cr. 1702, NS), and 8th Bt. (cr. 1831, UK).

Patrick Gibson (1782-1829), a native of Edinburgh, was an accomplished painter, etcher and art critic, who trained under Alexander Naysmyth. In Glasgow, a Gibson family of Hillhead, descended from Thomas Gibson in Meikle Govan, who died about 1544. By the end of the 16th century the family was styled 'of Over Newton'. Captain James Gibson, of this family commanded the ship *Carolina*, which transported Covenanters to America, and was also master of the *Rising Sun*, involved in the Darien Disaster. Andrew Gibson, first of Hillhead, died in 1733. His descendant, James (1800-62), left a daughter Mary, who married John Dougan, a surgeon.

# GORDON

The people who came to call themselves Gordons arrived in Scotland after the Norman Conquest, and following a period in England. They are recorded as having been in Berwickshire about the middle of the 12th century, and they took their name from Gordon, a place-name, probably *gor-dun*, meaning 'hill fort.' Nearby is Huntlywood and Huntlyburn, and when the Gordons went to Aberdeenshire they transplanted the name Huntly to the centre of the lordship of Strathbogie, given to them by Robert the Bruce.

The Gordons also held lands in Galloway, and Sir Adam de Gordon gave these to a younger son, who founded the family of Lochinvar, later Viscounts Kenmure. The 6th Viscount, William, a Jacobite, was attainted in 1716, and beheaded. The attainder was reversed in 1824, but the peerage became extinct in 1847. The Gordons in the south-west have always remained separate from their distant kinsmen in the north-east.

By marriage the Gordons in Strathbogie gained Aboyne. Sir Adam's great-grandson, another Sir Adam, was killed at Homildon Hill in 1402. The legitimate line of the family was carried on by the Gordons of Lochinvar, but the chiefship passed to his daughter Elizabeth, who married Alexander Seton. Their son Alexander was created Earl of Huntly about 1445, and assumed the surname of Gordon. He settled the Earldom on George, his second son, who became chief of the clan. Sir Adam Gordon had an elder brother John Gordon, styled 'of that Ilk,' but he left only natural sons, Jock and Tam, from whom several chieftains of the Buchan Gordons descended.

The 6th Earl of Huntly, George, was created Marquess of Huntly in 1599, and the 4th Marquess was created Duke of Gordon in 1684. The 13th Earl and 5th Duke,

Col. George, was made Baron Gordon of Huntly in 1807, and when he died in 1836, the dukedom and other titles became extinct. The Marquessate went to the Earl of Aboyne (cr. 1660), descended from a younger son of George, 2nd Marquess. The present Marquess is 'cock of the north' and chief of the Gordons. The Huntly estate passed in 1876 to the Duke of Richmond and Lennox, created Duke of Gordon that year. Aboyne Castle remains the seat of the Marquess and Earl of Aboyne.

From Jock Gordon, mentioned above, descended the Earls of Aberdeen (cr. 1682), through Patrick Gordon of Methlic, killed at Arbroath in 1445. John, 7th Earl and 1st Marquess (cr. 1916), was Governor-General of Canada, 1893-98. Another branch of the family are the Gordons of Abergeldy, Upper Deeside, descended from Sir Alexander Gordon, 2nd son of the 1st Earl of Huntly, and now represented by John Howard Seton Gordon. In the neighbourhood of Abergeldie, Gordons were once numerous, particularly around Khantore; in Glenmuick, and Glengirnock, where the farms are now derelict.

Two regiments were formed from the Clan Gordon: the old 81st, disbanded in 1783, and the 100th Regiment of Foot, raised in 1794, renumbered the 92nd. In 1881 the 75th (Stirlingshire) Regiment became the 1st Battalion of the 92nd, or Gordon Highlanders, formed as the 2nd Battalion. The uniform of the 75th was altered to the full Highland garb as worn by the 92nd. The Gordons have served in the Egyptian Wars, the South African War, and in the present century in both World Wars. In 1994, as a result of Government policy, they were amalgamated with the Queen's Own Highlanders.

# GRAHAM

The surname Graham appears in England at an early period, and those who came to bear it – from Grantham, in Lincolnshire – are usually stated to have been of Anglo-Saxon origin. It is more likely they came from Flanders and were descendants of the Counts of Hesdin. William de Graham accompanied David I. (1124-53) to Scotland on his return from England, and received from him the lands of Dalkeith and Abercorn. His son John was at the court of William the Lion in 1200 when William Comyn resigned his claim to certain lands in favour of the church of Glasgow. Sir Patrick, a descendant, was sent to negotiate the marriage of Prince Alexander of Scotland with Margaret, daughter of Guy, Earl of Flanders, in 1281. The family were prominent during the War of Independence.

Sir David Graham of Kincardine and Old Montrose was one of the Scottish barons engaged in arrangements for the release of David II, made prisoner at the Battle of Durham in 1346. His great-grandson, Patrick Graham, was made a Lord of Parliament before 1445, and his grandson, William, was created Earl of Montrose, 1504/5. The 5th Earl, William, was created 1st Marquess of Montrose in 1644, and distinguished himself as a soldier during the Wars of the Covenant. His kinsman, John Graham of Claverhouse, was the military leader who defeated the Covenanters at Bothwell Brig in 1679. The 3rd Marquess of Montrose was raised to the Dukedom in 1707. James, the 3rd Duke as an M.P., helped to repeal the legislation which made it unlawful to wear Highland dress.

Malise Graham, the first of his name to bear the title of Menteith, was a grandson of Sir Patrick Graham, ancestor of the Earls and Dukes of Montrose. He was styled Earl of Strathearn, but was deprived of that title and created Earl of Menteith in 1424. However, William, the 7th Earl, was served heir to David, Earl of Strathearn, and was styled Earl of Strathearn and Menteith. He was deprived of the titles and in 1633, created Earl of Airth, to which he appended "and Menteith." John, his eldest son, bore the junior title of Lord Kinpont, and suffered a fate which prompted Sir Walter Scott to write his *Legend of Montrose*. In 1646, when Montrose took the field against the Covenanters, he was joined by Lord Kinpont. When encamped at Collace, some angry words passed between him and a friend, James Stewart of Ardvoirlich. Stewart plunged his dagger into Lord Kinpont's heart and fled to the Covenanting Army, where Argyll gave him a command as Major. Lord Kinpont was interred at the Priory of Inchmahone, in the Lake of Menteith, and Stewart was pardoned the following year. Lord Kinpont's son succeeded as Earl, but left no issue and was succeeded by his sister Mary, who married Sir John Allardyce of that Ilk.

Although not a Highland clan, the Grahams owned lands along the fringe of Gaeldom. The Montrose line were feudal superiors of the Macfarlanes of Arrochar. The surname also appears in Border districts. Walter Graham, in Netherby, Cumberland, in 1596, was of the Menteith line, and the ancestor of the Grahams of Esk, baronets. The title was bestowed upon Richard Graham, Gentleman of the Horse to the Duke of Buckingham, in 1629. His grandson, the 3rd Baronet, also Sir Richard, was created Viscount Preston and Lord Graham of Esk. Those honours ceased on the death of the 3rd Viscount in 1739, but the baronetcy passed to his cousin, Rev. Sir William Graham. The representatives of the family now live at Long Island, New York.

# GRANT

The ancestors of the Grant chiefs were in French Flanders in the 11th century. The name simply means *le Grand*, or 'Big.' They came to England after the Norman Conquest and possessed estates in Nottinghamshire bordering those of the Bissets, who introduced them to the north. Sir Laurence le Grant was Sheriff of Inverness in 1285, and is probably the same man who appeared with Robert Grant that same year, as witness to an instrument by which John Byset, younger, was enabled to give the church of Conveth to the Priory of Beauly. It seems likely there had been intermarriage between the Bissets and the Grants.

Lands which the Grants held in the west of Stratherrick came later to the Lovat Frasers, perhaps by marriage, as the Frasers quartered the three antique crowns of the Grants with their own armorial bearings, three cinquefoils. The Grants also held lands in Urquhart and Glenmoriston, but gained a firm footing in Speyside through the marriage of Sir Ian Grant, their chief by 1434, and Maud, daughter and heiress of Gilbert of Glencarnie. Thus Freuchie became their principal seat.

The 4th laird, John Grant, succeeded his father in the lands of Glencarnie in 1553, and as baillie of the Abbey of Kinloss. From his second son Patrick, descended the Grants of Rothiemurchus, to which family belonged Elizabeth Grant (1797-1885), author of *Memoirs of a Highland Lady*, which gives vivid pictures of life in Strathspey in the first quarter of the 19th century. From the Rothiemurchus branch sprang the Grants of Ballindalloch. Other cadets included Arneidle, Easter and Wester Elchies, Lurg and Moyness, Duthil, Corriemony, Ballintomb, Kinchurdie and Gartenbeg. The Grants had occasional feuds with neighbours, and they fought alongside the Campbells of Argyll against the Gordons of Huntly at Glenlivet in 1594. During the persecution of the MacGregors the Grants sheltered many of them and incurred the wrath of the Privy Council.

The Grants of Freuchie came to be known as the lairds of Grant. Ludovick, second son of Sir James Grant of Grant, married Anne Colquhoun, heiress of Luss, and succeeded to the lands and baronetcy, but on the death of his elder brother Humphrey, unmarried, took up the succession, the Luss chiefship passing to his second son. Lewis Grant, his grandson, was created Earl of Seafield in 1811, and assumed the surname of Ogilvie in addition to his own. The present holder of the title is Ian Derek Francis Ogilvie-Grant, 13th Earl, who resides at Old Cullen, Cullen, Banffshire. The 7th Earl had been created Baron Strathspey (UK) in 1858, and his descendant, the 11th Earl, died leaving an heiress, Nina Caroline, who succeeded as Countess of Seafield. Her son Ian is the 13th Earl. The barony of Strathspey went to her uncle, Trevor, who thus became the 4th Baron, holder of the baronetcy (NS) and chief of the clan. His son Sir Donald Patrick Grant (1912-92), succeeded, and his children are now styled Grants of Grant.

Sir James Francis Grant (1863-1953), author or editor of a long list of historical works, was Lord Lyon King of Arms, 1929-45, and Dr Isabel Frances Grant (1887-1983), founded the Highland Folk Museum at Kingussie. She was the author of a number of important books and articles, including a brief history of *The Clan Grant* (1955). A biography and bibliography of her works appears in *Review of Scottish Culture*, No. 2, 1986.

# HAMILTON: EARLS AND DUKES

The noble family of Hamilton appear to have come to Lanarkshire from Northumberland in the 13th century. There, the Umfravilles held sway, and Gilbert was a popular name among them. Gilbert, progenitor of the earls and dukes of Hamilton may have been a scion of the Umfravilles and (surnames just emerging then) took his designation from Hameldone or Hamilton, a Northumbrian place-name. The earlier origins may go back to Flanders or France: perhaps to Amfreville in the Seine Valley.

Walter Fitz Gilbert is recorded in 1294, and in 1296 he swore fealty to Edward I of England. He did have English sympathies, but joined Robert the Bruce before Bannockburn, and in 1315 was granted the lands of Machan (Dalserf). Later he received the barony of Cadzow, in Lanarkshire, and Kinneil and other lands in West Lothian. He died about 1346, leaving by his second wife Mary Gordon, two sons, David, his heir, and John, ancestor of the earls of Haddington. The territorial designation of Hamilton was used before 1445, and the family gave the name to the town and parish, formerly Cadzow. In that year, James Hamilton was cr. a hereditary Lord of Parliament: his seat to be called Hamilton. He made a good second marriage; his spouse being Princess Mary, sister of King James III. The Hamiltons were now the nearest family to the royal house and began to take a more active interest in Scottish affairs. Honours came thick and fast. James, 2nd Lord Hamilton, was made Earl of Arran and on the death of King James V in 1542, became Governor of Scotland. In 1549 he was granted the Duchy of Chatelherault, in France. His son James was cr. Marquess of Hamilton, Earl of Arran and Lord Evan. James, the 2nd Marquess, was cr. Earl of Cambridge and Lord Innerdale in 1619, and two years later made a Knight of the Garter. The 3rd Marquess, in 1643, became Duke of Hamilton, Marquess of Clydesdale, Earl of Arran and Cambridge, Lord Evan and Innerdale. William, who became 2nd Duke in 1649, was cr. Earl of Lanark in 1639. This Duke joined General Leslie in his march into England in 1651, and was fatally wounded at Worcester.

Anne, Duchess of Hamilton in her own right, married William Douglas, Earl of Selkirk, in 1656. Life in her household is well told in Rosalind Marshall's book, *The Days of Duchess Anne* (Collins, 1973). King Charles cr. her husband for life, Duke of Hamilton and Marquess of Clydesdale. She resigned her titles into the hands of King William in 1698, who conferred them on her eldest son, James, Earl of Arran. James, 4th Duke, was opposed to the Union of 1707, but was chosen a representative peer and cr. Duke of Brandon. He was involved in a duel with Charles Mohun in 1712, and both parties were killed. The 5th Duke maintained great state in his new home of Chatelheraunt, near the old tower of Cadzow, and the 6th married Elizabeth, one of the beautiful Gunning sisters. James George, 7th Duke, became the male representative of the Earls of Angus. His guardian also asserted his right to the Douglas and Angus estates, leading to the 'Douglas Cause,' but the Lords decided in favour of Archibald, alleged twin son of Lady Jane Douglas. After the Napoleanic War the 10th Duke built a new palace at Hamilton, but it was demolished a century later. The 11th Duke married a cousin of Napolean III, and the 14th piloted the first aircraft over Everest in 1933. Angus Alan Douglas-Hamilton, 15th Duke of Hamilton and 12th of Brandon, resides at Lennoxlove, near Haddington. His brother, Lord James Douglas-Hamilton, is MP for West Edinburgh.

# HAMILTON: EARLS OF HADDINGTON

The Hamilton Earls of Haddington descend from John, younger son of Walter Fitz Gilbert, whose elder son was ancestor of the Earls and Dukes of Hamilton. John witnessed charters between 1365 and 1381, and he married Elizabeth, daughter of Sir Alan Stewart of Darnley, whose son John granted them Ballencrieff and other lands at Bathgate. Alexander, their son, came into possession of Innerwick, in East Lothian, through his marriage with Elizabeth, co-heiress of Thomas Stewart, 2nd Earl of Angus. Their eldest son, Hugh, carried on the Innerwick line. The earls of Haddington descend from a younger son, Thomas.

Thomas Hamilton acquired the lands of Orchardfield, then on the outskirts of Edinburgh, and married Margaret, daughter of Adam Cant, from whom he purchased the estate of Priestfield. Their elder son, Thomas, merchant-burgess of Edinburgh, exchanged with his cousin, James of Innerwick, the lands of Ballencrieff for those of Balbyne and Drumcarne, in Perthshire. He was killed at Pinkie in 1547. His eldest son, then a minor, was the father of Thomas, who became Earl of Haddington. This remarkable man passed advocate in 1587, and in his time held the offices of Lord of Session and Lord Advocate. In 1617, as Lord Binning, he entertained the king in that house from which he earned the *sobriquet* Tam o' the Cowgate. In 1619 he was cr. Earl of Melrose, Lord Byres and Binning, and in 1627 was advanced to the dignity of Earl of Haddington. He was married three times and had at least ten lawful children, the eldest being Thomas, the 2nd Earl of Haddington.

The 5th Earl married in 1674, Margaret, elder daughter of John Leslie, Earl (later Duke) of Rothes, who had married his mother's sister, and by arrangement their eldest son, John, became 7th Earl of Rothes, while the second, Thomas, became 6th Earl of Haddington. Thomas sold Byres to the Earl of Hopetoun, and became an agricultural improver, planting some 800 acres of his Tynninghame estate with trees. His eldest son, Charles, Lord Binning, author of several poems, was the father of Thomas, 7th Earl. Thomas, who became 9th Earl in 1828, served as MP for various English seats and in 1727 was cr. Baron Melrose of Tynninghame. This UK honour became extinct at his death in 1858, when he was succeeded as 10th Earl by George Baillie of Jerviswoode and Mellerstain, grandson of his brother George. After his succession, he obtained a royal licence to add the surname of Hamilton to that of Baillie, and to quarter the arms of Hamilton with those of Baillie. He was a representative peer of Scotland. His son George, when still Lord Binning, obtained a royal licence to assume the surname of Arden. He had married in 1854, Helen, daughter of Sir John Warrender of Lochend, Bt., by his wife, Frances Arden, daugher of the Lord Chief Justice, Baron Alvanley. Her brothers all died without issue and she became heiress to the Alvanley estates. Their children did not assume the name Arden, except for the youngest son, Henry Robert, who inherited the Alvanley estates. Lord Binning succeeded his father as 11th Earl in 1870, and he was a representative peer from 1874 to 1917. In 1902 he became a Knight of the Thistle. The earl was succeeded in 1917 by his grandson, George Baillie-Hamilton, who soldiered in both World Wars, and was a representative peer. He was a Trustee of the National Library and of the National Museum of Antiquities. His son, John George Baillie-Hamilton, the 13th Earl, succeeded in 1986, and lives at Mellerstain, Gordon, Berwickshire. His interests include natural history and field sports.

# HAMILTONS OF ABERCORN

Claud Hamilton, Lord Paisley, youngest son of James, 2nd Earl of Arran, by his wife, Lady Margaret Douglas, was ancestor of the earls of Abercorn. He married Margaret, only daughter of George, Lord Seton, and their eldest son was James Hamilton, Sheriff of Linlithgowshire. He had a charter of the lands of Abercorn and others, in 1601. He was cr. a peer by the title of Baron of Abercon in 1603, and advanced to the dignity of Earl of Abercorn in 1606. He was one of the 'undertakers' who received land in Ulster, and his eldest son James, became Lord Hamilton, Baron of Strabane, in 1616. He succeeded his father as Earl of Abercorn in 1618. As the Irish estates were willed to his younger brothers, he resigned his Irish title in favour of his brother Claud, in 1633. George, 4th Lord Strabane, was the father of Claud, 5th Lord Strabane and 4th Earl of Abercorn. Claud commanded a regiment of horses for King James, at the Boyne, and after the defeat was killed on his way to France. His estate and title of Strabane was forfeited, and the earldom of Abercorn devolved on his brother Charles.

Charles, 5th Earl of Abercorn, obtained a reversal of his brother's attainder in 1692. He died without issue and the honours devolved on James Hamilton, descended from Sir George Hamilton on Donalong, Tyrone, fourth son of the 1st Earl of Abercorn. His son, Col. James, was MP for Strabane and father of James of Donalong, cr. Baron of Mountcastle and Viscount of Strabane, 1701. He succeeded as 6th Earl of Abercorn and his son James was 7th Earl. James, 8th Earl, succeeded his father in 1744, and was cr. a peer of Great Britain as Viscount Hamilton of Hamilton, in the county of Leicester. This is interesting as by some authorities, Leicester was the home of the first Hamilton to come to

Scotland. James was a noted agricultural improver. He inherited the lordship of Paisley, but resided mainly at Duddingston, Edinburgh. He built an imposing mansion at Baron's Court, Strabane, but died unmarried, when his nephew John became 9th Earl of Abercorn. In 1790 he was cr. Marquess of Abercorn and made a Knight of the Garter. By his first wife Catherine Copley, he had several children, the eldest of whom, James, Viscount Hamilton, was the father of James, 10th Earl and 2nd Marquess of Abercorn. This nobleman was a fine scholar, educated at Harrow and Oxford, and received several honorary degrees. He was served heir of the body of the 1st Duke of Chatelherault, and as heir-male of the 1st Duke, asserted his right to the original title of 1549. James became Governor-General of Ireland in 1866, but left on the resignation of the Conservative administration in 1868. He was then cr. Marquess of Hamilton of Strabane, Tyrone, and Duke of Abercorn in the peerage of Ireland. James, 11th Earl, 3rd Marquis and 2nd Duke of Abercorn, was MP for Donegal, 1860-80, and High Sheriff of Tyrone, 1863. In 1901 he was appointed Special Envoy to several European and Scandinavian countries. His son James Albert Edward, 3rd Duke of Abercorn, was MP for Londonderry City, 1900-13, and was Governor of Northern Ireland, 1922-45. His son James Edward, 4th Duke, who died in 1979, was the father of His Grace, Sir James Hamilton, 5th Duke, who holds a number of other titles.

From the three noble houses treated, there are numerous cadet houses, including the Barons Dalzell, Hamilton baronets of Silvertonhill, Lanarkshire, and the Stirling-Hamiltons of Preston, East Lothian. Readers seeking knowledge of cadets are referred to *A History of the House of Hamilton*, a well-researched work by Lt. Col. George Hamilton (Edinburgh, 1933).

# HAY

The first of the Hay family to appear in Scottish records was William de la Haye, who probably came with his uncle, Ranulf de Soulis, who appears at the royal court as butler, about 1153. The office was then probably a life appointment, and William de la Hay held it during most of the reign of William the Lion (1165-1214). He became 1st Baron of Errol, and married Eva, heiress of Pitmilly. William predeceased her, dying about 1201. The family derived their name from La Haye, in the Cotentin peninsula of Normandy. The surname is written *de Haya* in Latin charters, to indicate it is *de la Haye*, and *de Haye*. It was rendered in Gaelic as *Garadh*, and into English as Hay.

William de la Hay was ancestor of the Hays of Erroll, and his second son Robert may have been the progenitor of the Hays of Yester. The Earls of Erroll descend through his grandson, Gilbert, and from his son William, descend the Hays of Leys and those of Megginch, ancestors of the Earls of Kinnoull. Sir Gilbert, 5th Baron of Errol was made Hereditary Lord High Constable of Scotland by Robert the Bruce in 1314. Sir William Hay of Lochloy, who died about 1420 and was buried at Elgin, was a kinsman and the ancestor of the Hays of Mayne. William Hay, the 9th chief, was belted Earl of Erroll in 1452. His wife, Lady Beatrix, daughter of James, 7th Earl of Douglas, was ultimately co-heiress of her brother, the last 'Black Douglas.' George 7th Earl, was prominent during the reign of Queen Mary. His grandson, Francis, 9th Earl, was a leader of the Counter-Revolution and with his allies, the Earls of Huntly and Angus, he entered into a treaty with King Philip II. of Spain, to depose Queen Elizabeth I. and place King James VI, who was to be converted, on the throne of a united Catholic Britain. Later, the king went against them and destroyed their strongholds, The Earl's castle of Slains has been a ruin ever since.

In 1745, Mary (1685-1758), Countess of Erroll in her own right, raised her followers for Prince Charles Edward Stewart. It was James, Lord Boyd, her great-nephew, who succeeded to the honours in 1758, and assumed the surname of Hay. His descendant, Diana Hay (1926-78), 23rd Countess of Erroll, married (as his first wife), the late Sir Iain Moncreiffe of that Ilk, a brilliant historian and genealogist, and their son, Sir Merlin Sereld Victor Gilbert Hay, 24th Earl and Lord High Constable of Scotland, is the present chief of the Hays.

Peter Hay of Megginch, who died in 1596, was the father of George, created Earl of Kinnoull in 1633. His grandson, George, 3rd Earl, accompanied Montrose to the north and was with him at Crathes after the Battle of Tippermuir in 1644. He visited France and spent some time in the household of his cousin, the Earl of Carlisle. The 6th Earl resigned his titles into the hands of Queen Anne, and obtained a charter in 1704, limiting the honours to himself during his life, and at his death to his kinsman, Thomas, Viscount Dupplin, descended from a younger brother of the 1st Earl. His son George became 8th Earl. The present Earl is Arthur William, born 1935.

John Hay of Yester appears as a Lord of Parliament in 1488. A descendant became Earl of Tweeddale in 1646, and his son John was advanced to the dignity of Marquess in 1694. The 13th Marquess is Edward Douglas John Hay, born 1947, who is Hereditary Chamberlain of Dunfermline.

# HENDERSON

The surname Henderson is cognate with Henryson, meaning simply 'son of Henry.' This being a prolific forename all over Europe in the Middle Ages, it was borne by many families. Henderson – with intrusive 'd' – became the most prolific form, but some families retained the Chrisitian name as a surname, hence Henry and again with intrusive 'd', Hendry. The surnames now appear all over Scotland, but at one time there were at least three quite distinct goups. People move about and mingle like clouds.

Henryson appears in Aberdeen as early as 1317, when John *filius* Henry appears as a burgess. In 1370, James Henrisson, an Aberdeen merchant, complained that his shop had been wrecked by the English. William Henrison was chamberlain of Lochmaben Castle, Dumfriesshire, in 1374, and Walter Henrison was 'sergeand' in Edinburgh in 1467. Robert Henryson, 1430-1505, was a well-known poet, along with William Dunbar and Gavin Douglas, one of the notable 'makars.' He was teaching law at Glasgow in 1462, and prior to his death he was a schoolmaster at Dunfermline. Many words of humanistic appearance were introduced by him, and he made good use of humour and alliteration. His finest poem was *The Testament of Cresseid*, which is a kind of supplement to Chaucer's work on the same subject.

The Hendersons of Fordell, in Dalgety parish, Fife, were the chief Lowland family of the name. Robert Henderson appears to have wadset the lands to Alexander Drummond of Ardmore, before 1478, but the subjects were redeemed by his son, James, King's Advocate, in 1510. His descendant, John was cr. a baronet (NS) in 1664. His line ended in an heiress, Isabella, who succeeded to Fordell in 1817, and married Admiral Sir Philip Durham. Isabella's kinsman, George

Mercer, on succeeding to Fordell, took the surname of Henderson. Georgiana Duncan, grand-daughter of his brother Douglas assumed the name of arms of Mercer-Henderson, and married in 1888, Sidney, Earl of Buckinghamshire, whose family inherited Fordell. Rev. Alexander Henderson, 1583-1646, minister at Leuchars, and a prominent Presbyterian leader at a difficult period, is supposed to have been a cadet of the Hendersons of Fordell. The old castle there was restored by the late Sir Nicholas Fairbairn, QC, MP, Solicitor-General, 1979-82, knighted in 1988.

A branch of Clan Gunn bears the name Henderson. According to tradition they are descended from Henry, a younger son of George Gunn, the 15th century chief who lived with 'barbaric pomp' at Clyth. After a devastating feud with the Keiths, a family dispute, probably about the succession, led to Henry separating himself from his brothers and settling in the lowlands of Caithness. In 1594 there is mention of a champion of the clan, Donald MacWilliam MacHendrie, who, says Dr Black, "may have had something to say in the matter of the Henderson patronymic," but the popular account is that they are descendants of Henry Gunn. A third distinctive group, a sept of the MacDonalds of Glencoe, Englished their name from *MacEanruig*. They claimed a fabulous descent from one Eanruig Mor Mac Righ Neachan: 'Big Henry, son of King Nechtan,' who succeeded to the Pictish monarchy about 706. A more acceptable claim would be descent from Dugal MacEanruig, who flourished about 1340.

In modern times, Dr Hamish Henderson, of the School of Scottish Studies, now retired, has done much to recover the folksongs of the travelling folk. During World War II he served as an infantryman in N. Africa, Sicily and Italy, and was mentioned in dispatches.

# HOGG

As the surname Hog (variants Hogg, Hogges, Hoge and Hoog), is found in early times in Scotland and England, and later in Ireland, it cannot be supposed that all who bear it descend from a common ancestor. In the eastern border counties of Scotland, where the name is most prevalent, the name almost certainly derives from the animal, the male of which, in its wild state typified courage and ferocity. It is worth noting that other families in the same area, such as the Gordons, Nisbets, Redpaths and Swintons, all displayed boars' heads on their seals and shields.

Early examples of the surname include Adam, son of Henry del Hoga (i.e., 'of the hog'), who was given as a bondman to the Abbey of Kelso by Andrew Fraser about 1280. The croft of Henry del Hoga is recorded as early as 1250, and about 1270, John de Grantham, son of Emma, heiress of Saloman del Hoga, made a grant from her lands at Berwick to the monks of Kelso. About 1280, there is mention of the croft which Adam del Hoga held in the time of Lady Alycie de Gordun. At one time it was thought that the Hogs of Harcarse and Bogend, in Berwickshire, descended from Hogs in Morayshire, and there is certainly a place there called Hogstoun. However, the name which evolved around what is now Gordonstoun was Ogstoun.

There was an aristocratic family of Hogs in Denmark, and at Frue Kirk, Aalborg, there is a fine monument dated 1647, commemorating Sir Erik Hog and his wife, Dame Sophia Lange. There the surname is said to mean 'falcon,' and to "go the whole hog," as the saying goes, the name must be written with a spole or spoke through the vowel.

It seems likely that the Hogs of Harcarse and Bogend descended from John Hog, an Edinburgh burgess who swore fealty to Edward I. in 1296. His descendants rose to prominence in the city and in 1359, Roger Hog loaned money to the Scottish king. Walter, son of Simon Hog, held the land called Hogistoun, adjacent to the burgh muir, in 1402. The law lord, Sir Roger Hog (1635-1700), a portrait of whom hangs in the little church of Fogo, was the grandson of Thomas Hog, a burgess of the Canongate, and ancestor of the families of Ladykirk and Cammo and of Newliston and Kellie. Roger Hog (1715-89), who purchased Newliston, Kirkliston, in 1753, because of his wealth and standing, was recognised as chief of the surname in 1783, when he matriculated arms: Argent, three boars heads erazed Azure and armed Or. His descendant, Major Roger Hog, last of Newliston, died in 1979, and the present chief appears to be Eric J. G. Hog, residing at Renoir, Paris, France.

One of the best-known Hoggs was James (1770-1835), 'The Ettrick Shepherd,' a son of Robert Hogg, tenant of the small farms of Ettrickhall and Ettrick house, in Selkirkshire. The parochial registers show that the spelling Hog was common up to about 1700, after which, as with the surnames Ker, Tod and others, the final letter was duplicated. Although he had little education, James Hogg rose to become a famous poet and novelist. He has been aptly named 'The Poet Laureate of Fairyland.' His best known poem is *The Queen's Wake*, containing the beautiful episodal tale of 'Kilmeny,' and his finest prose work is *Confessions of a Justified Sinner*. Two of his brothers, David (1773-1854) and Robert (1776-1833), emigrated to America in 1833, Robert dying at sea, and the families settled at Binghampton, in New York State. There are numerous descendants in various states.

In a renovated byre at Aikwood Tower, the border castle restored by Sir David Steel, MP, there is a permanent exhibition on the life and Work of "The Ettrick Shepherd".'

# HOUSTON

M any writers of books on tartans make the Houstons a sept of Clan Donald. This erroneous assumption arises from the fact that the patronymic of the MacDonalds of Sleat is *Clan Huisdein*, i.e., Children of Hugh, who was the son of Alexander, Earl of Ross and Lord of the Isles. The Houstons first appear in Renfrewshire, and if they must be allotted a tartan, it should be Stewart Ancient or the Lennox District tartan, as the Houstons of Houston were vassals of the Earls of Lennox.

Hugo de Pad'inan, progenitor of the Houstons of Houston, was granted a charter of the barony of Kilpeter, in Strathgryfe, by Baldwin de Biggar, towards the end of the reign of Malcolm IV. (1153- 65), or very early in the reign of William the Lion (1165-1214). He witnessed charters between 1165 and 1180. Hugo was of Flemish extraction, and before settling in Kilpeter had occupied some lands at Romanno, in Peeblesshire. It was from his grandson Hugh, son of Reginald, that the lands of Kilpeter became known as Houston, and the family so called. In 1225 he had a dispute with the monks of Paisley over his lands of Auchinhoss, and compromised through an agreement by which he was to pay the lordly ecclesiastics half a merk annually towards keeping the tomb of St. Mirin illuminated with wax candles.

Portraits of John de Houston, knight, the IXth Laird of Houston, and his lady, Dame Maria Colquhoun, who died respectively in 1400 and 1405, once graced the church at Houston, and have been cited as proving that painting was so prevalent in Scotland as to be employed in funeral monuments not only of great peers, but even of Knights of no great eminence nor fame. John, the XIIth Laird, had a charter of half of the lands of Lenny, in Mid Lothian, in 1468. His son Peter was slain at Flodden in

116

1513, fighting along with the men of Lennox on the right wing of the Scottish army. Patrick, son of Peter, also fell in battle at Linlithgow Bridge, in 1525. The Houstons were a turbulent family. Patrick Houston, XVIth of that Ilk, was implicated in the slaughter of Robert, son of John Mure of Caldwell, in 1550, and in 1564 appeared before the High Court in Edinburgh, for an assault on Andrew Hamilton of Cochno. Nevertheless he was knighted in 1556 by Mary Queen of Scots. Here it is worth mentioning that one Margaret Houston, Widow Beveridge, nursed the Queen through childbirth in 1566, and with a slap on the rump of Prince James, heralded the Union of the Crowns.

The XIXth Laird of Houston was created a Baronet of Nova Scotia in 1668. Sir John, the 3rd Baronet, suffered losses through being a Jacobite, and after his death at London in 1722, his estate of Houston was sold. The 4th Baronet, Sir John, died without issue, leaving his remaining estate to his kinsman, George Houston of Johnstone. The title however, passed to the heir male, Patrick Houston, who had emigrated to America, about 1735. There are descendants in Georgia, but they have not assumed the baronetcy since 1795. Some early Houstons migrated to Wigtonshire and from there into Ulster. Sam Houston (1793-1863), of Texas fame, was a descendant. The ancestors of Sir William Houston (1766-1842), created a Baronet in 1836, were at Cottreoch, in Wigtonshire. His heir, Col. Sir George, of the Grenadier Guards, married a daughter of Thomas Boswell of Blackadder, and assumed the additional surname of Boswall. The present Baronet is Sir Thomas A. Houston-Boswall, a fine arts specialist associated with two companies, who resides in New York. His son and heir (by his first wife, Lady Margaret) is Alexander Alford Houston-Boswall.

# INNES

The distinguished Innes family descend from Berowald the Fleming, who received a charter of lands in the district of Elgin called Innes (from which their surname is derived) and Easter Urquhart, from Malcolm IV. in 1160. One of the witnesses was William, son of Freskin the Fleming, to whom Berowald may have been related. A grandson, Walter of Innes, had a charter from Alexander II in 1226. Sir Robert Innes (1364-81), 8th of Innes, was the father of Sir Alexander, who married Janet, daughter of the Thane of Aberchirder. Sir Robert, 11th Laird, was Sheriff-Depute of Moray, and the father of four sons: Sir James, who entertained King James IV at his castle in 1490; Walter of Innermarkie, ancestor of the baronets of Balvenie; Patrick, ancestor of the Innes baronets of Coxon, 1686-1886; and Thomas of Elrick.

William, 15th of Innes or 'of that Ilk,' sat in the Reformation Parliament of 1560. His son Alexander was beheaded by the Regent Morton in 1578, and left a son, John, who resigned the chiefship to Alexander Innes of Cromney, grand-nephew of Alexander, 13th Laird. This chief was murdered by a kinsman. His son, Robert, founded the burgh of Garmouth in 1587. Robert, 20th chief, was created a baronet (NS) in 1625, and raised a regiment for Charles II. His grandson, Sir James, 3rd Bt., married about 1666, Margaret, daughter and co-heir of Harry Ker, only surviving son of Robert, 1st Earl of Roxburghe. His great-grandson, Sir James Innes, succeeded to the baronetcy in 1762, and after protracted litigation, became 5th Duke of Roxburghe in 1812. His son was created Earl Innes in 1837. Guy David (Innes-Ker), 10th Duke, is 5th Earl, 11th Baronet and 30th Chief, and lives at Floors Castle, Roxburghshire.

From Robert Innes, 2nd of Innermarkie, sprang the Innes family of Edingight, from whom descended Sir

Thomas Innes of Learney (1893-1971), who was Lord Lyon King of Arms from 1945 to 1969. He was probably the most colourful holder of the office since Sir David Lyndsay of the Mount, the Lord Lyon of 1538, and author of *A Satyre of the Three Estates*. Sir Thomas was the author of *Scots Heraldry, The Tartans of the Clans and Families of Scotland*, and other authoritative works. The holder of the office of Lord Lyon since 1981, is his third son, Sir Malcolm R. Innes of Edingight, who is also Secretary to the Order of the Thistle, and President of the Scottish Genealogy Society. Walter Innes, 5th of Innermarkie, was created a baronet (NS) in 1628. His son, Sir Walter, was an active Royalist during the Civil War. The Rev. George Innes, 4th Bt., was a priest of the Church of Rome, on whose death in 1698, the baronetcy devolved on his cousin, Sir James Innes of Balvenie and Orton. The 17th Bt. is Sir Peter Alexander Berowald Innes, a consultant civil engineer, who resides at Nations Hill, Kings Worthy, Winchester.

The Innes clan (recognised as such in 1579) produced two excellent antiquaries. Fr. Thomas Innes (1662-1744), a priest of the Scots College at Paris, produced in 1729, his *Critical Essay*, which laid the foundations for genuine Scottish historical research. He was descended from the Innes family of Drainie. Cosmo Innes (1798-1874), Professor of Constitutional Law at the University of Edinburgh, was the author of *Scottish Legal Antiquities* (1872), and other learned works. He was a cadet of the family of Innes of Luchars and Dunkinty, Keepers of Spynie Castle.

# IRVINE

The Irvines, Irvings, and Irwins (many other variants) are said to be of Celtic origin, and descended from Duncan, hereditary lay abbot of Dunkeld (of the kin of St. Columba), who was killed at Duncrub in 965. His son Duncan, Abbot of Dunkeld, is thought to have fought at Luncarty in 990. He had sons: (1) Crinan the Thane, who married the Princess Bethoc, heiress of Malcolm II, King of Scots, and had a son, King Duncan I, killed in 1040; (2) Grim, of Strathearn; and (3) Duncan of Cumbria. From the latter descended William Irvine, armour-bearer to Robert the Bruce, and Robert, witness to a charter to James Douglas, of lands in Roxburghshire, about 1320. From Robert descended the Irvines of Bonshaw. Their surname derives from an old parish in Annandale. William received a charter of part of the Forest of Drum, then in Kincardineshire. He was Clerk of the Rolls, 1328-31. His son William was one of the barons who sat in the Parliament held at Perth in 1369. He was probably dead by 1398, when his son Alexander had a charter of the Park of Drum, which remained with the family until 1737. He went to France in 1408 with the Earl of Mar, to join the Duke of Burgandy, and returned a knight, but was killed at Harlaw in 1411.

The Vth laird, Alexander Irvine, was deprived of his office of Sheriff of Aberdeenshire in 1471, for attacking with a force of men the house of Sir Walter Lindsay of Bewfort. His son and heir, Alexander, married Janet Keith, and had by her a son Alexander, and two daughters, Mary and Elspet. By Nan Menzies he had four natural children, David, Alexander, John and Agnes, for whom he made provision in 1493. The Irvines of Drum were the undoubted chiefs of the surname: recognised as such by Parliament in 1664, when a birth-brief was issued for Capt. John Irvine, soldiering in

120

France, son of Robert Irving of Fedderet. Alexander, XIIth chief, inherited debts and a reduced estate, and when he died in 1696, his kinsman and executor, Alexander Irvine of Murthill, intruded himself as laird of Drum. However, on the death of his grandson John, without issue, the rightful heir of entail, Alexander Irvine of Artamford, succeeded. The XXVth laird, Lt. Col. Charles Francis Irvine, served in the Gordon Highlanders in World War II.

The Dumfriesshire chieftains did not come into prominence until the 16th century. Christopher Irving of Bonshaw and a son were killed at Flodden in 1513. From the time of his successor, Edward, the family are well documented. Various members were involved in the municipal affairs of the town of Dumfries. Edward married Blanche Graham, and was succeeded in 1605 by his son William, who died about 1647. His descendants are represented by the Canadian branch of the family, descended from Aeamilius Irving, 1714-96, of Quebec, and from his father's younger brother, John Beaufin Irving, 1844-1925, whose son Sir Robert Beaufin Irving, 1877-1954, was Commodore of the Cunard-White Star line, and captain of the *Queen Mary*. William's second son, Francis Irving, married Agnes, daughter of Herbert Raining, Provost of Dumfries. His son John of Friars Carse, was Provost of Dumfries, 1634 and 1646, and a Covenanter. Richard Francis Irving, his descendant, emigrated to Australia in 1874. By his second marriage, with Annie M. Tindale, he had, with a daughter Heather, a son, Malcolm James Irving of Barwhinnock and Lango Downs, Charleville, Queensland.

The Bell-Irving family of White Hill, Lockerbie, can trace their descent from Richard Irving, who had a charter of lands in Hoddam, in 1549.

121

# JAMIESON

The surname Jameson or Jamieson'simply means 'son of James.' It is worth noting that a family named Jamieson or Neilson held the office of Crowner of Bute from early in the 14th century to the 17th, and this may explain why some authorities list Jamieson as a sept of the Stewarts of Bute. Some others, with less conviction make them a sept of Clan Gunn. As this was a prolific forename in mediaeval times, and the name of seven Stewart kings, there must be many unrelated families of the surname in various parts of Scotland.

Early references to the surname include Alexander Jemison, who had a safe conduct to trade with England in 1445. William Jamyson was a tenant in Pollock in 1472, and in the same year John Jameson was a freeman of Irvine. Robert Jacobi was in Brechin in 1493, but the surname James is rare in Scotland. James Jameson was reader at Kettins Church in 1563, and Sir Mark Jamieson was vicar pensioner of Currie in 1567.

George Jameson (1586-1644), a native of Aberdeen, was apprenticed to John Anderson, an Edinburgh painter, in May, 1612. He later applied himself to portrait painting, occasionally practising in history and landscape. He was patronised by the Campbells of Breadalbane, and among other work for them executed a large pedigree chart with miniature portraits, which is now in the National Portrait Gallery. Other portraits by him are possessed by the University of Aberdeen, and he has been called 'The Scottish Vandyke.'

A distinguished naturalist, Robert Jameson (1774-1854), was born at Leith. In boyhood he showed a marked interest in natural objects. He entered the Humanity Class at the University of Edinburgh in 1788. Later he studied medicine and visited London, where he met members of the Linneaen Society. He studied geology on the Orkney and Shetland islands, and on the island of Arran, and in 1804 was appointed Professor of Natural History at Edinburgh. He was the author of a number of scientific books.

John Jamieson (1759-1838), a native of Glasgow, studied Latin and Greek there, and became pastor of a Secession congregation at Forfar. He was translated to Nicolson Street Church, Edinburgh, in 1792. At an early stage in his career he received the degree of Doctor of Divinity from the College of New Jersey. Dr Jamieson was a prolific writer, but is best remembered for his *Etymological Dictionary of the Scottish Language* (1808).

There are several armigerous Jamieson families in Scotland. John Jamieson of Croy, merchant-burgess of Glasgow, had a grant off arms in 1865, and about the same time his nephew, Michael James Jamieson, matriculated arms. Michael's brother Robert Jarvie Jamieson followed in 1869. Douglas Jamieson (1880-1952), a grandson of John of Croy, was Solicitor-General for Scotland, 1933-35, and Lord Advocate, 1935. In the same year he became a Lord of Session. His daughter Barbara married Kenneth C. Cook, whose arms were registered at the College of Arms. Others who bear arms include Dr Arthur Jamieson of Barnach, chairman of the Glasgow & West of Scotland Family History Society, 1977-88, who matriculated at the Lyon Office in 1951.

James Jamieson, who died in 1736 in Essex County, Virginia, bore arms which indicate a Scottish origin, and others are found throughout America.

# JOHNSTONE OF ANNANDALE

Johnson or Johnstone is a surname with at least three derivations. Johnstone parish, in Dumfriesshire, means *John's Toun,* or the dwelling place of John, who, before his surname was stabilised, received a grant of the lands from Robert de Brus about 1170, after he had confirmation of lands in Annandale from King William the Lion. This was the foundation of the great Border clan of Johnstone. Some other Johnstones have a territorial origin: from Perth, often named St. Johnston, or from the lands of Jonystoun, now Johnstonburn, at Humbie, East Lothian. The surname Johnson, *John's son,* is sometimes confused with Johnston or Johnstone.

John, father of Gilbert, may have been a native settler who elected to hold his lands from the Bruce lords of Annandale, or he may have come with them from Yorkshire. Gilbert was succeeded by another Gilbert, witness to a transaction of 1249. Sir John of Johnstone appears in the homage roll of 1296. Gilbert of Johnstone also subscribed, and was probably a brother, as the two men are mentioned in a charter of the lands of Comlongan and Ruthwell, between 1315 and 1332. Gilbert was alive in 1347, and was the father or grandfather of Sir John Johnstone, on record between 1377 and 1398. Adam of Johnstone, who succeeded, is the first to be styled 'of that Ilk.' A descendant, John, had a brother James, who had a charter of the lands of Drumhaston, Skeoch and others, in 1545, on payment of 1,000 merks to John, the Commendator of Saulsett, and the convent there. It was in the time of John Johnstone of that Ilk, that the bitter feud with the Maxwells began, and it lasted nearly a century. He was twice married, first to Elizabeth Jardine, and next to Nicola Douglas, and had a large family, including James, his heir; Robert of Raecleuch and Capt. James of Loch-house. John, son of James, must have come of age about 1570, and was held responsible by the Government for the behaviour of his clan. His son James, however, continued the feud with the Maxwells. On a day fixed for a reconciliation in 1608, he was shot and mortally wounded.

James, son of James, was a minor when his father was killed, and in his time the feud was terminated. He was cr. a peer, as Lord Johnstone of Lochwood, in 1633. In 1643, he was cr. Earl of Hartfell, Lord Johnstone of Lochwood. His son James, 2nd Earl, resigned his titles in 1657 for a regrant, and became Earl of Annandale and Hartfell. He married Henrietta Douglas. Their eldest surviving son, William, succeeded, and in 1701 was cr. Marquess of Annandale and Earl of Hartfell. Henrietta, his eldest daughter married in 1699, Charles Hope, cr. Earl of Hopetoun in 1703, and when George, 3rd Marquess of Annandale died in 1792, he was succeeded in his estates by his grand nephew, James, 3rd Earl of Hopetoun. A long contest for the titles ensued, in which a contender was John James Hope Johnstone, 1796-1876, son of Adm. Sir William Hope and Anne, daughter of James, 3rd Earl of Hopetoun. The claim was renewed by his grandson, John James Hope Johnstone, 1842-1912, and Sir Fredrick Johnston of Westerhall, but no decision was reached, and the dignities became dormant. The Hope Johnstones continued at Raehills, and in 1986, Patrick Andrew Wentworth Hope Johnstone, son of Major Percy Wentworth Hope Johnstone of Annandale and Raehills, *de jure* 10th Earl of Annandale (who died in 1983) and his second wife, Margaret Jane Hunter Arundel, was recognised by the House of Lords Committee of Privileges as 11th Earl of Annandale (Hartfell included), and Lord Johnstone, and was summoned to the Upper House.

# JOHNSTONES: VARIOUS

The Johnstones of Galabank once entertained a claim to the Annandale peerage, and proved their descent from the barons of Newby and Graitney, who branched off from the Lockwood cadets of Annandale. Lt. Col. James Johnstone, of Fulford Hall, Warwickshire, who represented this family, served with the Durham Light Infantry in World War II.

A Johnston family of Beirholm, Annandale, descended from Gavin Johnston, who received a charter of the lands of Clerk Orchard, Thornick and Scaligholm in 1555. He was ancestor of Archibald Johnston, 1611-63, of Warriston, Edinburgh, a distinguished lawyer and stateman, who became Lord Advocate in 1646. He was unfortunately, induced to take office under Cromwell, who made him Lord Clerk Register. He also advanced him to the peerage as Lord Warriston. At the Restoration, having supported Cromwell and also the Covenanters, he fled to France. An act of forfeiture being passed against him, he was condemned to death. He was discovered at Rouen, and brought back to Edinburgh, where he was hanged without trial. A descendant, Sir Partick Johnston, was three times provost of Edinburgh, and was mobbed by the citizens for supporting the Union of 1707. However, he became a member of the first parliament of Great Britain. Lt. Col. George Richard Johnston, who represented this family, served in World War I with the Royal Horse Artillery. He became a qualified interpreter in six languages, and was granted arms by the Lord Lyon in 1950.

The Johnstones of Westerhall are an important branch of the Johnstones of Annandale, and descend from Matthew, second son of Sir Adam Johnstone of that Ilk. Matthew received a charter of lands in Westeraw, Lanarkshire, in 1455. The family had a long history as

MPs for Dumfries and other seats. Sir James Johnstone of Westerhall, MP, was knighted by Charles II, and his son, Sir John, MP, was cr. a baronet (NS) in 1700. He married Rachel Johnstone, co-heiress of Sheens, but dying without male issue the title devolved on his brother, Sir William, who married Henrietta Johnstone, the other heiress. He was also an MP, as was his son, Sir James, who was a claimant for the marquisate of Annandale in 1792. His brother, Col. John, was ancestor of the Barons Derwent. Sir William, 5th Bt., was a member of seven successive parliaments, and acquired the great Pulteney property through his first wife, Frances, whom he married in 1760, heiress of Daniel Pulteney. Their daughter Henrietta became Countess of Bath. The 9th Bt., is Sir Frederick Allan Johnstone, who succeeded to the title in 1952.

The Johnstons of Caskieben also possess a baronetcy (NS) conferred in 1626 on Sir George Johnston, Sheriff of Aberdeen. This family appear to be a collateral line of the Annandale Johnstones, and erroneously use the style 'of that Ilk,' which denotes paramount chiefship. The 11th Bt., emigrated to Alabama, USA, where his descendant, Sir Thomas, 13th Bt., became partner in a legal firm. His son, Sir Thomas Alexander Johnston, is the present Bt.

It is difficult to pinpoint Johnstons or Johnstones descended from those who took their name from Jonystoun, East Lothian, or from St. John's-toun (Perth). Gilbert, son of Thome Johnstone, who received the forfeited lands of Whiteriggs and Redmyre, in Kincardineshire, from Robert the Bruce, was probably of a family who took their name from St. John's-toun. Another was Christy Johneson, who took part in the clan battle on the North Inch, 1396. There has been much speculation about the identity of the two clans involved in that conflict.

# KENNEDY

**P**robably descended from the indigenous race who inhabited Galloway, the Kennedys appear on record as early as the reign of William the Lion (1165-1214). The name means 'son of Kenneth.' Gilbert MacKenedi witnessed a charter of lands in Carrick, about 1185, and it was around this time that Henry MacKenede was a leader in a rebellion in Galloway. In 1266, Fergus Makenedy rendered accounts to the Sheriff of Ayr for expenditure, on the King's ships. Alexander Kenedy, clerico, witnessed John Baliol's renunciation of a treaty with France in 1296, and swore fealty to Edward I the same year.

In the time of Robert II. (1371-90), the Kennedys of Dunure emerged as the principal family of the name, and they obtained the lands of Cassillis, possibly through marriage. An advantageous union was made by James of Dunure, who married about 1409, the widow of George Douglas, Earl of Angus, who was Princess Mary, daughter of Robert II. It was probably because of this marriage that several lines of the family assumed the double tressure on their seals. The celebrated James Kennedy, Bishop of St. Andrews, third son of James and the Princess, did so, and the Lindsay MS. of 1542's hows the arms of Kennedy of Girvanmains with the tressure. The eldest surviving son, Gilbert succeeded. David, the 3rd Lord, was created Earl of Cassillis in 1509, and was slain at Flodden. When his son Gilbert was assassinated in 1527, his brother William, Abbot of Crossraguel, became tutor to his nephew Gilbert, the 3rd Earl, whose son, also Gilbert, was a supporter of Mary, Queen of Scots. Tradition says the wife of John, 6th Earl, the Countess Jean (Hamilton) was the lover of John Faa, a Gypsy captain, about 1622, but here, chronology is the weak point, as she was then aged 15 and, although contracted, was not yet married. The 9th Earl, Thomas, erected the village of Straiton, in Ayrshire. Archibald, the 12th Earl, was made Marquess of Ailsa in 1831. His descendant, Charles Kennedy, 8th Marquess, succeeded to the title and estates in 1994, and resides at Cassillis House, Maybole.

An interesting group of Kennedys, said to be from Lochaber, settled around Dull, in Perthshire, about 1550. It seems likely they were of Celtic ancestry. There were moreover, Kennedys in Ireland, notably those who became baronets of Johnstown-Kennedy. The most famous Kennedy of Irish extraction was John F. Kennedy (1917-63), the assassinated USA President. The Kennedys of Underwood, Symington, descend from Robert Kennedy, of Liverpool, who purchased the lands and barony about 1785. Of this family, Neil James (1866-1958), assumed the additional surnames of Cochran and Patrick when he married Eleanora, the heiress of Dr Roger Cochran-Patrick of Woodside. From them descend the Kennedy-Cochran-Patrick family of Ladyland, Beith, Ayrshire. The Kennedys of Knockgray descend from John Kennedy of Dalmorton, whose son, Rev. Alexander Kennedy, minister of Straiton, 1691-1738, chaplain to the Earl of Cassillis, bought the estate. The Kennedys of Doonholm derive their descent from Robert Kennedy of Tilliepowrie, in Angus. Peter Norman B Kennedy of this family, is a company director and chairman of the Doon Fishery Board. Ludovic Kennedy, the writer and broadcaster who married Moira Shearer (King), the ballerina star of the film, 'The Red Shoes,' was born in Edinburgh in 1919. He is descended from Robert, brother of the 1st Marquis of Ailsa, by his wife Jane Macomb, and was recently knighted.

# KERR ORIGINS

It is often stated that the surname Ker, Kerr or Carr, is derived from a Lancashire place-name, meaning a copse or wood, and that the earliest so-named were of Anglo-Norman origin. However, the name was probably brought to Normandy or Brittany by Norsemen. The name 'Kari' is found in a saga of the 10th century.

While the two great families of Cessford and Ferniehurst, in Roxburghshire, are the best-known, there must be many Kerr families in Scotland who are not descended from those houses, but may have also Anglo-Norman ancestry. They appear in a number of lowland shires. The earliest on record is Johannes Ker, venator (i.e., 'hunter'), styled 'of Swynhope,' in Peeblesshire, who witnessed the perambulation of the bounds of Stobo manor, about 1190. William Ker was witness to an agreement between the burgh of Irvine, Ayrshire, and Brice of Eglunstone (Eglinton), during the reign of William the Lion, 1214-49. He is thought to have been descended from William Espec, a Norman baron who settled in Yorkshire in 1086. Thomas Kaurr was Sheriff of Roxburgh in 1264. The ship of Thomas Ker, an Aberdeen merchant-burgess, was plundered by the English in 1273. Thomas Kayr swore fealty to Edward I at Kinghorn in 1296, and was juror at Dyrsart in 1296. William Kerre of Ayrshire, Henry Ker of Edinburghshire, and Nicol Kerre of Peeblesshire, also signed the Ragman Roll in 1296. Wylliam Ker appears on an inquest of the lands of Lady Mary la Zuche, in Conynham, Ayshire, in 1296.

The Kers of Cessford and Ferniehurst descended from a family long settled at Altounburn, Roxburghshire. John Ker obtained a charter of all the lands and tenements of Moll and Aldtounburn, in the barony of Sprouston, resigned by John de Copeland in 1357. He was possibly the father of Henry Ker, who was Sheriff of Roxburgh in 1369. Robert of Aldtounburn the next on record received a charter of the lands of Smailholm in 1404. He had sons Richard and Andrew, successively of Aldtounburn. Andrew's son, Sir Andrew of Aldtounburn had two sons, Sir Walter of Cessford and Thomas of Ferniehurst. From them descended the Earls and Marquesses of Lothian, the Lords Jedburgh, Earls of Ancrum, and the Earls and Dukes of Roxburghe.

Kers and Kerrs appear in a number of counties from an early date. In 1358, Richard Kerr had a charter by William, Earl of Douglas, of the lands of Samuelston, now in East Lothian. George of Samuelston and Elizabeth Carmichael his spouse, witnessed a charter by George, Earl of Douglas, 1450. By the reign of James IV, 1488-1513, many are recorded in the *Register of the Great Seal*. Some of those in the west country may have been vassals of the Douglases. Henry Ker of Dundaff Hill, in Stirlingshire, was escheat for a period, and James Douglas received a charter of the property in 1364. Many Kerrs farmed in Lanarkshire, Renfrewshire and Ayrshire. The Kers of Kersland, Ayrshire, seem to stem from Robert Ker, who embraced the Reformation in 1560. He left three daughters, the eldest of whom, Janet, married (as his second wife) Capt. Thomas Crawford of Jordanhill, descended from the Crawfords of Kilbirnie. Their son Daniel Crawford, assumed the name and arms of Ker of Kersland. Much research on those western families was done by Dr William Hogarth Kerr, educated at Hamilton and Glasgow, who became a physician at Swansea, Wales, in 1919. He was the eldest son of Rev. Robert Kerr, 1857-1939, U.F. Church minister at Kirkmuirhill, Lanarkshire.

Ayrshire born John Kerr, a qualified CA, is a director of the Scottish Association of Young Farmers' Clubs. He was their Chairman of Council, 1976-77, and Chairman of the European Committee of Young Farmers, 1980-82.

# KER: DUKE OF ROXBURGHE

Sir Robert Ker, cr. 1st Earl of Roxburghe in 1600, was son of William Ker of Cessford and Caverton, Warden of the Middle March, by his wife, Janet, daughter of Sir James Douglas of Drumlanrig. His sister Elizabeth married in 1601, Sir James Bellenden, knight, of Broughton, and had a son William, cr. 1st Lord Bellenden in 1661, with destination to the heirs male of his body; but resigned his peerage and obtained a re-grant, confirmed in 1673, in favour of his cousin, John Ker, second son of the 2nd Earl of Roxburghe, who succeeded as 2nd Lord Bellenden, and continued that family. The 2nd Earl was son of Jean Ker, sister of William, Master of Roxburghe, who died in the lifetime of his father, the 1st Earl. She married John, 2nd Earl of Perth. Their eldest son, James, was ancestor of the Earls of Perth and Melfort, and their fourth son William Drummond, succeeded as 2nd Earl of Roxburghe, and assumed the surname of Ker. He fulfilled the stipulations of a deed of nomination, drawn up in 1648, and married his cousin, Jean, the daughter of Harry, Lord Ker, youngest son of the 1st Earl by a second wife.

The 2nd Earl had two sons, Robert, 3rd Earl, and John, who succeeded to the Lordship of Bellenden in 1671, and continued that family. The 3rd Earl was drowned in 1682, when the ship the *Gloucester*, carrying the Duke of York and some other noblemen, was wrecked off Yarmouth. By his Countess, Margaret Hay, daughter of the 1st Marquess of Tweeddale, he had three sons: Robert, 4th Earl; John, 1st Duke; and Lt.Gen. William, soldier and politician. The 4th Earl died unmarried and the honours devolved on his brother John, cr. 1st Duke of Roxburghe in 1707. His only son, Robert, 2nd Duke, in the lifetime of his father, was cr. a peer of Great Britain by the title of Baron Ker and Earl Ker of Wakefield.

His elder son, John, 3rd Duke, was a celebrated book collector and was installed as KG and KT. He died unmarried in 1804, when the honours devolved on his kinsman, John, 7th Lord Bellenden, 1728-1805. When he died there was a long contest for the succession between Maj. – Gen. Walter Ker, heir male of the 1st Earl; William Drummond, descended from Sir John Drummond of Logiealmond, as heir male of the 2nd Earl; and Sir James Innes, 6th Bt., son of Sir James Innes, 3rd Bt., of Innes, who married Margaret, daughter of Harry, Lord Ker, only son of the 1st Earl by his second marriage. The House of Lords decided in favour of the latter in 1812.

Sir James Innes, 1736-1823, the 25th feudal baron of Innes, sold his ancestral estates in 1767, and served in the 88th and 58th Regiments. He married first, in 1769, Mary, daughter of Sir John Wray of Glentworth, Bt., and Frances, heiress of Fairfax Norcliffe of Langton, Yorkshire, and assumed the surname of Norcliffe. She died without issue, and he married in 1807, Harriet, daughter of Benjamin Charlewood, of Windlesham, Surrey. They had an only son, James Henry Robert, 6th Duke. On succeeding to the dukedom, Sir James Innes assumed the surname of Innes-Ker, which has been in use since 1812. The 7th Duke was also James Henry Robert Innes-Ker, who married in 1847, Lady Anne Emily Spencer Churchill, daughter of John Winston, 7th Duke of Marlborough. She was Lady of the Bedchamber and Mistress of the Robes to Queen Victoria. The present and 10th Duke of Roxburghe is Guy David Innes-Ker, among whose other titles is 11th (Premium) Bt., NS, (1625 for Innes of New Innes), and Marquess of Bowmont and Cessford. He has been twice married. By the first Duchess, Lady Jane Grosvenor, he has issue. The heir is their elder son, the Marquess of Bowmont and Cessford.

# KERR: MARQUESS OF LOTHIAN

**M**ark Ker or Kerr, cr. 1st Earl of Lothian in 1606, was descended from Andrew Ker of Auldtounburn and Cessford, who died in 1444. Andrew's eldest son Walter, was the father of Sir Robert of Cessford, who died before his father, about 1500, leaving two sons, Andrew of Cessford, and George, from whom descended Sir Walter Ker of Fawdonside, who became heir male of Cessford, but resigned his rights in 1664. His line is extinct. Andrew of Cessford survived the Battle of Flodden, 1513, and was knighted. He married Agnes Crichton, and had three sons: Sir Walter of Cessford; Mark, commendator of Newbattle, father of the 1st Earl; and Andrew.

The first Earl of Lothian was an Extraordinary Lord of Session, 1589, and had crown charters of the lands of Newbattle and Prestongrange, erected into the Barony of Newbattle in 1591. He married Margaret Maxwell, daughter of Lord Herries, whom Scotstarvit alleges, caused her husband's death by witchcraft in 1609. Witch or not, she bore him three sons and five daughters. Robert, the eldest, succeeded his father as 2nd Earl, and married in 1611, Annabella, daughter of Archibald, Earl of Argyll. They had a daughter Anne, who married in 1630, her kinsman, Sir William Ker of Ancrum. Her father took his own life in 1624, and she was not allowed the earldom, but her husband, having redeemed Newbattle and other lands, was cr. Earl of Lothian and Lord Ker of Newbattle. He was descended from Robert Ker of Ancrum and Woodhead, third son of Sir Andrew Ker of Ferniehurst. Sir Andrew was grandfather of Sir Thomas of Ferniehurst, father of Andrew, cr. 1st Lord Jedburgh in 1621-22, and Robert (Carre), cr. Earl of Somerset in 1613.

William Ker, son of Robert of Woodhead and Arcrum, had by his wife Margaret Dundas, a son Sir Robert, cr.

Earl of Ancrum in 1701, and he had two sons, the above William, cr. Earl of Lothian in 1631, and Charles, 2nd Earl of Ancrum, who died without issue, when his title devolved on his nephew of the half blood, Robert, 4th Earl of Lothian. William, Earl of Lothian of the cr. of 1631, and Anne Ker, had issue, and their eldest son was cr. Marquess of Lothian and Earl of Ancrum, in 1701. William Henry, his grandson, 4th Marquess, fought at Fontenoy and in 1745 commanded the cavalry on the left wing of the Royal army at Culloden.

Schomberg Henry, 9th Marquess and Keeper of the Privy Seal, married in 1865, Lady Victoria, eldest daughter of the 5th Duke of Buccleuch, and died in 1900. He was a director of the Lothian Coal Company, which sunk the pit at Newtongrange, 1890-94, named after one of his daughters, the Lady Victoria Colliery. It was the jewel of the Scottish coalfied. The pit closed in 1981, and is now a mining museum. Robert, 10th Marquess, died unmarried in 1930, and was succeeded by his cousin, Philip Henry, who also died unmarried in 1940, when he was succeeded by his kinsman, Peter Francis Walter Kerr, 12th and present Marquess, descended from the youngest son of John, 7th Marquess. He served in the Scots Guards in World War II, after which he held some Government posts and was delegate to the Council of Europe and Western European Union in 1959. He married in 1943, Antonella, daugher of Maj.-Gen. Sir Foster Reuss Newland. Their eldest son and heir is Michael, Earl of Ancrum, who was admitted advocate at the Scottish Bar in 1970. He was MP for Berwickshire and East Lothian, in 1974; for Edinburgh South, 1979-87, and was elected for Devises in 1992.

# KIRKPATRICK

Everyone conversant with Scottish history will be familiar with the stabbing at the altar of the Greyfriars church of Dumfries, of Red John Comyn by Robert the Bruce, in 1306. This incident, mentioned in Barbour's *Bruce*, brought immediate excommunication. An old tradition says that when he left the chapel, Bruce exclaimed, "I doubt I have slain Comyn," and a faithful follower replied: "You doubt? Then I'll mak siccar," and rushed into the building and stabbed the unconscious Comyn to death. Someone did 'mak siccar,' and the story goes that it was Sir Roger Kirkpatrick of Closeburn. The crest of the family shows a bloody dagger, and their motto is I MAKE SURE, in remembrance of the slaying of John Comyn. It is worth noting however, that the seal of a later Sir Roger Kirkpatrick, 1498, is like the shield of today, but the crest was then a swan neck and head.

Ivo or Ivone, the earliest recorded ancestor of the Kirkpatricks, witnessed a charter before 1141. The family settled at Closeburn, Dumfries, on lands adjoining a chapel dedicated to St. Patrick: *Cell Patricii*, and took their name from the lands. Stephen, grandson of Yvo, is styled in a document of 1278, Stephanus Dominus Villae de Closeburne, filius at heres Domini Ade de Kirkpatrick. Sir Thomas, his son, died without male issue, and was succeeded by his nephew, Winfred, whose elder son, Sir Thomas, had a new charter of the lands of Bridburgh and Closeburn in 1409. Roger, his brother succeeded, and was the father of Thomas, his heir, and Alexander of Kirkmichael, ancestor of the Kirkpatricks of Conheath, and of branches of the family in Kildare and Antrim, Ulster. Thomas was knighted, and married Maria, daughter of the 1st Lord Maxwell. His grandson, Thomas, died sometime after the Battle of Solway Moss, 1542, and was succeeded by his cousin

Roger, whose great-grandson, Robert Kirkpatrick of Closeburn, by his wife Grizel Baillie, was the father of Thomas of Closeburn, cr. a baronet of Nova Scotia in 1685. The 10th Bt., Sir James Alexander Kirkpatrick, served in the RAF in World War II and was mentioned in despatches. His son, Sir Ivone, 11th and present Bt., resides in New Zealand.

That grand lady, the Empress Eugenie, 1826-73, was of Scottish extraction. Her grandfather, William, second surviving son of William Kirkpatrick of Conheath and Mary Wilson, became American Consul at Malaga, in Spain. He married Dona Francisca Marie, daughter of Baron de Grevignee, with issue, Maria Manuella; Carlota Catalina, and Henriquita. The eldest married Don Cipriano Palofoj, Count of Teba, later Montigo, and had two daughters, Maria Francisca and Eugenie Maria de Guzman. Maria Francisca married James Francis Raphael Stuart Fitz James, Duke of Alba and Xerica, and Eugenie married at Notre Dame in 1853, the French Emperor, Charles Louis Napolean III, 1808-73, third son of Louis Bonaparte, King of Holland. She was a great beauty, with auburn hair, fair complexion and blue eyes, and her upbringing was cosmopolitan. The Empress visited Scotland in 1860, calling upon the Duchess of Hamilton and the Duke of Atholl. At Edinburgh and Glasgow she was welcomed enthusiastically, and when at Dumfries, was presented with a genealogical chart of the Kirkpatrick family. Her only son, Napolean, 1856-79, Prince Imperial, was killed in Zululand.

Herbert James Kirkpatrick, 1910-77, son of Maj.-Gen. Charles Kirkpatrick, of Larchwood, Pitlochry, and Elsie Isobel Fasson, had a conspicuous career in the RAF, rising to the rank of Air Vice-Marshall. In World War II he was twice mentioned in dispatches and awarded the D.F.C. He was made C.B.E. in 1945 and in 1957, C.B.

# KNOX

John Knox, 1505-7, the priest who brought about the Reformation in Scotland, has stamped his name indelibly on the Scottish nation. The story is forcibly told in his *History of the Reformation of Religion in Scotland*, first published in 1573. He was born near Haddington, probably son of William Knox, a small farmer, and Marion Sinclair. William may have been descended from the ancient family of Knox of Ranfurly, in Renfrewshire.

The surname is mentioned in the reign of Alexander II. (1214-49), when Adam, son of Uchtred, had a grant of the lands of Knock, so named after a hillock called by that name (Gaelic *Cnoc*), in the Barony of Renfrew. John de Cnoc witnessed a document regarding the lands of Ingliston, in Renfrewshire, about 1260. In 1328, Alan de Knoc received payment from the royal exchequer, of 44s: 10d for conveying the royal stud to the Forest of Selkirk. A family of Knox appear in the north-east in the 15th century and have no known connection with the Renfrewshire family. Indeed, they derived their name from the Aberdeenshire place-name of Knock. They must have considered themselves as chiefs of the surname, as John Knox of that Ilk is mentioned in 1538. Another John Knox, 'grassman' of Knock, is recorded in the *Poll-Tax Record* of 1696. The Renfrew family must also have deemed themselves chiefs, since Johne Knox of that Ilk was an arbiter in a dispute between the town and the abbey of Paisley in 1408. Knollis seems to be a variant surname, and Sir William Knollis was Preceptor of Torphichen and Lord St. John of the Knights Hospitallers before 1500.

The Earls of Ranfurly descend from Marcus Knox, merchant-burgess of Glasgow (1585), through his son Thomas, who married Elizabeth Spang. Their son Thomas, a merchant in Belfast, matriculated arms at the Lyon Office in 1693, as the male representative of the Ranfurly family. He died in 1728, leaving only two daughters, and was succeeded in his lands of Dungannon, Co. Tyrone, by his nephew Thomas, son of his brother, John of Ballycruly. Thomas married Hester Echlin, and they were the parents of Thomas Knox, who was created Baron Wells of Dungannon in 1781, and Viscount Dungannon in 1791. His son, another Thomas, was made Baron Ranfurly in 1826, and created Earl of Ranfurly in 1831. The 7th Earl is Gerald N. Knox, residing at Nayland, Colchester, Essex. An Irish family, Knox of Palmerston, Killala, Co Mayo, appear by their arms to be related to the Earls, but authorities do not agree as to where they branched from the Knox family of Renfrewshire.

Jack Knox, RSA, RSW, son of Alexander Knox in Kirkintilloch, is a well-known artist, and has exhibited his work in Glasgow, Edinburgh, London and Aberdeen. He lectured at the Glasgow School of Art, in Renfrew Street, 1981-92. Some of his work is in permanent collections. David Laidlaw Knox, a Lockerbie man, was educated at Lockerbie and Dumfries academies, and the University of London. An economist and management consultant by profession, he was MP for Leek, 1970-83, and since then has been MP for Staffordshire Moorlands. Ian Campbell Knox, a freelance writer and director, who resides in London, was educated at Edinburgh and Anstruther. He has a number of BBC credits, including *Sweet Nothings*, 1983, and *Spender*, 1991. He gained a BAFTA award for the best play, *The Privilege*, in 1983, and this work also won an award that same year at the Bilbao Film Festival. Dr John Henderson Knox, Edinburgh, is *Emeritus* Professor of Physical Chemistry, University of Edinburgh, having held the Chair, 1972-84. He was educated at George Watson's College and at the universities of Edinburgh and Cambridge.

# LAMONT

The Lamonts derive their name from Laumon or Ladman, a chief who was living, c.1238-c.1294, in the Cowal district of Argyll. He was a grandson of Ferchar (from whom the Macerchars were named), who descended from Anrothan, son of Aodh O'Neill, King of Northern Ireland, 1030-33. Between 1230 and 1246, Duncan, son of Ferchar, and his nephew, Laumon, son of Malcolm, gave the monks of Paisley lands at Kilmun, and the patronage of the church of St. Finan (Kilfinan). The grants were confirmed by Engus, son of Duncan and Malcolm, son and heir of Laumon. The name Laumon is probably derived from Old Norse *Logamor*, 'lawman,' and may indicate his maternal descent.

The Lamonts became powerful, and their chiefs were called 'the great MacLamonts of Cowal.' Their territory stretched from the Dumbartonshire border to Loch Fyne, and probably included some islands. Malcolm, son of Laumon, married Christian, daughter of Alexander of Ergadia, only to learn that she was within the fourth degree of consanguinity, and in 1290, they obtained a dispensation. From the 13th to the 17th century the chiefs lived at Castle Toward. In 1446, the Campbells ravaged the district, killing numerous Lamonts, and the chiefs moved to Ardlamont. About 1463 the lands of the chief fell to the crown by non-entry, and the Lamonts of Inveryne held sway. John Lawmond had a dispute with the monks of Paisley in 1466 over the patronage of the kirk of St. Finan, and it was resolved on production of their old charters. He had a charter of confirmation of the lands of Ardlamont and others in 1472, when his wife was Agnes, 'Donaldis doc(h)ter.'

Sir John Lamont of that Ilk married Jean, daughter of Archibald, Earl of Argyll, who was killed at Flodden in 1513. In 1587, the Laird of Lamont appears in the roll of

'Landlords and Baillies,' upon whose lands dwelt broken men. Sir James Lamont sat in parliament, 1639-40, as one of the Commissioners for Argyll. He established a parochial school at Toward, in 1646. Not long after this, Campbell cadets in Cowal ravaged his lands, and "most barbariously, cruelly and inhumanly, murdered several, young and old, yea, and sucking children, some of them not one month old." Furthermore they carried people from Toward and Escog to Dunoon, and hung "near the number of thirty." The atrocities formed one of the charges against the 9th Earl of Argyll, as chief, in 1661, although not himself involved.

Archibald Lamont of Inveryne was MP for Argyll, 1685-86. He married Margaret Henry, but left no issue and he was succeeded by Dougal Lamont of Stinlaig, nearest heir male. His daughter Margaret married another cadet, John Lamont of Kilfinan, and their son Archibald succeeded to the estates, now smaller, because of the depredations of the Campbells. His descendant, Archibald James Lamont, 1818-62, married Adelaide Dawson, by whom he had a daughter Adelaide. He next married Harriet, daughter of Col. Alexander Campbell of Possil. Their elder son, John Henry Lamont, sold Ardlamont in 1894. He was awarded the chiefly arms as heir of line, and was allowed supporters as chief in 1909. On his death the chiefship passed to the Monydrain branch, of whom Ronald Coll Lamont, 24th chief, died in Australia. Following resignations by his daughter Marian, and her cousin Keith John Lamont, the chiefship was awarded in 1953 to their cousin, Alfred Grenville Lamont, residing in Australia. The present chief is Peter, son of the late Noel Brian Lamont. The last of the Lamont lairds with land in Argyll, were the Knockdow family, at Loch Scriven, 1431-1958.

# LANDSBOROUGH

The surname Landsborough or Landsburgh is not ancient, but several bearers of it have distinguished themselves. The nearest reference to it occurs in 1703, when Samuel McClamroh, at the University of Glasgow, appears as McLanburgh, and this may be a transitional stage. The original surname was in fact McClamroch, and was prevalent in the south-west of Scotland, especially in the district known as Glenkens. There were a variety of spellings: MacClameroch (1455), McClanrouth (1500), McClameract (1530), McGlainroch (1637), McKlamroch and even Mackclamyaugh (1684), McClamroh (1703), and Maclamrock (1747). The correct rendering is Maclamroch, son of the ruddy (or bloody) handed. As so often happened in Galloway, the 'c' in Mac was capitalised and attached to the suffix, while Mac was shortened to Mc. In a marriage contract of 1750, the laird of Stranfasket signed himself 'John McClambroch,' and his son signed as 'Alexr. McClamroch.' The meaning of the name is supported by the fact that the family crest was a hand couped, holding a bloody dagger. The McClamrochs of Craigenbay and the collateral line of Stranfasket were vassals of the Viscounts Kenmure.

It has been stated that the reason for the change to Landsburgh by the brothers and kin of Alexander McClamroch of Stranfasket was because he contracted debts through horse-racing and other habits, and lost the estate to John Newall, younger of Barskeoch, about 1759. Alexander borrowed heavily and even owed the Kirk-Session of Kells money. Moreover, he married in 1750, Margaret, daughter of Robert McMillan of Nether Holm, and uplifted her dowry of £100 Sterling in 1753, although she died in December, 1751, probably in childbirth. It would seem that his kinsmen were attempting to distance themselves from him, but it was probably the provisions to them by their father's bond of 6th August 1751, which finally ruined him.

Descendants of Alexander's brothers Andrew and John are of interest. Andrews sons moved to Otley, in Yorkshire, and founded families there. One member, Andrew, born in 1822, emigrated to Ohio, later to Iowa, U.S.A. John, a weaver, had a son, David Landsborough (1775-1854), who became minister of Stevenson parish, Ayrshire, and after 1843, pastor of a Free Kirk congregation at Saltcoats. He was an accomplished naturalist, and the author of *Natural History of Arran*, and other works. Three of his sons emigrated to Australia, and one of them, William (1825-86), explored in Queensland. He also crossed Australia from the Gulf of Carpentaria to Melbourne in 1862. William became a member of the Upper House of Legislature in Queensland in 1864, and was Government resident in Burke district, 1865-69. He received a gold watch from the Royal Geographical Society of London, a service of plate from the inhabitants of New South Wales, and a gift of £2,000 from the Legislature of Queensland. Many places in Australia have been named after William: as 'Landsborough Town,' Victoria; 'Landsborough County,' N.S.W.; and 'Landsborough River,' Westland, South Island, N.Z. He died on his estate, 'Lochlamborough,' near Brisbane. William's youngest brother, Rev. David Landsborough (1826-1912), was minister of Henderson United Free Church, Kilmarnock, and also a fine naturalist. His son, a third David, was a medical missionary in Formosa.

Robert McClamroch, who emigrated to Virginia about 1755, probably belonged to the Craigenbay line of the family. He was the ancestor of James G.W. MacLamroc, of Greensboro, N.C., an eminent lawyer and family historian.

# LEITH

Those who first bore the surname of Leith were of Flemish extraction, probably from Boulogne, and were perhaps of the same ancestry as the Setons and Bethunes. The surname is derived from the port of Leith, so closely connected with Boulogne as to share the arms of the cathedral there. They may have landed at Leith, but quickly settled in Aberdeenshire near the Leslies, who also came from Flanders.

The first Leith of note was William of Barns, Provost of Aberdeen, 1351-53, and 1373-74, who held the lands of Caprinton. He represented the town in parliament, 1357 and 1367, and was sometime Collector of Customs. To achieve such positions the family must have been established in Aberdeen before his time. William married Christian, said to have been a (?natural) daughter of Donald, Earl of Mar. The cross-crosslet in the Leith arms is probably derived from Mar. Stodart queries this marriage, and says it is likely the family held lands under the earls. Certainly in 1359, William received a charter of Rothens, Harebogge and Blakeboggis, in the Garioch, from Thomas, Earl of Mar. He held also the lands of Ruthrieston in 1473, when he appears as 'William de Leth,' and he died in 1480.

Laurence of Barns, son of William, had a charter of Caprinton in 1388, and was an alderman of Aberdeen in 1401. His brother John, armiger, who was ambassador to England, 1412-16, had a charter of Ruthrieston. The descendants of William are usually styled 'of Barns.' Laurence had sons Norman of Barns, Gilbert, alive 1505, and John, ancestor of the Leiths of Overbarns or Overhall. Henry Leith, Vlth of Barns, who died before 1499, had by his wife Eliza Gordon, George of Barns; William de Edingariock, who succeeded his nephew, John of Barns; and Patrick, ancestor of the Leiths of

Harthill. Patrick, son of Patrick, sold Edingariock. His brother Laurence, held Kirkton of Raine, sold by his son, John, who purchased New Leslie and Peill, where a new house was built by his son James, called Leith-hall, and this became the seat and designation of the family. From him descended the later lairds of Leith-hall, and the Leiths of Freefield. John, XXIInd representative of the family, was succeeded by his brother Gen. Alexander Leith, who married in 1784, Mary, eldest daughter of Charles Forbes of Ballogie. He was succeeded by his son Andrew, who assumed the name Leith-Hay, the designation of later lairds of Leith-hall. Gen. Alexander's second son, John James, was the father of Alexander, 1st Baron Fyvie, (1905), whose son-in-law, Charles Forbes-Leith, was cr. a baronet (UK). His grandson, Sir Andrew Forbes-Leith, 3rd Bt., lives at Dunachton, Kingussie.

From the Leith family of Harthill descended Alexander Leith of Treefield, who married Martha, daughter of John Ross of Arnage. Their son John Ross, 1777-1839, WS, was heir to his aunt, Christian Ross of Arnage, and assumed the surname of Leith-Ross. He married Elizabeth, daughter of William Young of Sheddocksley, Provost of Aberdeen. From Alexander Leith of Treefield, his half-brother, descended the later Barons Burgh. Armorial bearings for the Leiths of Harthill were rendered of old: Or, a cross-crosslet fitchée Azure, between two crescents and a fusil Gules. These were quartered with those of the family of Forbes of Yochone.

Ronald Leith, the talented organist and campanologist of St. Nicholas Church, Aberdeen, is a pillar of the Aberdeen & North-East Scotland Family History Society. As manager of their Family History Centre at 164 King Street, Aberdeen, he has done much to encourage the publication of genealogical material by the Society, and to enlarge their library.

# LESLIE

It was appropriate that in 1993, the anniversary of the death of the saintly Queen Margaret of Scotland, that an excellent history of the Leslies, by Alexander Leslie Klieforth, should appear. Titled *Gripfast: The Leslies in History* (Phillimore: Chichester), it is the best account of the Leslies since 1869. Their ancestor, Bartolph the Fleming, came to England in the retinue of Edward the Exile, who died soon after his return in 1057, and then to Scotland with Edward's daughter Princess Margaret and her brother Edgar. She married Malcolm Canmore, King of Scots. Klieforth says of Bartolph that he was probably the son of an Hungarian magnate, but he witnessed charters concerning the lands of Voormezele, in Flanders. His son Malcolm, was Constable at Inverurie, and his grandson, Norman, assumed the surname of Leslie from Lesslyn, in the Garioch, where the Leslies raised a motte. The ruined castle and the title of Baron was purchased in 1979 by David C. Leslie, an architect and burgess of Aberdeen, who has tastefully restored the building, which he and his wife Lesley Margaret (Stuart) run as a private hotel.

About 1458, George Leslie was elevated to the dignity of Earl of Rothes. His grandson, George, 2nd Earl, succeeded, and in 1490 was infeft in the barony of Ballenbreich and other lands. The Leslies obtained the lands of Balmuto and gave their name to a Fife town and parish. William, 3rd Earl, was slain at Flodden in 1513. The 6th Earl, John, signed the National Covenant in 1638. His son John, 7th Earl, was imprisoned as a Royalist during the Commonwealth period, but obtained a new charter of his honours in 1663. In 1680 he became a Duke. As he died without male issue only the Earldom passed to his daughter Margaret, who married Thomas, Earl of Haddington. Their eldest son became

Earl of Rothes, and their second son, Earl of Haddington. John, 10th Earl, died without issue, and the title passed to his sister Jane (1750-1810), who married George Raymond Evelyn Glanville. Their son George succeeded as 11th Earl. The 21st Earl is Ian Lionel Malcolm Leslie, who is chief of the clan and resides at West Tytherley, in Wiltshire.

Sir Alexander Leslie, a famous general during the Civil War, was created Earl of Leven in 1641. His title is now united with that of Melville. The family muniments are in the Scottish Record Office. Ronald, 11th Earl, founded the Thistle Chapel at St. Giles Cathedral, Edinburgh. The 11th Earl of Leven and 13th Earl of Melville, is Alexander Robert Leslie Melville, who served in the Coldstream Guards during World War II, and resides at Glenferness House, Nairn. Two sons of Sir Partick Leslie of Pitcairlie and Lady Jean Stewart, were raised to the peerage in the 17th century. The eldest son Patrick, was created Baron Lindores, but this title has been extinct since 1775. His brother, General David Leslie, served in the German Wars under King Gustav Adolph of Sweden, and returned to Scotland when the Civil War broke out. He commanded the Scots cavalry at Marston Moor in 1644, when the Royalists were defeated. In 1661 he was created Lord Newark. This title has been extinct since 1694. Another notable branch of the family are the Leslies of Balquhain, Aberdeenshire, with their important cadet, the Leslies of Wardis, whose Barontcy (NS, 1625) is dormant. The heir presumptive is Percy Theodore Leslie, residing at Kingston Hill, in Surrey. The Leslie baronets of Glaslough, Ireland, descend from the Wardis family.

# LINDSAY

The Scottish House of Lindsay, of which the Earl of Crawford and Balcarres is chief, was founded early in the 12th century by Sir Walter de Lindsay, who accompanied Prince David (later David I.) when he took possession of the Principality of Cumbria. He was one of the advisors at an inquisition of the property of the See of Glasgow, about 1120. Sir Walter was of Flemish extraction: a descendant of the Count of Alost. If, as some believe, the surname is derived from De Limesay, Pays de Caus, near Pavilly, there must have been a Norman connection. Others derive the surname from Lindsey, in Lincolnshire.

Sir David Lindsay of Glenesk, born 1359, succeeded to the lordship of Lindsay and barony of Crawford, on the death of his cousin James, and in 1398 was created Earl of Crawford. David Lindsay of Edzell succeeded as 9th Earl on the death of his namesake, the 8th Earl, through the exclusion of his son Alexander, the 'Wicked Master,' in 1542, but re-conveyed the Earldom to the son of the latter, also David, 10th Earl. David of Edzell's second son by Catherine Campbell, was John, founder of the family of Balcarres. He was a statesman during the reign of James VI, and on his appointment to the Court of Session became known as Lord Menmuir.

David, second son of Lord Menmuir, who had purchased Balcarres and Pitcarthy, in Fife, in 1587, was created Lord Lindsay of Balcarres in 1633. His son Alexander was created Lord Lindsay of Balneil and Earl of Balcarres in 1651. Alexander, his great grandson became the 6th Earl of Balcarres and was always known by that dignity, but became Earl of Crawford, *de jure*, in 1808. Succeeding Earls of Crawford and Balcarres have played important roles in Scottish history. The 28th Earl of Crawford and 11th Earl of Balcarres, David Robert

Alexander Lindsay, was a Trustee of the Tate Gallery, 1932-37, and of the National Gallery for several terms. He became a Trustee of the British Museum in 1940, and of the National Library of Scotland in 1944. He was senior Vice-President of the Scottish Genealogy Society from its foundation in 1953 until his death in 1975. Many honours were bestowed upon him, not least G.B.E. in 1951 and K.T. in 1955.

One of the most famous names in Scottish history is that of Sir David Lyndsay (ca.1485-1555), of the Mount, Lord Lyon King of Arms from 1542 to 1555, and previously Lyon Depute. He was a poet and satirist. His *Satyre of the Thrie Estaitis* is still performed on stage. His nephew, Sir David Lindsay of the Mount, also held the office of Lord Lyon, as did this man's son-in-law, Sir Jerome Lindsay of Annatland. By Agnes Lindsay (his second wife), Sir Jerome had a daughter Rachel, who married in 1640, Capt. Bernard Lindsay, of Leith. Their eldest son Robert was the progenitor of Lindsays in Virginia and North Carolina.

There are many branches of the family, and about 200 recorded spellings of the surname, of which 84 are given in Lord Lindsay's admirable *Family of Lindsay* (1840). Some McClintocks ('sons of Findan's gillie') found around Lorne and Luss, are said to have Englished their name to Lindsay. The Lindsays of Dowhill, Kinross, descend from Sir William Lindsay of Rossie, half-brother of the 1st Earl of Crawford. Sir Martin Alexander Lindsay (1905-81), 22nd of Dowhill, was created a baronet in 1962. His son Sir Ronald Alexander Lindsay, the 2nd Bt., resides at Reigate, in Surrey.

# LIVINGSTON

Leving or Leuing, ancestor of the Lowland Livingstons, is said to have come to Scotland from Hungary in the retinue of the Saxon Princess, Margaret, who married Malcolm, Kings of Scots, in 1057. Like others who came to Scotland at that time, they seem to have been sometime in Flanders awaiting a ship. Leving appears to have had some relationship with the East Flanders family of Gavere, closely allied to Count Lambert of Lens. The arms borne by Leving's descendants are: Argent, three gillyflowers (carnations) Gules, within a double tressure flory-counter-flory, Vert, the very device in that unusual green tincture, of the family of Gavere.

The descent from Leving to Sir Andrew Livingston, Sheriff of Lanark, and ancestor of the earls of Linlithgow, is nebulous. Levin' s son Thurston, had sons Alexander and William. About 1290, one William de Levystone witnessed a charter by Malcolm, Earl of Lennox, and in the Ragman Roll in 1296 appears Andrew de Levingston, Lanarkshire, Sir Archibald de Levingeston, Edinburghshire, and Master Archibald de Levingston, chevalier. Their designations indicate relationships, and there can be no doubt that the place-name of Livingston derives from Leving. By his wife Elena, the Sheriff of Lanark had a son William of Gorgyn (Gorgie), Edinburgh, who held those lands before 1328. His son William, married Christian, daughter and heiress of Patrick de Callander, on whose forfeiture he had a charter of the barony of Callander, Stirlingshire, in 1345. William was one of the commissioners appointed to treat with the English for the release of David II in 1357, and his son Patrick was one of the hostages for the ransom.

Sir John Livingston, IIIrd of Callander, who was killed at Homildon Hill in 1402, left a son and heir, Alexander, and was also ancestor of the Livingstons of Kinnaird, Westquarter and Barnton. Alexander's grandson, James of Callander, was cr. Lord Livingston of Callander in 1455. Alexander, 5th Lord Livingston, accompanied Queen Mary to France in 1548, and his daughter Mary was one of the Queen's 'Four Maries.' His son, William, 6th Lord, entertained the Queen at Callander House in 1565, and again in 1567. The 7th Lord, Alexander, was also high in favour with the royal family. He was cr. Earl of Linlithgow in 1601. His second son Alexander succeeded and James third son, a distinguished soldier, was cr. Earl of Callander in 1641. The 4th Earl of Callander, James, succeeded as 4th Earl of Linlithgow in 1695, but becoming involved in the Jacobite rising of 1715, his estates and honours were forfeited. The Kilsyth branch, cr. Viscounts, 1661, suffered a similar fate. The Kinnaird line, cr. Viscounts Newburgh in 1647, ended in an heiress. Also extinct are the Livingstons of Dunipace and of Teviot.

The people who have been termed the 'Highland Livingstones,' have a different origin from the Lowland families. A member of this group is called in Gaelic, *Mac-an-leigh*, 'son of the physician.' From this we have the surname Macleay. The Macleays of the north-west are said to be descended from *Ferchar Leighiche*, who had land in Appin in 1386. He was of the famous MacBeths, physicians to the Lords of the Isles. *The Mac-an-leighs* of Appin, followers of the Stewarts of that place, Anglicised their name as Livingstone, of whom was Blantyre born David Livingstone, 1813-73, the celebrated missionary and African traveller. This family of Livingstone, called the Barons of Bachul, received in early times a grant of lands in Lismore, which they held as keepers of the bishop's crozier.

# MacALISTER

Under their own patronymic, Clan Alister of Kintyre are the senior cadet branch of Clan Donald. They descend from Alasdair (or Alexander) *Mor*, younger son of Donald of Islay, grandson of Somerled, and great-grandfather of John, 1st Lord of the Isles. They were given lands in Kintyre, and after Alasdair was slain in battle with a relative, Ronald of the Isles, they cultivated the friendship of their kinsmen the MacDonalds and the powerful Campbells. This allowed them to survive, in Kintyre. Alasdair's descendant, Charles, son of Ean-Dubh (Black John), was appointed Steward of Kintyre in 1481. Angus Vic Ean-Dubh, his son, styled 'of the Loup,' Loch Tarbert, is on record in 1515. His son, Alasdair was forfeited for abiding from the raid of Sulloway, but had a remission in 1450. The MacAlisters supported Clan Donald in their feud with the MacLeans, and in 1591, Gorrie Mac Eachine Vic Alester Vic ean-Dubh, received a charter of the lands of Loup and others from the Earl of Argyll. His son Alasdair was a supporter of James VII, and fought at Killiecrankie and the Boyne. He married Jane, daughter of Sir James Campbell of Auchinbreck, Bt. Among their family were Hector and Charles, successively lairds of Loup, and Duncan, whose son Gen. Robert MacAlister commanded the Scots Brigade in Holland. In 1792, Charles MacAlester of Loup married Janet, heiress of Kennox, and moved to Ayrshire. Their grandson, Charles Sommerville MacAlester, was awarded arms in 1846 as chief of the clan. His son, Charles Godfrey Sommerville MacAlester of Loup and Kennox, barrister-at-law (Inner Temple, 1892), died without issue in 1931, and his nephew of the same name, son of William, succeeded.

The MacAlisters of Glenbarr, Argyll, an old cadet branch, descend from John MacAlister of Ardnakill, who married Flora, daughter of Lachlan MacNeill of Tearfergus. Their son Ranald married in 1742, Anne, daughter of Alexander MacDonald of Kingsburgh, and had seven sons. The youngest, Col. Matthew MacAlister, 1758-1824, fought against Hyder Ali and was imprisoned at Seringapatam for nearly four years. He was the first MacAlister of Glenbarr. By his second wife, Charlotte Brodie, he had a son Keith, father of Matthew, IIIrd of Glenbarr. By his second wife, Edith Dudgeon, Matthew had a son, Ranald MacDonald Brodie MacAlister of Glenbarr and Clachaig. The MacAlister-Hall family of Torrisdale, Carradale, Argyll, descend from William Hall, 1785-1865, of Dalintober, Campbelton, who married Grace, daughter of Peter MacAlister. Their grandson, Major William Hall of Torrisdale served with distinction in the South African War, 1900-1, and in the First World War. He matriculated arms in 1895 and later assumed the additional surname of MacAlister. His son, Donald Stuart MacAlister-Hall of Torrisdale, married in 1939, Caroline Mary Begg. Donald Diarmid, their eldest son, was born in 1940.

The Alexanders, who settled in Clackmannanshire in the 16th century, claimed descent from Clan Alister. These Alexanders of Menstrie became Viscounts in 1630 and Earls of Stirling from 1633 to 1739; also Viscounts Canada. Sir William, the 1st Earl, a poet and courtier, was granted lands comprising modern Nova Scotia and New Brunswick. This historic deed is in the Sigmund Samuel Canadiana building of the Royal Ontario Museum. He was instrumental in founding the Order of Baronets of Nova Scotia. At Menstrie Castle there is a commemoration room, one wall of which is adorned with the arms of 107 baronets of Nova Scotia, grouped round a portrait of Charles I.

# MacARTHUR

For long it was argued that the MacArthur Campbells of Strachur were not only of the same stock as the House of Argyll, but represented the senior line of the family. The claim to chiefship has long been abandoned, but there is no doubt they were of the same stock and migrated from the district of Lennox, part of the old British kingdom of Strathclyde, into Argyll. It has also been maintained that the Campbells and related groups were Celts, but their armorial bearings proclaim their descent from the Baldwins, Counts of Flanders. The House of Argyll descended from Gilleasbuig or Archibald, who held the lands of Menstrie and Sauchie, in Stirlingshire, in 1263, whose descendants obtained the lands of Loch Awe. Duncan Dhu, probably his brother, was the father of Arthur, from whom the MacArthurs of Innestrynich, on the shores of Loch Awe, took their name. The Campbells of Strachur, were known as MacArthur Campbells, to distinguish them from the descendants of Gilleasbuig, and from their kinsmen at Innestrynich, but are always named as Campbells in historical documents. There seems originally to have also been some link with the MacAulays of Ardencaple, in Dumbartonshire.

Arthur Campbell, progenitor of the Strachur line, signed the Ragman Roll in 1296, but afterwards espoused the cause of Robert the Bruce. He probably fought at Bannockburn in 1314 along with the followers of his kinsman, Sir Neil Campbell of Loch Awe. Arthur was made constable of Dunstaffnage Castle, with the Mains thereof, and Bruce also gave him the lands of Torinturke and others in Lorne, also Kinlochlyon and Auchingewall, for the service of a gallery of 20 oars. The (MacArthur) Campbells had a long association with Strachur, and are now represented by Ian Niall

MacArthur Campbell, XXIVth of Strachur, who resides at Newtonlees, Kelso.

John MacArthur of Innestrynich, contemporary with Arthur (MacArthur) Campbell of Strachur, fell victim to a campaign by King James I to rid the Highlands of chiefs considered too powerful. The historian Tytler calls him "a potent chief," and he is said to have been the leader of 1,000 men. In 1427 his lands were forfeited and he was beheaded. Duncan Makarthure de Turrywadiche, witness to a charter in 1529, received a charter, to him, his spouse Janet Campbell and son John, of the 2-merk land of Auchencrywe, in the barony of Phantilands, from Malcolm son of Eugene Makcorquidill, in 1542. Nigel MacArthur, Notary Public, witnessed a charter of lands at Roseneath, in 1558, and a few clergymen were probably of *Clann-Artair-na-tir-a-cladich ile* – 'of the shoreland,' but when their chief lost his lands, most clansmen became rentallers.

One family of MacArthurs became hereditary pipers to the MacDonalds of Sleat. Charles MacArthur, piper to Sir Alexander MacDonald, perfected his piping under Patrick Og MacCrimmon. His brother Neil was the father of John MacArthur, grocer-burgess of Edinburgh, who became first piper to the Highland Society of Scotland, founded in 1784, and he died in 1792. There was another MacArthur family at Kilmuir, Skye, one of whom was a piper.

Arthur MacArthur, who emigrated from Glasgow to Massachusetts in 1825, was the father of Arthur MacArthur, 1845-1912, a soldier who reached the rank of Lt. General. His son, Gen. Douglas MacArthur, 1880-1964, commanded the US forces in the Far East in World War II, and occupied Japan.

# MacCRIMMON

There is scarcely a family of the Western Isles that has aroused so much controversy as the MacCrimmons. They may have been in Harris and Skye from the early years of the McLeods, and were one of the lesser families on their lands. Dr G.F. Black derives their name from Old Norse: *Hromund (Hro(p)mundr)*, 'famed protector'. The eponymous ancestor is given as Finlay a Breachain, (Finlay of the plaid). It cannot be said that the next few generations, doubtless Norse/Celtic, are well documented, but it seems likely they were pipers to the MacLeod chiefs.

Donald Mor MacCrimmon, piper to Rory MacLeod (1595-1626), is credited with having developed the advanced piping called piobaireachd. His son Patrick Mor and his grandson, Patrick Og, composed many pipe tunes and improved others. The sons of Patrick Og, Malcolm (c. 1690-1769) and Donald Ban (c. 1710-46), were both pipers, sometime in Harris, and the latter was sometime piper to a MacLeod Independent Company raised to keep peace in the Highlands. Malcolm's sons, Iain Dubh (1731-1832) and Donald Ruadh (1742-1845), were both pipers. Iain Dubh witnessed the decline in piping caused by the Jacobite Rising of 1745, and perhaps annoyed by a chief in need of cash, he decided to emigrate, but could not leave his native land. His younger brother, Donald Ruadh, went to America, and had a colourful military career for which there is ample evidence.

The MacLeods of Harris and Dunvegan fostered piping and there are many proofs in their accounts. In 1706 it is on record that Patrick Og MacCrimmon was paid 228 merks, and in 1711 there is an entry for "two pypes brought to MacCrimmon, MacLeod's principal pyper." Patrick Morrison, merchant, was paid for "livery cloths to MacCrimmon," in 1714. According to tradition, a MacCrimmon college of piping was established as far back as the time of Alastair Crotach MacLeod, who died about 1547.

The whole concept of a MacCrimmon college was censured in 1980 by Alastair K. Campsie in his book, *The MacCrimmon Legend*, but it certainly existed: perhaps not always at Boreraig. While Campsie has credited Dr Samuel Johnson, who visited Dunvegan in 1773, with "acuity," he skips smartly over the great man's words: "There has been in Skye, beyond all time of memory a college of pipers, under the direction of MacCrimmon, which is not quite extinct." His comments on what he calls the "alleged" indenture by which Simon, Lord Lovat, sent a piper, David Fraser, to be "perfected" under Malcolm McGrimon in 1743, show his ignorance of documents of this kind. He stated that the authenticity of it was "conjectural," but the manuscript was unearthed in the Scottish Record Office in 1981, and certified as genuine by archivists. Despite his nit-picking, it does prove the existence of a school of piping.

Lt., later Capt. Donald Ruadh MacCrimmon, and his sons Patrick and Donald are well-documented. Donald emigrated to Ontario, Canada, about 1820, and his family carried on the piping tradition. His descendant, Malcolm Roderick MacCrimmon, an expert piper in Alberta, was in 1941 made hereditary piper by Dame Flora MacLeod of MacLeod (1878-1976). He has passed on the position to his son Iain Norman, b. 1952, who lives at Monifeith, in Angus. Initially taught at Edmonton by Harry Lunan, he now plays for the City of Dundee Pipe Band, and also composes. Who said *MacCrimmon no More?*

A genealogical account of the family appears in *Notes and Queries* of the Society of West Highland and Islands Historical Research, February, 1995.

# MacDONALD OF MacDONALD

Clan Donald is the largest of Highland clans and has played a conspicuous part in Scottish history. The old seanachies proclaimed descent from Conn of the Hundred Battles, who flourished in Ireland about AD 125, and from Colla Uais, a Celtic prince with influence in the Western Isles before the establishment of the Scots kingdom of Dalriada by Fergus mac Erc, about 503. There is more support for descent from Angus, a brother of Fergus, who also founded a dynasty in Argyll called the *Cinel Aonghais*, credited with intermarriage with the Pictish royal house.

The clan of Angus were driven out of Islay (to which island they later returned) by the Vikings about 850, and settled beside kinsmen in Argyll. By the 1100s the Scots were resisting the Norsemen, and eventually the mighty Somerled drove them from the mainland. A son of Gillebride, who had probably some Norse blood, he also – perhaps to end feuds with the Norse kings of Man and the Isles – married Ragnhild, a natural daughter of Olaf of Man. At times Somerled, aided by his brother-in-law, Malcolm McHeth, who married a natural daughter of Alexander I, King of Scots, 1107-24, came into conflict with the Scottish kings, and in 1164 he invaded Renfrew, where he was killed: some say assassinated by a page. His mainland possessions were divided among his sons, Reginald of Islay and Kintyre, Dougal (ancestor of Clan MacDougal) of Mull and Lorn, and Angus of Arran and Bute. There were also some natural sons. Reginald's son Donald was the name father of *Clann Domhnuill*, and was 'Regulus' of Argyll and the Isles. His great-grandson, 'Good' John of Islay, ruled as Lord of the Isles for half a century, and was confirmed in his mainland possessions. He married first, Amie MacRuaridh, from whom descended the MacDonalds of Clanranald and

Glengarry, and secondly, Lady Margaret, daughter of Robert the Steward, who, after becoming King Robert II in 1380, induced him to settle the Lordship on a son of this union, Donald Og, who also laid claim to the Earldom of Ross.

Under the Lords of the Isles evolved a remarkable culture. They had a 'parliament' or council, which met at Finlaggan, in Islay. Their lieutenants were the MacKays of the Rhinns; their record keepers the MacPhees of Colonsay; their pipers, MacArthurs; their bards the MacMhuirichs, and their physicians the Beatons or McBeths. Alexander, Lord of the Isles, was made Earl of Ross, but the inbuilt power of the lords was seen as a threat to the kingdom of Scotland, and John his son, was forfeited in 1493. After the fall of the Lordship, the representation passed to the Glengarry line of the family, who favoured the spelling MacDonell, more in line with Gaelic phonetics. Some writers say the Dunyveg line should have succeeded; others that the Clanranald lairds were heirs of line. Aneas, 9th of Glengarry, a Royalist, became Lord MacDonell and Aros at the Restoration in 1660. At his death in 1680 Glengarry passed to his cousin, Reginald of Scotus, and the high chiefship to the Sleat line of the family descended from Hugh, son of Alexander, Lord of the Isles, probably by a daughter of Patrick O Beolan. The Sleat chieftains were baronets, and in 1776, the 9th Bt., was cr. Baron Macdonald in the peerage of Ireland. In 1947, the 7th Baron, Alexander Godfrey, was officially confirmed as Chief of the Name and Arms of MacDonald. Lord Godfrey, the 8th Baron, resides at Kinloch Lodge, Isle of Skye, and the old family territory is owned by the Clan Donald Lands Trust. There is an excellent Clan Centre at Armadale, Skye.

# MacDONALD OF THE ISLES

The MacDonalds of Sleat, who style themselves 'MacDonald of the Isles,' descend from the same ancestor as the clan chief, Lord MacDonald. Their history requires explanation. The lairds of Sleat, in Skye, are generally held to have been the clan chiefs from the latter part of the 17th century, and premier baronets of Nova Scotia from 1625. The story of the division into two families begins with Sir Alexander MacDonald, 9th Bt., which in 1776 was elevated to the peerage of Ireland as Baron MacDonald of Slate, in Antrim. He married in 1768, Elizabeth Diana, eldest daughter, and in her issue co-heir of Godfrey Bosville of Gunthwaite, Yorkshire, by his wife Diana, daughter of Sir William Wentworth, Bt. They had, with other children, Alexander Wentworth, 10th Bt. and 2nd Lord MacDonald, who died unmarried, and his brother, Godfrey, 11th Bt. and 3rd Lord MacDonald, who succeeded his brother in 1824.

Sir Godfrey, in the death of his maternal uncle, William Bosville of Thorpe and Gunthwaite, succeeded to these estates for life, and assumed the name Bosville in lieu of MacDonald, in 1814. On the death of his brother he assumed the name MacDonald after that of Bosville, and succeeded to the baronetcy and the Irish Barony. His Lordship married, apparently by declaration in Scotland, Louisa Marie La Coast, natural daughter of the Duke of Gloucester and Lady Almeria Carpenter, daughter of the Earl of Tyrconnel. They had three children, Alexander William Robert, William, and Louisa, before their marriage at Norwich, 29th May, 1803, and had ten other children, including Godfrey William Wentworth. Under Scottish law the first three children were legitimate in view of the subsequent marriage of their parents. Alexander William Robert entered into possession of the Yorkshire estates, but did

160

not assume any title. The father sought to separate the Skye and Yorkshire inheritances of MacDonald and Bosville. This would make Alexander William Robert owner of the Yorkshire lands, with the arms of Bosville, and Godfrey William Wentworth, proprietor of the Skye estates, with the territorial barony, the Irish peerage and the chiefship of the clan. A special act of Parliament was passed in 1847 to regulate the position.

Although the squires of Thorpe, father and son Godfrey Wentworth Bayard Bosville, did not assume any title, when the grandson, Alexander Wentworth Bosville MacDonald, petitioned the Scottish Court of Session in 1910, they were found to be *de jure*, 12th and 13th baronets. Alexander therefore became the 14th Bt. and 22nd chief of the MacDonalds of Sleat. He and his children all assumed the surname 'MacDonald of the Isles.' This has been criticised, since younger children do not normally use the family designation. The present Sleat chieftain is Ian Godfrey Bosville MacDonald, 17th Bt., residing at Osmigarry Lodge, Kilmuir, Isle of Skye. He is a chartered surveyor, with farming interests at Humberside.

Godfrey William Wentworth's line of the family had been chiefs of Sleat, and they continued as barons. The latter married in 1845, Marie Ann, daughter of George Thomas Windham of Cromer Hall, Norfolk. Their sons Somerled James, 1849-74 and Ronald Archibald, 1853-1947, were 5th and 6th Barons. Ronald was succeeded by his grandson, Alexander Godfrey MacDonald, 1909-70, to whom, in 1947, the ancient arms of MacDonald of MacDonald were restored by Letters Patent. His son, Godfrey James, is the heir.

# MacDONALD OF CLANRANALD

The Clanranald line of the MacDonalds looms large in the history of the West Highlands and Islands. Like the MacDonells of Glengarry, they descend from John, Lord of the Isles, and his first wife, Amie MacRuairi. Ronald, the eldest surviving son, from whom the generic appellation arose, was the father of Allan of Garmoran, who left at least three sons. Roderick, the eldest son, by his first wife, Margaret, daughter or grand-daughter of Donald *Balloch*, progenitor of the MacDonalds of Dunyveg, died in 1481, and was succeeded by Allan, numbered 4th of Clanranald by the clan genealogists. Allan married Florence, daughter of Alexander MacDonald of Ardnamurchan, and had two sons, Ronald Bane and Alexander. Ronald had charters of lands in Uist, Eigg and Arisaig. His son Dugal was murdered, and left issue, but was succeeded by his uncle, Alexander, styled 'Captain of Clanranald' in 1498. His son, Ian or John of Moidart, called Moidertach, legitimated in 1530, became 8th chief. He was imprisoned in Edinburgh Castle in 1540, and at that time Hugh Fraser, 3rd Lord Lovat, invaded Moidart and installed his uncle (of the half-blood) Donald *Gallda* MacDonald, in Castle Tirim, situated on a prominence in Loch Moidart.

John escaped, and aided by the Camerons, defeated and killed Donald *Gallda* at Loch Lochy in 1544. By his first marriage, to Margaret, daughter of MacDonald of Ardnamurchan, he left a son, Allan, 9th of Clanranald. From his second marriage to a daughter of Angus MacDonald of Knoydart, he had with other issue, a son John, from whom descended John MacDonald of Glenaladale, who led colonists to Prince Edward Island, Canada, in 1771. Allan married (?Flora), daughter of Alastair MacLeod of MacLeod, and had five sons. From

Ranald, fifth son, descended the MacDonalds of Belfinlay, Balivanich and Boisdale. Flora MacDonald, 1722-90, the heroine of the '45 Jacobite Rising, was a daughter of Ranald of Balivanich and his second wife, Marion MacDonald, descended from the Griminish family. Allan was succeeded by his third son, Angus, whose issue failed, and his brother Donald became 11th of Clanranald and Moidart. He was knighted in 1617, and succeeded by his son John, a Royalist, who married Sarah, daughter of Sir Rory *Mor* Macleod of Dunvegan. Her dowry was a fully equipped 24-oared galley, and 180 head of cattle.

The Clanranald family were involved in the '15 and '45 Jacobite Risings. Allan, 14th chief, was killed at Sheriffmuir, in 1715. His cousin, Donald, 16th laird, fought under Dundee at Killiecrankie in 1689. Donald, his son, took no active part in '45, but it was in Clanranald country that the Young Pretender landed in 1745. Ranald, 18th chief, gave a bond which enabled Prince Charles to leave Edinburgh, although it seriously affected the family fortunes. He fought in the Rising and later in the American Revolution. Under his son John, over 300 people emigrated from the impoverished Clanranald estates to Prince Edward Island in 1790. Ranald, 20th of Clanranald, was forced to sell his estates between 1813 and 1830. Although the family believed they were heirs of line of the Lords of the Isles, in 1810 he matriculated arms as chief of Clanranald. The present and 24th chief is Ranald Alexander, who also matriculated in 1956. He was chairman of the Museum of the Isles, 1980-89, and is an executive chairman of the Clan Donald Lands Trust. He married in 1961, Jane Campbell-Davys, and has issue. The chief resides at Wester Lix House, Killin, in Perthshire. The old family home was Arisaig House, in Lochaber.

# MacDONNELL OF GLENGARRY

The MacDonells of Glengarry and the MacDonalds of Clanranald descend from John, Lord of the Isles (d. about 1387) and his first wife, his cousin Amie MacRuari. Ranald, their second son, from whom Clanranald is named, had several sons, including Allan of Garmoran, from whom descended the chiefs of Clanranald, and Donald, Steward of Lochaber, progenitor of the MacDonells of Glengarry. A dispute for precedency long agitated the two houses. Donald died in 1420, having had at least three sons: John, who left no issue or was passed over in the succession; Alexander, who held lands in Morar and Glengarry, and died in 1460; and Angus. John, son of Alexander, held Glengarry, and was succeeded by his son Alexander, styled in 1501, Alastyr MacEan vic Allyster. He married Margaret, daughter of Sir Alexander MacDonald of Lochalsh, included with him in a crown charter of Glengarry and Morar, with parts of Lochalsh, Lochcarron, and Lochbroom (including Strome Castle), in 1538/9. They had five sons and were succeeded by Angus, laird of Glengarry by 1565, numbered 7th in the clan genealogies.

Donald MacDonell, 8th of Glengarry, had a charter of Glengarry in 1627, incorporating the lands into a free barony. Relations with the collateral line improved after his marriage to a MacDonald of Clanranald. Their son Aneas or Angus, a Royalist, who adhered to Montrose throughout his campaign, was cr. a peer at the Restoration of Charles II in 1660, by the title of Lord MacDonell and Aros. He married Margaret, daughter of Sir Donald MacDonald of Sleat, 1st Bt. In 1672, the Privy Council charged him to find caution according to the laws for "the whole name and clan." When he died in 1680, Glengarry passed to his cousin, Reginald or Ranald

MacDonell of Scotus, and the representation became vested in the Sleat line. The peerage became extinct.

Ranald MacDonell, 10th of Glengarry, was succeeded by his son Alastair, a noted Jacobite, was cr. a peer in 1716 (as Lord MacDonell) by the exiled James VIII. John, son of Alastair, and his son Alastair, took part in the '45 Rising, and spent some time as captives in the Tower of London. The latter died unmarried in 1761, and was succeeded by his nephew, Duncan 14th of Glengarry. His son, Alexander, raised a fencible regiment in 1794, by which time he was chief. He treated the men shabbily when they were discharged in 1802, and they emigrated to Glengarry County, Ontario, Canada, where they joined other clansmen who emigrated in 1792. They distinguished themselves in another regiment, the Glengarry Fencibles, during the War of 1812. Alastair attempted to live in the grand style of his ancestors, and his character is drawn as 'Fergus McIvor' in Sir Walter Scott's *Waverley*. He matriculated arms in 1777, and the following year killed Lt. MacLeod, of the Black Watch in a duel. Alexander was pardoned, and in 1802 married Rebecca, daughter of Sir William Forbes of Pitsligo. His son, Aneas, succeeded him in 1828, and in 1840 was forced to sell the ancestral lands and emigrate to Australia. Only Knoydart remained, and after his death in 1852, his widow, Josephine Bennett, and the other trustees evicted the tenants. Knoydart was later sold to a family of Bairds. The present octogenarian chief is A/Cdre. Donald MacDonell, 22nd of Glengarry (and 12th Titular Lord MacDonell), who served in the RAF and Fleet Air Arm, then became an industrialist. In 1981 he retired to Fortrose. His heir is Aneas Ranald Euan MacDonell, Yr. of Glengarry, born 1941, who lives in London.

# MacDOUGALL

The MacDougalls of MacDougall and Dunollie descend from Somerled, King of the Isles: progenitor also of the MacDonalds. His son Dugall (or Dougall) was ruler of the south isles, having been given Argyll and Lorn, with the islands of Mull, Lismore, Kerrara, Scarba, Jura, Tiree and Coll. His chief fortresses were Dunstaffnage and Dunollie, still the residence of the MacDougall chiefs. Parts of their territory was held under the kings of Norway. Dugall, name-father of the clan, had three sons, Duncan, Gillespic and Dugall, who, along with King Haakon, attacked Bute, which had fallen into Scottish hands. At this time the Norwegian king was still prepared to intervene in the islands. About 1249, Dugall's son Duncan had a temporary commission from Haakon to govern all the islands from Man to Lewis. The islands were finally ceded to Scotland in 1266. Duncan was the first to assume the surname of MacDugall (MacDougall). Alastair, his son, attended the council at Perth in 1284, as a baron of the realm, and when Argyll was made a sheriffdom in 1292, he was appointed sheriff.

In favourable circumstances, Robert Bruce, crowned King of Scots in 1306, could expect support from Gaeldom, but his slaying of John Comyn altered matters. Comyn's kinsman, Alastair MacDugall, defeated him at *Dal-Righ*, the same year. It was on this occasion that John of Lorn, son of Alastair, in attempting to seize the escaping king, grasped and held the famous reliquary brooch still owned by the family. Bruce confronted the MacDugalls again in 1308, and obtained the submission of Alastair. It was untrustworthy, as his son John adhered to Edward of England. Bruce, better organised in 1309, broke the power of the MacDugalls at Brander Pass. The Campbells, not then a powerful family, received part of their estates, and Sir Neil Campbell was given the king's sister Mary in marriage. However, the MacDugalls made a pact with their kinsmen the MacDonalds, in 1354, and re-entered Gaelic society. Their position was strengthened by Robert the Steward before becoming king, and some of their lands were restored. Ewen, VIth chief, married Joanna, daughter of Sir Thomas Isane, by the Princess Mathilda, daughter of Robert the Bruce, but died without issue.

John, son of Allan, succeeded his cousin, and in 1451 the Stewart lord of Lorn granted him lands around Oban Bay down the coast to Loch Melfort. By the 16th century the chiefs were acknowledging Campbell of Argyll as their superior. After the execution of Archibald Campbell in 1685, it seemed as if the MacDugall chiefs would recover their old territory, but the Campbells rallied. James VII, however, gave the chief a charter of part of Lorn. John MacDougall of that Ilk fought at Sheriffmuir in 1715, and was forfeited. As a prisoner he just escaped transportation, and the estates were restored to his son Alexander, who wisely heeded the advice of John, Duke of Argyll, and kept out of the Jacobite rising of 1745.

The MacDougall chiefs came to serve in the armed forces. Sir John MacDougall, 1789-1865, was in the Royal Navy and rose to the rank of Vice-Admiral. His heir, Capt. Alexander, served in the Royal Artillery, and another son, Charles, was in the Navy. Capt. Alexander's heir, Lt. Col. Charles MacDougall, served in the Bengall Staff Corps. Alexander James, XXIXth chief, served in the Royal Army Medical Corps in World War I. He was succeeded by his daughter Coline, 1904-84, 30th chief. She married in 1949, Leslie Graham Thomson, RSA, who assumed the surname of MacDougall.

# MacDUFF

The early members of the Clan MacDuff are literally seen through the mists of time. Although indistinct, the vital thread links us with Ethelred or Aedh, a son of Malcolm III and Queen Margaret. Born probably about 1170, and debarred from the throne either through infirmity or as an abbot, he married a grand-daughter of Queen Gruoch (the Lady MacBeth of Shakespeare), herself the heiress of the line of King Dubh (or Duff), killed in 967. Aedh was Earl of Fife, and among his children was probably a son Dubh (or Duff), who died in his father's lifetime, leaving two sons, Constantine, 2nd Earl, who died about 1129, and Gillemichael MacDuff, 3rd Earl, who did not long survive him. Gillemichael had two sons, Duncan, 4th Earl, and Hugh, whose son Michael was ancestor of the Wemyss family (still representers). Hugh may also have been ancestor of the Duffs of Banffshire.

Duncan, who died in 1154, was made hereditary earl by David I, in return for military service. The position of the earls as magnates of the important province of Fife, and their privileges later enshrined in 'the law of Clan MacDuff' all reflected compensation for exclusion from kingship. The 'law' gave them the honour of enthroning the king at his coronation; leading the vanguard in battle, and remission for homicide, with sanctuary at 'MacDuff's Cross.' Duncan was succeeded by his son Duncan, father of Malcolm, 6th Earl, who was succeeded by his nephew Malcolm, 7th Earl, who married Helen daughter of Llewellyn, Prince of Wales, with issue two sons, Colban, 8th Earl, and MacDuff of Reres. Colban had a son Duncan, and also a daughter Isabella, who, extending the 'Law of Clan MacDuff,' crowned Robert Bruce in 1306. Duncan, son of Colban, had a son Duncan, 1285-1353, who was followed by his daughter Isabella, Countess of Fife. When she died childless about 1389, the earldom passed by an entail made by her father, to Robert Stewart, Earl of Menteith. His third son Robert succeeded but as he was forfeited the earldom became annexed to the crown.

The genealogy of the Duffs becomes credible after a grant to David Duff, of the lands of Muldavit and Baldavy, in Banffshire, in the reign of Robert III, 1390-1406. After the direct line of Craighead-Muldavit expired, Alexander Duff of Keithmore's son, Alexander, assumed the chiefship. He had three sons, Alexander of Braco, who died in 1718 without male issue; William of Dipple, and Patrick, from whom descended the Duffs of Hatton and Fetteresso. William of Dipple, a wealthy landowner, was succeeded by his son, William, who was cr. Baron Braco of Kilbryde, in 1735, and Viscount MacDuff and Earl Fife, both in the peerage of Ireland, 1759. He erected Duff House, 1740-45. During the '45 he was on the government side. His son James, 2nd Earl Fife, was cr. a peer of Great Britain, 1790, as Baron Fife. He made additions to his estate and changed the name of the town of Doune to MacDuff, and procured for it a burgh charter. He died in 1809, when the title Baron of Fife expired, and the other honours devolved on his brother. Alexander, 6th Earl, was cr. Duke of Fife in 1889, on his marriage to Princess Louise, daughter of King Edward VII. All the peerages, save the Dukedom, and the representation of Duff of Braco, became dormant in 1912, but the present and 3rd Duke, James Carnegie, who succeeded in 1959, was already 11th Earl of Southesk, and has other honours.

Other surnames associated with the Clan MacDuff are Abernethy, Spens or Spence, Fife, and of course Wemyss.

# MacDUFFIE/MacFIE

The ancestors of the MacDuffies probably came to Scotland as early as the 12th century. Some authorities give them a Norse origin, but it is almost certain they were Celts from Ireland, where variants such as MacAfee, MacHaffie and Duffy are common. Skene suggests the "clan *Mhic Duibside* or Macduffys" derived their name from *Duibhside*, who appears in the 'Annals of Ulster' in 1164, as Ferleighinn or lector of Iona. Another possibility is that they descend from Murdoch, son of Fearchar Ruadh, son of Cormac, Bishop Dunkeld, who died in 1177, and derive their name from Duffie (*Dubhshithe*), third in the descent from Murdoch. The name MacDuffie means 'son of the dark spirit,' and possibly they were in Easter Ross before settling in Colonsay and Oransay, where a member of the family was a clergyman. The Augustinian priory of Oransay was traditionally founded by John, Lord of the Isles, before 1353.

No certain genealogy can be drawn before Christinus (some say Gillespic), who flourished towards the middle of the 15th century. He seems to have had three sons, Donald, Niall and Malcolm. 'Donaldi Mcduffee' appears as a charter witness in 1463, and again, as 'Donaldo Christini Makduff,' in 1472. His youngest brother, Malcolm, 'Lord of Dunevin,' succeeded as chief, and he is named on a graveslab at Iona to his wife's brother, Ian MacIan of Ardnamurchan. Malcolm also appears as "son of Christinus MacDuffie" on a cross at Oransay. It was possibly the MacDuffie/MacDonald marriage which resulted in some clansmen settling in Lochaber. The MacDuffie chiefs were keepers of the records for the Lords of the Isles, but unfortunately those registers have perished.

The name McDuffie was often shortened to MacFie.

Other variants are MacFee, MacPhie and MacFeye. Murroch was the name of the MacDuffie chief in 1531, and he was probably grandson of Malcolm. In 1609, Malcolm MacFie of Colonsay was one of twelve chiefs and gentlemen who met at Iona with Andrew, Bishop of the Isles, and formulated the 'Statutes of Icolmkill.' In 1615 Malcolm joined Sir James MacDonald of Islay, who had escaped from imprisonment at Edinburgh, and was one of the leaders in his rebellion. He and eighteen others were delivered by Coll Kitto MacDonald (*Colla Coitach*) to the Earl of Argyll for trial by the Privy Council. Coll however, was delated in 1623 for the murder of Malcolm MacFie, Donald Oig MacFie (brother of Murdock in Islay), Dougald MacFie and others. Malcolm left a widow, Marie MacDonald, and children Donald Oig, Katherine and Finvola. MacFies at this time scattered to Mull, Jura, Gigha, and other islands.

Subsequent chiefs were dispossessed for a time by Coll Kitto MacDonald then placed themselves under the protection of the MacDonalds of Islay. Their ancestral islands afterwards passed to the Duke of Argyll, who exchanged Colonsay and Oransay for Crerar, in South Knapdale, with Donald MacNeill, some of whose descendants shed lustre on the islands. The names of the MacFie chiefs since 1623 appear to be Donald Oig, Dougald, Donald, Angus and Malcolm, 1786-1854, whose son John emigrated to Canada before 1847, settling in Mariposa Township, Victoria County, Ontario, where he had a family. Many clansmen remained in Scotland, and among these were the MacFies of Dreghorn, Midlothian, and those of Langhouse, Renfrewshire. The latter family were prominent landowners, and their cadets included the MacFies of Gogarburn and Borthwick Hall, Midlothian, and of Airds, Argyll.

# MacFARLANE

The MacFarlanes of Arrochar, or of that Ilk, were proud of their descent from Gilchrist, a younger brother of Alwyn, Earl of Lennox, who flourished during the reign of Alexander II. (1224-49), and were granted by his brother a charter of the lands of Upper Arrochar and Luss, with some islands in Loch Lomond. For centuries the lands were known as Arrochar McGilchrist. Later lairds appear to have been the male representatives of the Celtic Earls of Lennox, but the title of Earl was assumed by Sir John Stewart of Darnley about 1473, and recognised by 1488.

A fighting race, the MacFarlanes fought in the War of Independence, and were involved in the conflict at Dalrigh, near Tyndrom, in 1306, when MacDougall, Lord of Lorn, gained the celebrated reliquary brooch of Lorn, worn by Robert the Bruce. From Parlane, the fourth chief, the surname arose. However, some members of the clan kept the surname of McGilchrist. This patronymic is now, but not always correctly, believed to be a sept of the Ogilvys and MacLachlans.

Under Duncan MacFarlane of that Ilk, the clan suffered losses when they fought along with the MacDougalls against the Stewarts and MacLarens at Stalc, in Appin, in 1468. The clan lost its chief, Sir John, at Flodden in 1513. His son Andrew earned the soubriquet of 'The Wizard.' He had learned many sleight of hand tricks when he visited the Continent, and these "astonished and frightened the country people who ascribed these things to witchcraft." Andrew is regarded as the composer of the famous clan pibroch, 'Thogail nam bo theid sinn,' to which words were later added to note the clan's reputation as cattle lifters. These include: "Wasps o' the west, be sparin' o' rest, when to the west fare we; That ye shall be shorn o' fleece and o' horn, 'tween this and the morn, swear we." Those raiding exploits led to the moon being called 'Macfarlane's Lantern.'

The clan fought at Glasgow Muir when their superior, the Earl of Lennox, took up arms in 1544 to oppose the Regent Arran. Hollinshed described them as "well armed in shirts of mail, with bows and two-handed swords." Many clansmen fought at Pinkie in 1547, where their chief, Duncan was slain. They distinguished themselves at Langside in 1568, when they supported the Regent Moray against the Queen's party. It is said that the Regent gave them their crest, a crown, with an armed warrior and the motto THIS I'LL DEFEND. The armorial bearings remained largely unchanged until Walter MacFarlane, the famous antiquary, re-matriculated in 1750. The motto of the clan was 'Loch Sloy,' from their rallying place, the loch of that name, opened as a reservoir by Queen Elizabeth (now the Queen Mother) in 1952.

Walter MacFarlane (1698-1767) was an unusual clan chief, with antiquarian leanings. He became a competent Latinist and palaeographer, and a zealous collector of historical material, most of which is preserved in the National Library of Scotland. He married Lady Betty Erskine, some thirty-five years his junior, in 1760. Walter was succeeded by his brother Dr William who sold the estate of Arrochar in 1784. He is supposed to have then emigrated to America, but this is an error caused by a misreading of a document of that time. Dr William died in 1791. The last chief, James, died about 1866. His sister Jane Watt MacFarlane, married James Scott, an architect and builder, and the heir to the chiefship may be among their descendants.

# MacGILLIVRAY

When King Alexander II. (1214-49) subdued Argyll in 1222, the forebears of the MacGillivrays were one of the principal tribes he dispersed. Some settled in Mull and others probably in Lochaber and Morvern. By some accounts their chief around 1263 was Gabra or Gillebride, who migrated into Strathnairn, "from the west" and placed himself and his followers under the protection of Farquhar, a Mackintosh chief who was killed in 1274. Thus, by Celtic law, they were indigenated into Clan Mackintosh, and subsequently, by MacIntosh inheritance, into the Clan Chattan.

Duncan MacGillivray, who flourished about 1500, is considered to be the first of the family styled "of Dunmaglass." He appears to have been a tenant, but his followers became known as *Clan Mhic Gillebrath*. In 1609, Farquhar of Dunmaglass was a minor, and his uncle, Duncan, along with two others, took burden "for the haill kin and race of MacGillievray," and signed the famous Clan Chattan Bond. In 1626, Farquhar was granted a feu charter of Dunmaglass by John Campbell of Calder.

The MacGillivrays took an active part in the Jacobite rising of 1715, and the chief, Capt. Farquhar of Dunmaglass, and his brother Lt., later Capt. William, served in the Clan Chattan Regiment. The Mackintosh chief remained loyal to his Hanovarian commission in 1745, but his wife Christian raised the clansmen for Prince Charles. Alexander, the MacGillivray chief, leading Clan Chattan, fell near the well which still bears his name. After the '45 two important members of the chiefly line emigrated to Georgia. Lachlan MacGillivray became an Indian trader and married Sehoy, half-breed daughter of Capt. Marchand and a Creek princess. Their son Alexander (1758-93), was educated by his kinsman,

174

Rev. Farquhar MacGillivray, in Charleston, and became a member of the Council of the Creek Nation at the age of 22. He kept the Creeks out of the War of Independence and enabled them to survive better than any other tribe against the ruthless white man. Another clansman, William McGillivray (1764-1825), son of a tacksman, emigrated to Canada and engaged in the fur trade. His story as chief superintendent of the North-West Company is told by Marjorie W. Campbell in her biography, *McGillivray: Lord of the Northwest* (Toronto, 1962).

Dunmaglass was in a precarious financial state when William MacGillivray succeeded his brother who was killed at Culloden Moor, and he obtained a captaincy in the Gordon Regiment. His son, John Lachlan, served in the 16th Light Dragoons, and died without issue in 1852. The estates then passed to his fourth cousin, John MacGillivray (1777-1855), also a Nor Wester in Canada. He did not actually come into possession of the estates because of prolonged litigation. It was another MacGillivray in Canada, Lt. Col. George B. MacGillivray, a newspaper proprietor, who matriculated posthumously in 1967 the arms for Farquhar, chief in 1672 when the official Lyon Register commenced. Capt. Neil John MacGillivray, who succeeded his father in 1855, was involved in much litigation and was forced to sell Easter Gask and Wester Lairgs, leaving only Dunmaglass. His son, John William MacGillivray, the last chief, was obliged to sell the remaining parts of his inheritance. He went to India, where he lived comfortably, but died without issue.

# MacGOWAN/SMITH

From early times there have been workers in metal, and in the Scottish burghs they were members of the Incorporation of Hammermen, which included those working with gold, silver and copper. Among their ranks were blacksmiths, whitesmiths, coppersmiths, and even clock and watchmakers. Little wonder then that Smith is the most prolific surname in the country.

The Gaelic form is *gobha* or *gobhainn*, and usually relates to blacksmith. MacGown is simply *mac a ghobhainn* or *MacGhobhainn*, 'son of the smith.' An exception is found in Dumfriesshire in the reign of David II, 1329-32, and it appears that a clan MacGowan existed in the vicinity of the River Nith. The clan was represented by Donald Edzear, a descendant of Dunegal of Strathnith (Nithsdale), whose home was at Morton. Dr Black suggests this may indicate descent from Owen the Bald, king of the Strathclyde Britons. Curiously, many people surnamed MacGowan appear in records of the south-west and unless other evidence is forthcoming, we must look upon them as descended from smiths. Gilbert Makgowin, a follower of the Earl of Cassilis, was respited for murder in 1526. In 1626, the Earl of Cassilis gave a precept for infefting John McGowne as heir to his father in the 5-merk land of Skeoch, at Whithorn. John McGowan, son of William McGowan, Town Clerk of Whithorn, was admitted Writer to the Signet in 1713. The surname appears elsewhere. In 1503, Gilcallum McGoun had a remission for rapine and other crimes on the lands of the Abbot of Cupar. William McGown, a follower of Ross of Pitcalny, is recorded in 1592, and Murchiey McGowne in Fanmore, Mull, appears in 1629. In modern times Iain Mac a Ghobhainn, otherwise Iain Crichton Smith, a native of Lewis, is a distinguished writer in prose and verse. Ian Duncan McGowan has been Librarian of the National Library in Scotland since 1990.

Smith or Smyth is rendered in old Latin writs as *Faber* and *Ferro*. Adam Faber held a croft on the lands of Swaynstoun, about 1225, and William faber de Karel was a witness about 1250. Thomas Smyth, Scotsman, had a safe conduct into England in 1398. Patrick Smyth, a Scot, was in custody in the Tower of London in 1401. Elizabeth and Margaret Smythe were heirs portioners of Alexander Smythe in Greinholme, 1621. The surname increased around Glengarry in the first half of the 18th century, when the woods there were used in the smelting of iron ore from Lancashire. It is said that in 1841 census enumerators in Lewis who could not understand some of the Gaelic names, entered them as Smiths. There were Smiths there before 1841, and a number had emigrated to Canada. Others who were smiths kept 'Gobha' in their names. John *Gobha* Murray, of Tolsta, Lewis, emigrated to Compton County, Quebec in 1855.

Adam Smith, 1723-90, the famous political economist and moral philosopher whose book The *Wealth of Nations*, published in 1776, is still hailed as a landmark in the study of economics, was a native of Kirkcaldy. Donald Alexander Smith, 1820-1914, from Archieston, in Moray, had a remarkable career in the fur trade in Canada, starting as a junior clerk with the Hudson's Bay Company, and rising to high office. He was Deputy-Governor, 1888-89, and was cr. Baron Strathcona and Mount Royal, in 1897. He was Governor from 1889-1914. John Smith, 1938-94, QC, from Dalmally, Argyll, qualified as an advocate, but turned to politics. He was an MP from 1970-94, latterly for Monklands East, and Leader of the (Labour) Opposition from 1992.

# MacGREGOR

The crest of the MacGregors bears the proud motto 'My Race is Royal,' and for centuries the ancestor was believed to be Alpin, the King of Dalriada slain in battle with the Picts in 832, and whose son Kenneth united the Scots and Picts in 844. However, the old genealogies of the clan cannot now be accepted. It is possible their name derives from the shadowy figure of Gregor of the Golden Bridles, who lived in the 14th century. Clan leaders often took their designations from an ancestor noted for some outstanding exploit or trait. Gregor was quite possibly of royal descent, but it is uncertain if the bloodline was Scottish or Pictish.

Gregor's son, Iain 'Cam,' who died in 1390, held the glens of Orchy, Strae and Lochy, on the opposite watershed of Strathfillan and Glendochart. He had three sons: Patrick, who held the ancient homeland of Glenorchy and lands of Strathfillan; Ian Dhu, ancestor of the MacGregors of Glenstrae; and Patrick, progenitor of the MacGregors of Brackley, Roro and Glengyle. Patrick's son Malcolm lost the Strathfillan lands to the Campbells of Breadalbane, and the Glenstrae line came to be recognised as chiefs, but not universally. Some authorities say they never had a chief in olden times.

The MacGregors lost possession of all of their lands except Glenstrae to the Campbells of Argyll and Breadalbane, but the Earls of Argyll were also feudal superiors of Glenstrae. The Campbells annoyed and oppressed the MacGregors, reducing them to a state of lawless insubordination. Naturally, they retaliated against the possessors of the soil, but were represented in Edinburgh as having an untameable ferocity which nothing could remedy save "cutting off the tribe of MacGregor, root and branch." An enactment of 1488 injured the clan, but they were still numerous over a wide area, and it seems that their fighting spirit and pride of race sustained them.

By the slaughter of Drummond of Drummondernoch in 1589, and their part in the Conflict of Glenfruin in 1603, the former leading to an incident related in Scott's *Legend of Montrose*, the very name of MacGregor was proscribed in 1603 by the Privy Council. They were forced to adopt other names such as Murray, Graham, Stewart, Grant and even Campbell. A later act pronounced death on any who had borne the name if they assembled in groups of more than four. Remarkably they fought under Montrose, and this led to a relaxation in 1661. The surname was not fully restored until 1774.

In 1714 the Balhaldie line – cadets of Roro – claimed chiefship, but were frustrated. At length the Brackley line, with others, entered into a deed recognising John Murray (later MacGregor) of Lanrick as chief. The position was not conceded by the MacGregors of Glengyle, from whom the celebrated Rob Roy MacGregor *alias* Campbell was descended, but the chiefship being *de jure* and *de facto* vacant, he was recognised by the Lord Lyon and matriculated arms in 1775, with heretable destination as chief of the clan. Several books have been written about Rob Roy MacGregor, one by Sir Walter Scott. The best is *Rob Roy MacGregor: His Life and Times*, by W. H. Murray (1982). The present chief is Brigadier Sir Gregor MacGregor of Macgregor, 6th Baronet (cr. 1795) of Lanrick and Balquhidder, who has had a distinguished military career. The heir is his son, Major Malcolm Gregor Charles MacGregor. There is a flourishing clan society, and the magazine, *The Quaich*, published at Edinburgh, is brimful of information about MacGregors.

# MACKAY

The surname Mackay is derived from the Gaelic *MacAoidh*, 'son of Aodh.' Aoidh was a popular Celtic name, meaning 'Fire.' Early chroniclers wrote the name Ed, Eth or Heth. It was often simply spelt Y or Iye, hence MacIye, which owing to the intrusion of 'k' became Mackay, which is somewhat misleading. There is some confusion about the family origins, but a distinct trace of some connection with the Kings of the Scots. Aethelred, son of Malcolm III and Queen Margaret, was otherwise known as Aedh, Abbot of Dunkeld, and 1st Earl of Fife. He died in 1128. Malcolm McHeth, Earl of Ross, was possibly his son. A competent historian has however suggested that Malcolm was a natural son of King Alexander I, 1107-24, son of Malcolm III. Some idea of his standing may be gleaned from the fact that he married a daughter of Somerled, *regulus* of Argyll.

When the MacWilliams attempted to gain the throne, Malcolm MacHeth was associated with them. He was captured in 1134, and imprisoned at Roxburgh. His eldest son Donald, was also kept there after 1156, and the fact they were not executed tends to support the idea they stemmed from the royal family. They were released in 1157, and Malcolm was restored to his earldom. It does not appear that his offspring succeeded him, and there were further uprisings along with the MacWilliams family. As they sought the crown, it seems probable the MacHeths were attempting to regain the earldom, Kenneth MacAht, grandson of Donald, rebelled in 1215, and was killed at Coupar. It seems likely the family held Strathnaver at that time.

Iye MacEth in Strathnaver, may be considered the first chief of Mackay. In 1263 he was chamberlain to the Bishop of Caithness, whose daughter he married. Their son Iye Mor obtained land at Durness from the Bishop.

His son Donald married a daughter of Iye MacNeil of Gigha, and had a son Iye, who was murdered along with his son Donald at Dingwall in 1370. He was succeeded by his grandson, Angus, who had grants of extensive lands in Sutherland and Caithness. Strathnaver itself was known as *Duthac Mhic Aoidh*, or 'The Mackay Country.' About 1415, Angus *Dubh* Mackay of Strathnaver married Elizabeth, sister of Donald, Lord of the Isles, and grand-daughter of King Robert II. Subsequent chiefs strove hard to keep their estates from being absorbed by the Earls of Sutherland. Eventually however, the power of gold prevailed.

In 1626 Sir Donald Mackay, a fine soldier, was cr. a baronet of Nova Scotia, and two years later made Baron Reay. He raised 'Mackay's Regiment,' in the Danish and Swedish services, that did much to advance the Protestant cause in Germany. A younger son of the 2nd Lord Reay, being maternally a nephew of the Scots-Dutch General Hugh Mackay of Scourie – who commanded the army of William of Orange at Killiecrankie in 1689 – entered the Danish service himself and became a Brigadier-General. His grandson, Col. Angus Mackay, married the eventual heiress of the Barons van Haeften of Ophemert, whose castle was inherited by the Mackays. In 1875, Baron Mackay van Ophemert succeeded his distant cousin, Eric, 9th Baron Reay, as 10th Lord Reay and chief of the clan. The present 14th Baron Reay and chief of the clan is Sir Hugh William Mackay, who is also Baron Mackay of Ophemert.

The Mackays of the Rhinns, in Islay, were lieutenants of the Lords of the Isles, and were sometime at Ugadale, in Kintyre.

# MacKENZIE

Unlike clans such as Chisholm, Fraser and Gordon, the MacKenzies were of Celtic origin and probably descended from Gilleoin of Aird. The surname in Gaelic means 'son of Coinneach', or of Kenneth, meaning fair or bright. The earliest known Kenneth was closely related to the Earls of Ross, and in 1267 resided at Eilean Donan, Loch Duich, one of Scotland's most photographed castles. Succeeding generations were vassals of the Earls, but the MacDonalds, Lords of the Isles, gained the superiority through marriage.

About 1463, Alexander MacKenzie had grants from John, Lord of the Isles, of lands including Garve and Kinlochluichart, and the family were styled "of Kintail." He was succeeded by his son Kenneth, who had a charter of confirmation under the Great Seal, of Scatwell and others lands, 1508/9. After the forfeiture of the Lordship of the Isles in 1493, the MacKenzies rose to prominence in the north-west.

In 1508, Kintail was erected into a barony, and this gave the chief jurisdiction over his clan. New lands were obtained between 1528 and 1542, and more land and influence was gained in the 16th century through good marriages. Later, further tracts of land were acquired by less honourable means. A feud with the MacDonells of Glengarry led to the acquisition of lands in Lochalsh and Loch Carron. Further accessions gave the chiefs land across to the east coast. King James IV, ostensibly to civilise the Island of Lewis, gave rights to a group of Lowlanders called the Fife Adventurers, who soon found themselves in trouble with the MacLeods of Lewis. The King prevailed upon MacKenzie of Kintail to intervene, and by some duplicity he eventually received a grant of Lewis.

The descendants of Kenneth MacKenzie obtained two

Earldoms, Seaforth and Cromartie, and there were numerous cadets who founded landed families and left thousands of descendants. The Earls of Seaforth were Royalists, and suffered losses in the Jacobite Rising of 1715. The title and estates were forfeited. In the '45 Rising, the Earl of Cromartie was involved, and his followers were defeated at Dunrobin in 1746. His title and estates were forfeited. The lands were restored to his son, Lord MacLeod, whose daughter Isabella inherited these in 1796. Her husband, Edward Hay, assumed the surname and arms of MacKenzie. They left an only child, Anne, cr. Countess of Cromartie in 1861, who married Lord Elibank. Their daughter Sibell became Countess, and married Lt. Col. Blunt-Mackenzie. The male line of the Seaforth family having failed in 1818, their son, Roderick, 4th Earl of Cromartie, was recognised as chief of Clan MacKenzie by the Lord Lyon in 1979. John Ruaridh, his son, the 5th Earl, is the present chief.

MacKenzies who achieved lasting fame include Coinneach, the Brahan Seer, who lived in the 17th century. Many of his prophecies came true. Sir George MacKenzie (1636-1691), of Rosehaugh was a distinguished lawyer and founder of the Advocates Library in Edinburgh, since 1925 the National Library of Scotland. Sir Alexander MacKenzie (1764-1820), emigrated to New York with his father, Kenneth, from Stornoway, about 1772, and became a fur-trader in Canada. He ranks as one of that country's greatest explorers, having made historic journeys to the Arctic Sea and the Pacific Coast, and wrote an account of his epic voyages. He retired to Scotland in 1808 and purchased the estate of Avoch, Ross-shire.

# MacKINNON

Many of the genealogies in the Gaelic manuscript of 1467 are suspect, but the MacKinnon descent given there, from Cormac, son of Airbertach, cannot be easily dismissed, as it is has received support from West Highland monuments. Finguaine, son of Cormack, may be accepted as the name-father of the clan, and ancestor of Nial, down to whom the manuscript brings the line. Nial was probably related to Lachlan Mackinnon, who in 1409 witnessed a charter by his superior, the Lord of the Isles, to Hector MacLean of Duart. Either him, or a later Lachlan was the father of John MacKinnon, last Abbot of Iona, who died in 1500, and whose tomb effigy survives, as well as part of a sculptured cross erected by Lachlan at Iona in 1489.

Although one of the lesser clans in Mull, the MacKinnons held important posts under the MacDonalds of the Isles. They were sometime Masters of the Household, and were entrusted with the supervision of weights and measures. They exchanged their lands in the south of Mull for Mishnish in the north, and at the same time came to possess Strathordil, in Skye. The MacKinnons were loyal to their superiors and took part in attempts to restore the Lordship of the Isles. Ewen, their chief in 1513, was a member of the council of Donald *Dubh*, the claimant. Although the clan was noted as troublesome in 1587, the chief accepted the Statutes of Iona in 1609, and bound himself to keep good order. There was some unrest in 1696, when the Royalist chief, Sir Lachlan, died leaving a son who was a minor. His kinsman, MacKinnon of Corriechatachain, helped to stifle the disturbance.

John Dhu MacKinnon was out with his clansmen in the '15 Jacobite Rising, and was pardoned. He joined Prince Charles in 1745, and was taken prisoner. John was later released and died in 1756. His son found the estate in debt and sold the lands. He held Strathaird until 1791, and left a son John, last of the line. John died in 1808, and William A. Mackinnon, M.P. for Dunwich, descended from a cadet in Antigua, obtained a decree of Lyon Court in 1811, recognising him as chief. MacKinnon of Corry asserted a claim but the matriculation was not reduced. William A. MacKinnon was succeeded by his son, Major Alexander F. MacKinnon (1848-1947). His grandson, Alastair Neil Hood Mackinnon (1926-83), had no surviving male issue, and the chiefship passed to his brother, Lt. Col. Ian K. Mackinnon, who has no children. The heir to the chiefship is his neice, Anne Gunhild, styled Madam Mackinnon of Mackinnon.

Col. Daniel Mackinnon (1791-1836), of the chiefly line, wrote a history of the Coldstream Guards, published in 1832. William Alexander Mackinnon, (1830-97), son of a Skye minister, became Surgeon-General in the army, and founded the Mackinnon Scholarship in the University of Glasgow. Another William Mackinnon (1823-93), a merchant in Glasgow, founded the British East Africa Company and was created a Baronet in 1889. Professor Donald Mackinnon, who died in 1914, held the chair of Celtic Languages in the University of Edinburgh from 1882 until his death. Lachlan Mackinnon, author of the quaint *Recollections of an Old Lawyer* (1935), represented an eminent Aberdeen legal family. Rev Donald Mackinnon (1890-1966), Free Church minister at Portree, later at Kennoway, Fife, was a noteable genealogist. The clan sennachie, Charles R. Mackinnon of Dunakin, Skye, wrote a useful work titled *Scotland's Heraldry* (1962). Numerous Mackinnons from Skye, Mull, Rum (clearance, 1828), Arran and other islands, emigrated to Canada.

# MacINTOSH

In Gaelic, the surname Macintosh is *Mac-an-Toisich*, meaning 'son of the chief (or thane),' and the principal family is said to have descended from Shaw, a younger son of Constantine, 3rd Earl of Fife (MacDuff), who died before 1130. The peerage writers are silent about Shaw, but heraldic evidence gives some credence to the story. Different chiefs gave their style to other Macintosh families. Those of Tininie, in Atholl, descended from the thanes of Glentilt, and the Toshes of Monzievard in Strathearn, are said to have descended from the thanes of Strowan. The Mackintoshes of Mackintosh have favoured the 'k' in the name, and after the marriage of the 6th chief, Angus, to Eva, the heirtrix of Clan Chattan, in 1291, came to represent the old Clan Chattan.

In 1234, Ferquhard, son of Shaw, witnessed a charter of the Bishop of Moray, and held the office of seneshal. His extensive lands comprised Petty and Breachley, with the forest of Strathdearn. Another Ferquhard, 9th chief of Mackintosh, abdicated in 1409, and gave up all claims of his issue in favour of Malcolm Beg, a strong chief whose leadership inspired confidence. As 10th chief, he had a dispute with the Cummins about the lands of Meikle Geddes and Castle Rait, but obtained a charter of those subjects. The rival claims may have brought about the famous conflict at Perth in 1396.

William (1521-1550), the 16th chief, styled of Dunachtonmore, had the misfortune to quarrel with his superior, the Earl of Huntly, and was tried at Aberdeen for conspiring against him. A packed jury found him guilty, and he was put to death. For the next two centuries the Mackintoshes had feuds with the Gordons, the Camerons and the Macdonells of Keppoch. In 1688, Lachlan, 19th chief, took part in the last clan battle, against the MacDonells at Mulroy. His son Lachlan was created Lord Mackintosh, but died childless in 1731. For the next century no son succeeded his father, and his successor, William of Daviot, 22nd chief, is notable as having supported King George during the '45, while his wife took the field for Prince Charles. His successor, Sir Aneas, created a Baronet, died in 1812, without issue. By an entail the estate descended to Alfred Donald (1851-1938), who, by tanistry, settled the duthus of Moy and the chiefship on his cousin, Vice-Admiral Lachlan Mackintosh, the 29th chief. The chiefship of Clan Chattan passed from Alfred Donald to his grand-daughter, Arabella, but as she did not bear the ancient name the honour passed to Duncan Alexander Mackintosh of Torcastle, descended from Angus, 25th chief, and he thus became the 31st Captain of Clan Chattan. Lachlan Ronald, son of the Vice-Admiral, is the 30th chief of Clan Mackintosh. He sold a large part of the family estates, but has retained Moy Hall.

A branch of the Mackintoshes, sometime at Spittal, in Old Aberdeen, went to England, and a descendant, Harold Vincent Mackintosh (1891-1964) became a Knight in 1922, a Baronet in 1935, and in 1957, Viscount Halifax. His son, Sir John, was head of the well-known confectionary firm of Mackintosh. The 3rd Bt. is Sir John Clive Mackintosh. One of the most colourful clansmen, Waldo E. Mackintosh, Chief of the Creek Indians, who visited Moy in 1964, descended from John Mackintosh of the Borlum line of the family, who emigrated to Georgia before 1775. His grandson, William, became a Creek chief, and ancestor of Waldo, known to the Creeks as *Tustunuggee Mico*.

# MacLACHLAN

The MacLachlans are one of the oldest clans in Scotland. The ancient traditional genealogies bring them from the O'Neill kings in Ireland, through Niall of the Nine Hostages, who flourished around 400 and this is the oldest traceable family in Europe. Their descendant, Anrothan, is said to have married in the 11th century, into one of the old dynastic families of Dalriada, and acquired lands in Cowal. The evidence for this is very weak, but Gilpatrick, said to be his great-grandson, witnessed a charter whereby his cousin, Laumon (father of the Lamont Clan) gave church livings, lands and fishings to the Abbey of Paisley about 1238. Gilpatrick had a son Lachlan, from whom not only the clan is named, but Lachlan Water and Lachlan Bay, the village of Strathlachlan, and the barony of Strathlachlan, with its Castle Lachlan.

Richard, son of Lachlan is mentioned in 1327 as custumar of Stirling, and the following year he appears as 'Ricardus filius Lochlane,' Sheriff of Stirling. Lachlan seems also to have had a son Gillescop: possibly also Ewen, who swore fealty in 1296. A younger Gillescop requested the barony of Kilbride, in Strathlachlan, from Edward I, but adhered to Robert the Bruce, and was present at his first parliament in 1308. In 1314 Gillescop granted to the Preaching Friars at Glasgow, 40s. sterling yearly from the ferms of his pennylands of Kilbride. Later MacLachlan cadets held local benefices. In 1410, Iain MacLachlan, the chief witnessed a charter, from which it appears that his cousin, Allan, crowner of Glassary, was ancestor of the MacLachlans of Dunadd. A 'nobleman,' Donald MacLachlan, seemingly of the chiefly line, had a dispensation in 1411, to re-marry Affrica Nigelli, related to him in the fourth degree of affinity. Ferquhard, natural son of another Ferquhard

MacLachlan, was bishop of the Isles, 1530-44. The MacLachlans of Coire-uanan held the position of standard-bearers to the Camerons of Lochiel. Of this family was MacLachlan of Drumblane, in Menteith, and others of the surname in that district.

The MacLachlans prospered through their attachment to Bruce, also because of intermarriage with the Campbells. In 1536, Lachlan MacLachlan of that Ilk had a safe conduct to France in 1536, along with the Earl of Argyll, in connection with the marriage of the Scottish king and Madeleine de Valois, daughter of King Francis I. By the time the chief's lands were enumerated in a statute of 1633, these contained thirty farms in Strathlachlan and the vicinity of Loch Fyne, with the patronage of the kirk of Kilmory. They were erected into a free barony in 1680. In 1666, Archibald MacLachlan of that Ilk, signed the great bond at Inveraray, by which 10s was to be paid out of each merkland in Argyll, for maintaining an armed watch. In 1679, Capt. MacLachlan, as laird, raised 50 men for his company in the Ardkinglas Regiment of 854 men. He died in 1687. The MacLachlans were Jacobites, and involved in the risings of 1715 and 1745. The chief, Lachlan, was fatally wounded at Culloden. Because of this he was not attainted, and in 1747 his son Robert, aided by the Argyll family, was able to take possession of the estates.

William MacLachlan, 1856-1942, the XXIInd laird, married Frances, Widow MacNicol, daughter of Albert Macpherson of Cluny. Their daughter Marjorie is the present chief. She married in 1948, George S. Rome, who assumed the surname of MacLachlan. They have three sons and three daughters.

# MacLAREN

The MacLarens formed a small clan in west Perthshire, mainly in the parish of Balquhidder, and in parts of Comrie and Callander. Loch Voil and Loch Earn were parts of their territory. Their surname derived from Lachrain or Lawrence, Abbot of Achtow in the 13th century. In those times the Celtic church permitted their clergy to marry. At an early period MacLarens were allodial holders of land under the Celtic earls of Strathearn, and they were probably of the same stock. Indeed the arms of the earls from the middle of the 12th century, with the two chevronels, are similar to those borne by the MacLaren chiefs. It seems highly probable they were all descended from the ancient dynastic rulers of Fortrenn (Strathearn and Menteith), one of the seven provinces of Alba.

The Ragman Roll was signed in 1296 by Conan de Bethweder (Eoan of Balquhidder) and his cousin, Lorin de Ardbethey (Ardveach). A third name, Morice de Tyry, has been confused with MacLarens in Tiree, but he belonged to the Perthshire family of Tyrie. It was several centuries later before MacLarens appeared in Tiree. The distinguished mathematician, Colin MacLaurin, 1698-1746, son of Rev. John MacLaurin of Kilmodan, claimed descent from the Tiree family, and his son, John of Dreghorn, Ayrshire, a Lord of Session, recorded arms in 1781, blazoned Argent, a shepherd's crook Sable.

Clan Labhran was never strong after the fall of the earldom of Strathearn and when their jurisdiction became vested in the crown, the chieftains never obtained charters to the lands they held. Eventually the superiority was held by the Murrays of Tullibardine, Lord Drummond and Campbell of Glenorchy. Reduced to rentallers, with no ancestral castle and no tenant cadets of their own, they had little use for a charter chest, and it is not surprising that so little is known about them. Although 'Clanlawren' is credited with having a captain or chief in 1587, his jurisdiction must have been limited. Local feuds with the Buchanans, MacGregors and Campbells did nothing to strengthen the clan, and they were forced to seek the protection of the Campbells of Glenorchy, later of Breadalbane. Some even settled in Breadalbane. In 1769 there were fourteen MacLaren tenants on the south side of Loch Tay, and three on the north side.

The MacLarens supported Montrose and Dundee in their campaigns, and along with their Jacobite friends the Stewarts of Appin, were 'out' in the '15 and '45 risings. At Culloden in 1746, thirteen were killed, fourteen wounded, and a few taken prisoner. Their leader, Donald of Invernenty, made a daring escape when being taken to Carlisle for trial. At one period they had been accused of resetting MacGregors, but in 1736, bad feelings were aroused, and Robin Oig, a son of Rob Roy MacGregor, shot and killed John MacLaren of Wester Invernenty while he was ploughing. He became a fugitive and was executed in 1754, for the abduction and forcible marriage of Jean Key, heiress of Edinbellie. In spite of all their troubles, the chiefly line of Achleskyne held on to their farm until 1892, and in 1957, the recognised chief, Donald, 1910-66, son of Rev. Duncan MacLaren, of Turriff, purchased Creag an Tuirc and matriculated arms. His lady, Margaret (Miller) wrote a readable clan history, published in 1960. The senior branch of Ardveach tenanted their farm until 1888. Invernenty was next in importance. The distinguished Barons Aberconway descend from John Maclaren, who farmed on the Island of Lismore, in Loch Linnhe.

# MacLEAN

In old writs the MacLeans appear as MacGillean, 'son of Gillean,' and derived their name from 'Gilleain-na-Tuaighe,' or 'Gillean of the Battle-Axe,' a renowned Celtic warrior of the 13th century, probably descended through a Celtic Abbot of Lismore from a branch of the old royal house of Dalraida. They may have been followers of the Lord of Lorn, and settled early in Morvern, but they became attached to the MacDonald Lords of the Isles. They clearly had some close blood relationship before 1367, when consanguinity caused Lachlan *Lubanach* MacLean of Duart to petition the Pope for a dispensation to marry Mary, daugher of MacDonald of the Isles. It is possible the earlier link was through the MacRuaris, since the MacLeans have always shown a sable galley in their armorial bearings. Lachlan and his brother Hector of Lochbuie, sons of John *Dubh*, received their lands in Mull from the Lords of the Isles. In 1488 the service due for the lands in Mull held by Hector Maclean of Duart was a galley of 22 oars. This underlines the importance of their sea-power.

Hector of Lochbuie had a son, Charles, who was the progenitor of the MacLeans of Dochgarroch and Glen Urquhart. Fearchar, son of Charles, also had a son Charles, who was a close friend of his kinsman, Lachlan *Bronnach*, the grandson and successor of *Lubanach*. Lachlan's son, Donald, obtained Ardgower from Alexander, Lord of the Isles, thus founding that important line of the family, now represented by the veteran soldier, diplomat and author, Sir Fitzroy Hew MacLean of Dunconnel, who was cr. a baronet in 1944. He resides at Strachur House, Argyll. Twice married Hector Og MacLean of Duart had four sons: Hector of Duart; Lachlan, cr. a baronet in 1631 (NS), who succeeded his brother; Donald of Brolas; and John, ancestor of the Counts MacLean of Sweden. The MacLeans of Duart and Lochbuie were ardent Jacobites and Sir John of Duart, the 4th Bt., led the clan at Killiecrankie and Sheriffmuir. He was sometime in France, where his son Sir Hector, 1703-50, was born. The latter was apprehended in 1745, suspected of enlisting men for the French service and carrying Jacobite documents. He spent over two years in prison, and died at Rome, unmarried. The title devolved on his kinsman, Allan MacLean of Brolas. Sir Fitzroy Donald MacLean, 1835-1936, during his long life, succeeded in re-purchasing and restoring the ancient stronghold of Duart. He was succeeded by his grandson, Sir Charles, whose son Sir Lachlan Hector MacLean, 12th Bt., is the present clan chief. He lives at Arngask House, Glenfarg, Perthshire. Donald MacLaine of Lochbuie, born 1816, a rich merchant in Batavia, Java, bought back the estate of Lochbuie, and it remained with his descendants until the 1920s.

The MacLeans of Dochgarroch have been influential in the north from the middle of the 16th century. They are now represented by Rev. Donald MacLean, Hazelbrae House, Glen Urquhart. His wife Loraine is a keen historian and honorary secretary of the Highland Family History Society. Present day MacLeans who have achieved eminence include Ranald Norman Munro MacLean, who was called to the Scottish Bar in 1964, and since 1990 has been a Senator of the College of Justice. John David Ruari McLean, residing at Carsaig, in Mull, is an expert typographer, who advises HM Stationery Office, and is a Trustee (appointed by the Crown) of the National Library of Scotland. The well-known journalist and broadcaster, Jack McLean, an Ayrshire man, has been a columnist with *The Scotsman* and *Glasgow Herald*, and in 1989 was adjudged Scottish Feature Writer of the Year.

# MacLEOD

The MacLeods can claim Viking ancestry. Olaf the Black (1177-1237), eldest son of Godfrey, King of Man and the Isles, by his third wife, Christina, daughter of Farquhar, Earl of Ross, had a son Leod, fostered by Paul Balkeson, Sheriff of Skye, who bequeathed to him his lands of Harris and North Uist. From his maternal grandfather, he received part of the Barony of Glenelg, and by his marriage to the heiress of MacRiald Armuin, he obtained Dunvegan, Bracadale, Duirinish, Trotternish and other lands in Skye. His sons Tormod (Norman) and Torcul (Harold), were the progenitors of the MacLeods of Harris and Dunvegan, and those of Lewis. It is not certain which of them was the elder, but in time the MacLeods of Dunvegan became recognised as chiefs of the clan. Leod died about 1280.

In 1343, Torquil MacLeod, the Lewis chief, had a grant of four davachs of land in Assynt, "together with the fortress on the island." His descendants were loyal to the Lords of the Isles, and although the chief made his submission to the King of Scots after the forfeiture of the Lordship in 1493, the family joined in attempts to restore the principality. Towards the end of the 16th century the Macleods of Lewis were weakened by a curious fratricidal conflict, and this may have been a factor in the decision of King James to colonise the island with Lowlanders. In 1597 the chiefs, having failed to produce their charters (which they had), he granted Lewis for a substantial rent to a company called the Fife Adventurers. The scheme failed, but MacKenzie of Kintail bought them out and obtained possession of Lewis. The chiefly line became extinct, but came to be represented by the MacLeods of Raasay.

The MacLeods of Dunvegan rose to strength. Malcolm, son of Norman, had a grant of parts of Glenelg in 1343. He was the progenitor of the old MacLeods of Berneray, and those of Gesto. Alastair *Crotach*, the chief who died in 1547, is credited with having established a college for his MacCrimmon pipers and he built for himself a sculptured tomb at Rodil, in Harris. One of the greatest MacLeod chiefs was Rory 'Mor,' who was knighted about 1613. He was a patron of the arts and lived at Dunvegan, where he supported pipers, harpers and bards. The clan took no part in Montrose's campaign, but supported the Royalists at Worcester. Perhaps because of the ingratitude of the Stewarts, the clan took no part in the Jacobite Risings. Although he had talks with Jacobite agents, Norman, the prudent chief of 1745, did not bring out his followers. Other MacLeods, notably those of Raasay and Galtrigal, were involved.

On the death of Sir Reginald MacLeod of MacLeod in 1935, the chiefship devolved on his elder daughter, Flora, in terms of an entail. This remarkable woman was the last person to be born at 10 Downing Street, London. Her maternal grandfather, Stafford Henry Northcote, was Chancellor of the Exchequer, 1874-80. She married Hubert Walter, who died in 1933, and on becoming chief resumed her maiden name. Her second daughter, Mrs Joan Wolrige Gordon, had twin sons, John, the present MacLeod chief, and Patrick, of Hallhead and Esslemont. Flora (D.B.E., 1953) instituted 'MacLeod Days' during Skye week in 1950, and in 1956 a clan 'parliament' at Dunvegan. As a result the castle has become a world centre for the clan. It houses precious relics such as the Fairy Flag, the mediaeval Dunvegan Cup, and the famous drinking horn used when the chiefs are inaugurated.

# MacMILLAN

The MacMillans descend from Gilchrist, one of six sons of Cormac, Bishop of Dunkeld, about 1107, son of Airbertach, who belonged to one of the dynastic families of Dalriada. Gilchrist, called *An Gillie-Maolin*, 'the little tonsured one,' was a monk of the Celtic church at Kintrae, Old Spynier, in Moray, and he may have built a Culdee shrine at Kilmallie (*Cill-Maolin*), where he left descendants. About 1160, Malcolm IV, King of Scots, removed the MacMillans from Lochaber to Lawers, in Perthshire, to make room for the Gilliechattan family, and some also settled in Knapdale, Argyll. A return to Lochaber is said to have been made about 1300, when a MacMillan in Breadalbane fled there after killing his father-in-law. This might be a distorted story, as about 1335, John, son of Malcolm Mor MacMillan, 1st of Knap, and six of his followers, sought refuge in Lochaber after the killing of Marallach Mor at Kilchamaig, Loch Tarbert. According to the late Rev. Somerled MacMillan, they and their sons were none other than the Clan Qwhevil, outlawed in 1392, who proved victors over the Clan Ha (*Clann Sheadhgh*, 'offspring of Shaw,' i.e., the people who adopted the surname of Mackintosh), at the clan battle of the North Inch, Perth, in 1396.

The headship of the MacMillans was vested in the lineal descendants of the above Malcolm Mor MacMillan. Gilchrist, grandson of his son John, was the father of Ewen, the first to be styled 'of Murlaggan,' in Lochaber. The family were kindly tenants there for centuries, until forced to leave by Donald Cameron, XXIInd of Lochiel. About 1760, John MacMillan of Murlaggan gave up his farm through reduced circumstances, and it was taken by Alexander MacMillan, of the Glenpean family. Archibald, his eldest son, along with his cousin, Allan MacMillan of Glenpean, emigrated to Canada in 1802,

196

with over 400 other tenants. In Lochaber were numerous cadets: Glenpean, Glendessary, Kenmore and Sallachan, Lagganfern and others.

The direct line of the Knap family failed, and Duncan MacMillan of Dunmore, Loch Tarbert, came to represent the family. He registered arms in 1742. His son, Alexander of Dunmore, settled his estates on his cousin, Duncan, of the Laggalgarve family, by whom they were lost. In 1951, the representative of the line was Sir Gordon Holmes MacMillan, 1897-1986, of Finlaystone, Langbank, Renfrewshire, then recognised as chief in 1951. His son, George Gordon MacMillan of MacMillan and Knap, is the present chief.

The MacMillans of Galloway are well-known. The MacMillans of Holm and Dalquhairn, and of Glencrosh, descended from John MacMillan of Brockloch and Holm of Dalquhairn, who died in 1830. His son Robert was the father of John of Holm of Glenquhairn and Glencrosh, who died in 1895. His eldest son Robert inherited Holm of Glenquhairn and younger sons Thomas and John James, were joint proprietors of Glencrosh. Hugh P. MacMillan, 1873-1952, son of Rev. Hugh MacMillan, Greenock, was a distinguished lawyer and judge, and was cr. a Life Peer in 1930.

Malcolm MacMillan, a tacksman on the island of Arran, was father of Duncan, whose son Alexander, 1817-96, founded with his brother Daniel, the publishing house of Macmillan. Of this family came Harold Macmillan, Prime Minister of Great Britain, 1957-63. cr. Earl of Stockton. The 2nd Earl is his grandson, Alexander Daniel Alan Macmillan, chairman of Macmillan, whose son and heir is Daniel Maurice Macmillan, Viscount of Ovenden.

# MacNAB

The MacNab chiefs descended from the Celtic hereditary abbots of Glendochart, in Perthshire. MacNab in Gaelic means 'son of the Abbot.' The abbots themelves were descended from the heirs of St. Fillan mac Feradach, who died in 703, a disciple of Ailbe of Emly. He founded his abbey in the upper part of Glendochart, which became known as Strathfillan. When the Celtic church was dismantled, the MacNabs continued to hold their lands as the barony of Glendochart. They were probably kin of the people who became Dewars. The MacNabs chose the wrong side during the War of Independence, but about 1365 their chief Gilbert received a crown charter of the lands of Bovain, in Glendochart.

Alexander MacNab, who died before 1407, received from Robert, Duke of Albany, a charter of the lands of Ardchyle, Invermonichele, Bovain and Downich. His son John was one of the jurymen in 1428 who declared the rights and duties of the hereditary keeper of the *coygerach* or quigrich of St. Fillan. Patrick MacNab, his grandson, disponed to his son, Finlay, in 1487, the above named lands. Finlay's grandson, another Finlay, is styled 'of Bovain,' in 1503. He married Mariota Campbell, to whom he granted a life-rent charter of the lands of Ewer and Leiragan, about 1522. The IXth laird, John MacNab, married Eleyn Stewart, and died before 1558.

Finlay, Xth chief, resigned his lands in favour of Colin Campbell, VIth of Glenorchy, who received a crown charter in 1553. In 1559 Colin conveyed the lands to Finlay MacNab. Finlay married Katherine, natural daughter of John Campbell of Glenorchy, about 1548, and his son Alexander succeeded him. Finlay, son of Alexander, was the last of the family to bear that forename. He became involved in the Civil War, and deserted the Campbells to join Montrose. His son Ian *min Macanaba*, 'smooth John' led the clan, and was killed in Breadalbane in 1653.

Major John MacNab, XVth laird, served in the Hanovarian army in 1745, and was taken prisoner at Prestonpans. He was released after the Jacobite defeat at Culloden. His eldest son, Francis, 1734-1816, XVIth laird, is well known from his full length portrait by Sir Henry Raeburn. Francis was never married but had a number of natural children. He inherited an encumbered estate, but continued to live the life of a feudal lord at Kinnell House. When he died, the chiefship devolved on Archibald, 1777-1860, son of Dr Robert MacNab of Bovain. He married Margaret Robertson, and had six children, who all predeceased him except Sarah Anne, who died in 1894, unmarried. Archibald, to avoid arrest for debt, emigrated in 1823 to Renfrew County, Ontario, where he obtained a grant of land and attempted to establish a feudal lordship. This involved him in numerous problems, and he fled to the Orkneys, later to France, where he died at Lanion. His cousin, Allan Napier MacNab, became Premier of Upper Canada.

James W. MacNab, 1831-1915, of Arthurstone, became recognised as *de jure* chief, as was in time his grandson, Lt. Col. James Alexander MacNab, who transferred his rights to his uncle, Archibald Corrie MacNab, 1886-1970, who had prospered as a civil servant in India, and bought back 7,000 acres of the old clan territory. He married Alice MacLeod, and in 1949 was recognised as chief. Having no children, he was succeeded as XXIIIrd chief by his nephew, James Charles MacNab, XXIIIrd chief, or 'The MacNab.'

# MacNACHTAN

The MacNachtan or MacNaughton clan is of undoubted antiquity, but its history has been much neglected. The name means 'son of Nechtan', an ancient Pictish name which also appears in the Cinel Loarn, a branch of the Scots of Dalriada, perhaps through marriage with a Pictish princess. A similar name, *Naiton*, was known among the Britons of Strathclyde. The resemblance to MacNaught, MacNitt and MacKnight, prolific surnames in the south-west, is noteworthy. Families such as McNaught of Kilquhanity and McNeight of Barns, may have no connection with the MacNachtans found in Argyll, Perthshire, and Fife, and probably earlier around the Moray Firth and on the island of Lewis, where a castle was built and named Macnauchtane. There is however, a place called Macnaughton, near Irongray, in Dumfriesshire. The MacNachtans were thanes of Loch Tay, possessing land between there and Lochawe. The earliest reference to them makes their eponymous ancestor *Neachtain Mor*, of the Cinel Loarn, who lived about the beginning of the 9th century. The earliest printed source says they descend from Nauchtan, an eminent man in Argyll in the time of Malcolm IV, who received lands at Lochawe.

Malcolm, the first chief, was father of Gillechrist, Ath and Sir Gilbert. Gillechrist was of baronial rank, and gave a church at the head of Loch Fyne to Inchaffray Abbey, in Perthshire, about 1246. His brothers gave a church on an island in Loch Awe, to the same abbey. Gillechrist possessed Dunderave, on Loch Fyne, and about 1267 had a charter appointing him hereditary keeper of the royal castle of Fraoch Eilean. The family lands made up part of the twelve baronies which were formed in 1292 into the new sheriffdom of Argyll. They came to hold land in Glenshira and Glenlyon, from whence they spread to Kenmore and Fortingall. On

Loch Tayside, as late as 1769, there were thirteen MacNaughton crofters, including John of Portbane, whose descendants lived at Remony, Pitlochry and Aberfeldy. Numerous MacNaughtons went to the USA in the 18th century and to Canada in the 19th.

Donald MacNachtan of Dunderave, Loch Fyne, opposed Robert the Bruce, who deprived him of some lands when he became king in 1306. However, his son Alexander, received a charter of entail in 1343, of lands which had belonged to the deceased John, son of Duncan, son of Alexander of Islay, and some which had belonged to John, son of the parson. These were presumably kinsmen, and the lands helped to restore the family fortunes. Alexander, 6th chief, was the father of Duncan, the next chief, and by Mariota de Cardney, mistress of Robert II, had a natural son, Donald (?1385-1440), parson of Weem, who was Bishop Elect of Dunkeld, 1436/37, but was not confirmed. A MacNachtan chief is said to have died at Flodden in 1513, but this has not been proved. Gilbert MacNachtan of Dunderave appears in the *Treasurer's Accounts* during that year. In 1617, Alexander MacNachtan had a commission to raise 200 bowmen to serve in the war against France. The last MacNachtan of Dunderave lost his lands and died at Edinburgh in 1773, without issue. A scion of the family had absconded to Ireland before 1630, and in 1818 his descendant, Edmund MacNaghten, at the desire of 400 clansmen, petitioned Lyon Court for the chiefship, and was recognised. He was succeeded by his brother Francis, cr. 1st Baronet of Dunderave, Co. Antrim, in 1836. The 4th Bt., Sir Edward, a distinguished lawyer, was made a Lord of Appeal and a Life Peer in 1887. The present chief is Sir Patrick MacNaghten, 10th Bt., of Dunderave, Bushmills, Co. Antrim.

# MacNEIL

There are reasonable grounds for accepting that the MacNeills descend from Aeod Athaeuch, who ruled in Aileach before 1033, whose ancestor was Niall of the Nine hostages, the high king who ruled at Tara, in Ireland, around the year 400. They may have arrived in the Western Isles as early as the 11th century, and married into the old royal house of Dalriada. The genealogies of the MacNeills of Barra may however, be viewed with some reservations; so also their claim to chiefship of the name and clan from an early date. Possibly their residence in Barra resulted from marriage to a MacRuari heiress of the old Norse/Celtic sea kings, before 1427, when Gilleonan, son of Ruari, son of Murchard MacNeill, obtained a charter of the island, and of Boisdale, in Uist, from Alexander, Lord of the Isles. The sable galley of the MacNeill arms certainly suggests some link with the MacRuaris.

The genealogy is fairly accurate from the time of Murchard and his son Ruari, said to have been chief of Clan Niall. As late as 1530, Torquil MacNeill of the collateral line of Gigha, was referred to by the Privy Council as "chief and principal of the clan and surname of Macnelis." The power of the Gigha line waned in the days of Campbell expansion into the Inner Hebrides, and evidently that of the MacNeills of far off Barra, in the Outer Isles, increased, and that line has long been recognised as chiefs of the name and clan. The MacNeills of Colonsay are a branch of the MacNeills of Gigha and Taynish, whose pedigree has been proved back to Torquil MacNeill who had a grant of Gigha and Danna in 1440 by Alexander, Lord of the Isles, and at the same time, certain lands in Knapdale, with the constabulary of Castle Sween. Recent research suggests he was descended from Malcolm MacNeill, who flourished around 1300, and who, by some accounts, was also the ancestor of the MacLeans of Lochbuie and Duart. Another branch of the MacNeills of Taynish are those of Kippilaw, later of Nonsuch. An early member was Lachlan of Tearfargus and Losset, in Kintyre, who was the first chieftain of the clan to record his arms in Lyon register.

By the time of the Jacobite Risings, the MacNeils of Barra were the clan leaders. Roderick Dhu MacNeill of Barra, known in song and story, supported Dundee in 1689 and The Old Pretender in 1715. His son, Roderick also fought in the '15. In the '45 he was captured and taken to London, but was released in 1747. The MacNeil ownership of Barra continued until 1838 when it was sold by General Roderick MacNeill. He died without issue and the chiefship passed to his kinsman, Hector Edward, son of his third cousin, Hector MacNeil of Ersary, who had emigrated to America. The recovery and restoration of Kisimul Castle, the island stronghold of the MacNeills, and part of the old clan country in 1937, sounds like a fairy story, but is very real. This was accomplished by Robert Lister MacNeil, 1889-1970, upon whom the chiefship devolved by tanistry (established in Lyon Court, 1915). With the help of his second wife, Marie Stevens, he purchased Kisimul, and made the castle his second home. The present chief is his son Ian Roderick MacNeil, a distinguished lawyer.

Several members of the Colonsay family were also eminent in the legal profession. Duncan MacNeill, 1793-1867, became Lord Justice General and Lord Colonsay. A younger brother, Archibald, 1803-70, WS, was one of the Clerks of Session, and for a time Keeper of the Registers of Scotland.

# MACPHERSON

Macpherson means 'son of the parson.' Clerical celibacy was late in being enforced in the Highlands, and in any case was often ignored by old families who traditionally filled sacred offices in their own territory. Many people called *Mac a Phearson*, descended from different parsons. Thus Macphersons appear in different parts of Scotland.

The principal kindred of the name are the famous *Clan Mhuirich*, who were of Celtic origin and migrated from Lochaber into Badenoch, and gradually settled mainly in Strathnairn and Strathdearn. Their eponymous ancestor was Muriach, chief of the old Clan Chattan, whose younger son, Ewen *Ban*, was Prior of Kingussie about 1173. The descendants of three brothers, Kenneth, Iain (or John) and Gillies, traditionally offspring of the parson, formed the three great sections of the clan, the *Sliochd Choinnich*, the *Sliochd Iain*, and the *Sliochd Ghill-iosa*, from all three of which sprang numerous cadets. Kenneth's descendants included families in Cluny, Nuide, Blairgowrie, Dalraddie and Brin, and the Cluny line came to be officially recognised as chiefs of the clan, although their position was later challenged. His son Duncan, Parson of Laggan about 1438, was father of Donald *Mor*, who appears to have been the first to adopt the surname of Macpherson. He was succeeded by his son Donald *Dall*, 5th chief, and his second son, Gilliecallum *Beg* was ancestor of the Macphersons of Breakachy. Andrew, 8th chief, who defended Ruthven Castle against the Earl of Argyll in 1594, had a son, Lt. Col. Ewan, who died before his father, leaving two sons, Andrew, 9th chief, and Duncan 10th chief, who recorded arms in 1672. He left an heiress, Anna, who married Archibald, son of Sir Hugh Campbell of Calder. When it appeared by the marriage settlement that Duncan intended his son-in-law to succeed him, the clansmen, fearing that the estate would be taillied away to a stranger, signed a protest in 1689 in favour of William Macpherson of Nuide, the heir male, whose son Lachlan became 11th chief. His natural brother was Andrew, father of James Macpherson, 1736-96, the alleged translator of the Ossianic poems. Ewen, the 12th chief, fought for Prince Charles Edward Stuart in the '45, and was sometime in hiding with a price on his head. His estates were forfeited, but restored to his son Duncan. Three sons of Ewen, 14th chief, succeeded in turn, and their nephew, Ewen George, became 18th chief. Cluny was the home of the chiefs until 1932, and passed from the clan just over ten years later. Ewen George emigrated to Adelaide, Australia, where he died without male issue. Eventually the chiefship became vested in the Newton of Blairgowrie line of the family, now represented by William MacPherson of Cluny and Blairgowrie, a distinguished soldier and jurist, who became a Judge of the High Court of Justice (England and Wales), in 1983. A Clan Macpherson Association was formed in 1947, and in 1952 the first ever purely clan museum was opened at Newtonmore.

Of several branches of the family flourishing today, may be mentioned that of the chieftain of Pitmain (of the *Sliochd Iain*), Michael Alastair Fox Macpherson, who is a director of several companies, and has a home at Duror of Appin. This Macpherson family, and a number of others are armigerous. Thomas Macpherson, 1888-1965, of Drumochter, was MP for Romford Borough, 1945-50. In 1951 he was cr. Baron of Great Warley, Essex. His son, James Gordon Macpherson, 2nd Baron, a company chairman, served with the RAF, 1941-46, and owns a large estate in Inverness-shire.

# MacQUARRIE

Although a small clan, the MacQuarries or MacQuarrys have made their mark in places far from their homeland: the isle of Ulva and adjacent part of Mull, in the Western Isles. The surname is derived from the Gaelic 'son of Guaire,' itself an old personal name meaning proud or noble. According to the old genealogies, Guaire was brother of Fingon, name-father of the MacKinnon chiefs, and descended from Cormac, son of Airbertach, descended from one of the dynastic families of Dalriada. The MacQuarries, like larger clans, intermarried with neighbouring families and founded cadet houses.

Two charters of John, Earl of Ross and Lord of the Isles, were witnessed by John McGeir of Wlua, in 1463. This is probably John Makquhory of Wlway, who died about 1473. When rebellion broke out under Donald Dubh of the Isles in 1503, Makcorry of Vllowa (Dunslaf, son of John) and others were frequently summoned before parliament to answer for treasonable acts, but did not compear. In 1509, along with others he was ordered to pay Duncan Stewart of Appin and his tenants for cattle and goods they had taken. Dunslaf or *Donn-sleibe*, 'Lord of the Hill,' had a natural son, John, legitimated before 1540. He had a remission from Queen Mary in 1546 for assisting the English in burning the islands of Bute and Arran.

In 1630, Donald Makquoyrie in Ulway was served heir to his grandfather Hector, in the lands in Ulva, the isle of Staffa (famous for its coastal caves), and some lands in Mull. He married Christian, daughter of Lachlan Oig Maclean of Torloisk, and was succeeded by his eldest son Alan, who was involved in the Civil War and lost his life at Inverkeithing in 1651. In 1689, during the time of his son Alan, the family writs were burned, and this suggests he was involved in the Revolution. John, the next laird, seems to have lived quietly in Ulva. Lachlan, his son, entertained Johnson and Boswell at his Ulva home on the night of 16-17 October, 1773, and the moralist found the chief intelligent, polite and much a man of the world. However, Lachlan was forced to sell his encumbered estate in 1777, retaining only Little Colonsay, which was sold later. He became an officer in the 74th Regiment, and died in 1818, reputedly a centenarian. Lachlan married twice and left a large family. His eldest daughter, Marie, married Gilleon MacLaine of Scallastle, Mull (a cadet of Lochbuie), and became known as 'mother of heroes,' four of her sons having fought in the Napoleanic Wars. The main cadets of the clan were the MacQuarries of Ormaig, Laggan and Bellighartan. Some MacGuires descend from MacQuarries.

The most famous clansman was Major-General Lachlan Macquarrie, who after a relatively obscure army career, was Governor-General of New South Wales, Australia, from 1809 to 1821. When he and his Scottish entourage took over, the colony was little better than a prison camp, but by about 1815 progressives began to see Australia as a field for free settlement, rather than a penal colony. Macquarie had seen the influence of rum, sugar and slavery in the New World, and his Calvinistic beliefs resulted in his reducing the number of licensed premises in Sydney from 75 to 20! He set about building roads, constructing public buildings and churches, and he encouraged convicts to become good settlers when emancipated. His popularity is reflected in the naming of Macquarie River and other places in Australia. His brother Charles, also a soldier, was for several years laird of Ulva. The population was reduced and the clan became scattered.

Much research about the MacQuarries has been done by Edinburgh historian, Robert William Munro.

# MACRAE

The name MacRae is a personal one, not a patronymic like MacDonald. It is probably of ecclesiastical origin, and in Gaelic is rendered *MacRath*, 'son of grace.' It appears in Ireland and Scotland from the 5th century to the 13th as such, and originated independently in more than one place and time, with people in no way connected to each other.

Macraith de Ospitali witnessed a gift of the church of Dunrod by Fergus, Lord of Galloway, to the canons of Holyrood, confirmed during the reign of Malcolm IV (1153-65). Macracht decanus de Carric, on record about 1202, was possibly the same person. Alexander Macrad witnessed a charter of lands of Lus to Maldoon, son of Gillemore, by Maldouen, 3rd Earl of Lennox, about 1225. Macrath ap Molegan of Dumfriesshire rendered homage in 1296, and had his lands restored. In 1376, Patrick McRey was a tenant in Tibbers Penpont. Christinus MacRath, the first of the name on record at Inverness in 1386, was probably ancestor of a tribe which moved from Clunes, in the lordship of Lovat, to Wester Ross, when there was pressure on land. After this time MacRaes appear also in Perthshire, and in the south-west.

In Kintail the MacRaes were at first vassals of the Earls of Ross, then became loyal supporters of the Mackenzies: in fact formed a bodyguard for the chief and were called his 'shirt of mail.' In the 15th century the MacKenzie chiefs moved to Kinellan, in Strathpeffer, leaving the MacRaes as constables of Eilean Donan Castle, in Loch Duich, and as chamberlains of Kintail. Some were clergymen in the district. Rev Farquhar MacRae, 1508-1662, was vicar of Kintail for 44 years, and progenitor of the MacRaes of Conchra.

At the Battle of Auldearn in 1645, the MacRaes fought under the MacKenzie chiefs in the army of Montrose, and it is recorded that more of them fell than the Maclennans, who were the MacKenzie standard bearers. At the beginning of the 18th century, one Duncan MacRae, a clansman of immense strength and a poet, gained local fame when he recovered stolen cattle from reivers in Lochaber. He was killed along with other MacRaes at Sheriffmuir in 1715. The MacRaes, perhaps because they lacked a chief, took no part as a group in the '45, although individuals served with other units. A large number of them enlisted in the Seaforth Highlanders when that regiment was formed in 1778, and took part in a mutiny at Leith, claiming they had only joined for a limited period and not for service overseas. In 1781 they agreed to embark for the East Indies.

MacRae of Inverinate, in Kintail, claimed chiefship, and Sir Colin MacRae, 1844-1925, WS, of this line of the family, petitioned Lyon Court in 1909 for official recognition, but the claim was opposed by MacRae of Conchra, who alleged there was no chief. No decision was made. Sir Thomas Innes of Learney, 1893-1971, Lord Lyon, 1945-69, considered the idea of "no representer" to be untenable. The Inverinate and Conchra families are both armigerous. Lt. Col. John MacRae, of the Conchra line, purchased the ruined castle of Eilean Donan, and completed its restoration in 1932. It is one of the most photographed buildings in Scotland. Unfortunately, the MacRaes are now thin on the ground in Kintail, but found all over Scotland, and because of much emigration, are very numerous in the USA, Canada, Australia and New Zealand.

# MacWILLIAM/WILLIAMSON

The earliest MacWilliams of note were of the blood royal. Malcolm Canmore, King of Scots, who reigned 1057-93, had a son Duncan, by some historians son of his first wife, Ingebiorge, widow of the northern jarl, Thorfin, and by others (including Lord Hailes) considered to be illegitimate. He was probably a hostage in England from 1072-1087, and knighted by King William Rufus on his release. Duncan expelled his uncle, Donald Bane, who had asserted his pretensions to the throne after the death of King Malcolm and the saintly Queen Margaret in 1093, their children being all under age. In 1094 Duncan reigned, but he was assassinated and Donald Bane again occupied the throne until ousted in 1097 to allow Edgar, son of Malcolm and Margaret, to be King of Scots.

The descendants of Duncan II, in more than one generation put forward a claim to the Scottish crown. Duncan's son William Fitz Duncan, claimed the throne. He appears to have had two sons, William and Donald, surnamed MacWilliam. Donald invaded Ross and Moray, but was defeated and killed at Mangarve, Inverness, by forces led by Roland of Galloway, in 1187. Donald MacWillian left at least two sons, Donald *Ban*, slain in an insurrection in Moray in 1215, and Guthred. The latter led a revolt in the north in 1211, and was captured by an army containing 100 knights and 100 serjeants, commanded by an English nobleman, possibly Saier de Quincy, Earl of Winchester. Guthred was executed at Kincardine and hung up by the feet. It seems there was a government attempt to exterminate the MacWilliams, and there is a confused account of a rising in 1230, and of an infant of the race having its brains dashed out against the market cross of Forfar.

The name William became prolific in England after the

Norman Conquest, and in spite of the fate of the above MacWilliams was also popular in Scotland, resulting in various families of MacWilliams, Williamsons, and Wilsons, not of common ancestry. Many MacWilliams and Williamsons existed in Glenlivet, and are found there in old records as MacWillie, McKullie, and MacVillie. In the south-west, the name often took the form of Macuilam and MacQuilliam. The Glenlivet tribe became attached to Clan Macpherson. Others are supposed to be of MacFarlane ancestry, but this is disputed. It is also said that a branch of the MacLeods of Dunvegan, descended from William 5th chief, who died in 1409, took the name MacWilliam, and were known as *Clan Man Mhic Uilleim*. The Robertsons of Pittagowan, early in the 16th century, were known as MacWilliams.

In 1317, John Williamson held land in Peebles, and Adam, son of William Williamson, rendered the accounts there in 1343. Between 1620 and 1680, the burgh was frequently represented by Williamsons. James Williamson, the Provost in 1638, signed the National Covenant, and James of Hutcheonfield recorded arms, 1672-78. He purchased the estate of Cardrona, on which many later members of the family resided. Major-General William Williamson, who died in 1815, served with the H.E.I.C.

Thomas Williamson, an archer in the Scots Guard in France in 1495, acquired property there, and in 1506 married Marguerite, heiress of Guillaume Raoult, seigneur of Mesnil Hermey, and his descendants flourished in the land of their adoption. The pedigree of this family traces Thomas from Duncan Williamson, who in 1381 married Alice Mackenzie of Kintail.

John David McWilliam, educated at Leith Academy, Heriot Watt University and Napier University is Labour MP for Blaydon.

# MATHESON

The Mathesons claim descent from a local dynast called Gilleon of the Aird, also progenitor of the Mackenzies, who flourished in the first half of the 12th century. He is believed to have belonged to a branch of the old royal house of Lorn. Those Mathesons of the north-west, who point to Lochalsh as their homeland, are known in Gaelic as *MacWhathain*, collectively as *Mathanach*. The old genealogies give the meaning of the name as 'son of the bear.' The clan should not be confused with the Lowland Matthewsons, sons of Matthew, who appear in Galloway, Ayrshire, Kintyre, and Fife, where around Kilconquhar there was a notable family of Matthewson clockmakers in the late 18th and early 19th century.

It seems that the earliest reference to a Matheson is in 1264, when Kermac MacMaghan in Inverness received twenty cows of the fine of the Earl of Ross, for services rendered. In the sagas he is called Kjarmak, son of Makamel (Cormac Manmathan). Matheson has been adopted as the English form of the name. The old genealogies give the descent of the chiefs as Christin, father of Kenneth, father of Mahan, father of Kenneth, father of Murdoch, father of Duncan, father of Murdoch, father of Murdoch of Bower, chief in 1427. John, a succeeding chief, was appointed constable of Eilean Donan Castle, and successfully sustained attacks by Donald Gorm MacDonald of Sleat, in one of which however, in 1537, he was killed. The Matheson possessions were greatly reduced, and his son Dugal had no more than a third of Lochalsh. He engaged in squabbles with his turbulent neighbour, Glengarry, in whose dungeon he died. His son Murdoch Buidh, in an effort to avenge his father, gave up all his farms except Balmacara and Fearnaig, to Mackenzie of Kintail, for a sufficient body of men to attack his enemy, but met with little success.

Murdoch had two sons, Roderick of Fearnaig and Dugal of Balmacara, Chamberlain of Lochalsh in 1631. The former had an only son, John, who was father of John Mor of Fernaig, who made money in cattle droving and became owner of Bennetsfield in the Black Isle in 1688. His son was Alexander, whose son John fought at Culloden in 1746. His grandson John died in 1843, leaving the estates embarrassed. His successors were his nephew and his nephew's son who died in 1899, leaving the barren chiefship of the clan to his cousin, Heylin Fraser Matheson, Housemaster of Eastbourne College, whose son, Col. Bertram Matheson was confirmed as chief in 1963.

John Matheson, 1st of Attadal, was great-grandson of Dugal of Balmacara, and was succeeded by his son, Alexander, who died in 1804. His son John had to dispose of the estates. He married Margaret, daughter of Capt. Matheson of Shinness, head of the Sutherland branch, and their eldest son, Alexander, along with his uncle, Sir James Matheson, made fortunes in the India and China trade. Alexander was enabled to purchase Lochalsh, the ancient family *duthus*. Sir James (1796-1887) purchased the island of Lewis. His property passed to his nephew, Donald Matheson. In 1882, Alexander was cr. a baronet (UK). The 5th Bt., Sir Torquil George, 1871-1963, was nominated by the chiefs as *Tanastair*, and the chiefly arms tailzied accordingly. His elder son, Sir Torquil Alexander Matheson, is the 6th Bt., and present chief of the clan. He married in 1954, Serena Mary Francesca, only child of Sir Michael Peto, Bt., and they have two daughters. The family reside at Standerwick Court, Frome, in Somerset.

# MENZIES

The surname Menzies is of Norman origin, being originally de Meyners, and in all probability derived from Mesniers, north of Rouen. In England it assumed the form of Manners, and is found there about 1180. Robert de Meyners witnessed charters between 1217 and 1249, when he was appointed Great Chamberlain of Scotland. He granted the lands of Culdares, in Glenlyon, to Sir Matthew of Moncreiffe, ancestor of the late Sir Iain Moncreiffe of that Ilk, who possessed the deed. Robert also held lands in Rannoch. Members of his family may have married into the royal family, and the names David and Alexander favoured by them, crop up in the Menzies pedigree. Sir David de Menzies was one of the retinue of the Scottish Queen in 1248.

Letters patent were granted to Alexander de Meygneys by Edward I in 1297, and he is probably the man who witnessed the grant of the office of High Constable of Scotland to Sir Gilbert Hay in 1314. Alexander de Meyneris held the lands of Durisdeer, in Nithsdale, but resigned these in the hands of Robert the Bruce, who gave them to James, brother of Walter the Steward. Thomas de Meineris was one of those who signed the Declaration of Independence in 1320, and he was probably the knight to whom Bruce granted the lands of Unwyn (?Oyne), in the Garioch, and other lands in Atholl. Bruce also granted to Alexander Menzies the barony of Glendochart and some land at Finlarig. Robert Maynhers had a charter of half of the barony of Culter from Robert II in 1385. David de Meygnes was one of the hostages for King James I in 1425.

John de Mengues, who died in 1487, was succeeded by his son Sir Robert, who obtained a new grant of the family estates erecting them into the barony of Menzies. In 1586, Barbara Stewart, 'Lady Weyme,' widow of James Menzies of that Ilk, bound herself to keep faith with George, Earl of Huntly, during the ward and non-entry of her son Alexander. In 1665, Sir Alexander Menzies of that Ilk was cr. a baronet (NS). The dignity became extinct in 1910 on the death of the 8th Bt., Sir Neill James Menzies. The Steuart-Menzies family of Culdares, descended from Patrick Steuart of Cardney, who married Agnes, daughter of Col. James Menzies of Culdares, brother of the 1st Bt. It was a Menzies of Culdares who introduced the larch tree to Scotland in 1738. The lineal heir, Ronald Steuart Menzies, 1884-1961, petitioned Lyon Court in 1957, and obtained the name and arms of Menzies of that Ilk. His son, David Menzies of Menzies, the present chief, lives in Australia. The clan has other links with Australia. Sir Robert Menzies, 1894-1978, born in Victoria, was Prime Minister, 1939-41, and 1949-66. His ancestors hailed from Weem, in Perthshire. Moreover, Sir Douglas Ian Menzies, 1907-74, was Justice of the High Court of Australia.

Two brothers, Gilbert and William, possibly sons of Sir Robert Menzies of Weem, migrated to Aberdeen early in the 15th century. Gilbert became Provost of Aberdeen in 1423, again in 1439, and obtained the estate of Pitfoddels in 1457. From him and his wife Isabel Liddell descended a long line of lairds who wore the provost's robes over the next 200 years. John Menzies of Pitfoddels, elected County Convener of Aberdeenshire in 1810, gave his estate of Blairs to the RC Church, and the mansion became Blairs College.

Castle Menzies, the old home of the chiefs, became ruinous, but between 1972 and 1977, essential restoration was done by the Clan Menzies Society. Prince Charles slept here in 1746, and interesting relics of yesteryear survive. These include a death-mask of the Prince, and an ancient claymore used at Bannockburn in 1314.

# MILLER

Miller or Miller is an occupational surname, derived from miller (Latin *molendino*), and appears all over the country. At one time on large estates tenants were bound to grind their grain at a particular mill, and to uphold the mill, repair dam dykes, lades or aqueducts, and even to supply the millstones. This was termed thirlage, and the system ensured that the miller (an important person in the community) would continue in business. Indeed at some sites generations of millers are found. Surnames such as Milne usually refer to people who lived near a mill.

The earliest references are found in Latin documents, hence an inquest at Dumfries Castle in the reign of Alexander III, 1249-93, records the death of Adam Molendinarius. Probably Miller did not become a hereditary surname until much later. John and Henry Millare were jurors at an inquest regarding fishing in the Tweed, in 1467. Margaret Myllar was a tenant of the Bishops of Glasgow in 1509 and Robert Millare held lands at Irvine in 1540. John Millar, 1735-1801, son of Rev. James Millar, minister at Shotts, was admitted advocate in 1760, and became an eminent lecturer on law in the University of Glasgow. He wrote several legal works, important in his time, including the *Distinction* of *Ranks in Society*, which was translated into French. Hugh Miller, 1802-56, born at Cromarty, began life as a stone-mason and devoted his winter months to writing, reading and natural history. He became Scotland's first geologist, and among his works are *My Schools and Schoolmaster* (1854), and *Testimony of the Rocks* (1857).

Several Miller families became landowners. Among these are the Millers of Glenlee, in Galloway. The progenitor was Matthew Miller, who married Agnes, Daughter of Rev William Guthrie, of Fenwick. William, his second son, WS (1719), had three sons, John, Professor of Law at Glasgow, who died unmarried in 1780; Thomas; and Patrick of Dalswinton, a pioneer of steam navigation, and owner of Ellisland Farm, tenanted by the poet Burns. Thomas of Glenlee, the second son, qualified as an advocate in 1742. He was Sheriff of Kirkcudbright, 1748-54; Solicitor-General, 1759; Lord Advocate, 1760, and became Lord President of the Session in 1766. Thomas was cr. a baronet in 1789. He was succeeded by his son, Sir William, 2nd Bt., who also became a Lord of Session. The 5th Bt., Sir William Frederick Miller, served in the South African War and in World War I as a staff captain. Sir Frederick, the 7th Bt., served in World War II, and his son, the 8th Bt., is Stephen William MacDonald Miller of Glenlee, a physician at Shebbear, Beaworthy, in Devon.

A Miller family, styled 'of Monk Castle,' Ayrshire, stemmed from William Miller, a merchant in Glasgow. His brother Alexander, also a merchant, purchased the lands of Monk Castle and Craigmill, but those subjects passed to William, who was served heir in 1725. William Miller, Vth of Monk Castle, married Anna Maria, daughter of Admiral Campbell, Portuguese Navy, and had a son, William Augustus Cunninghame Miller. Another interesting family, of whom came George Miller, a civil engineer, bought the estate of Leithenhope, Peeblesshire, in 1852. Sir William Miller, MP of Berwickshire, 1873-74, purchased the estate of Manderston, near Duns, and was cr. a baronet in 1874. His son, Sir James, 2nd Bt., built the magnificent mansion there, now owned by Sir Adrian Baillie Palmer, 4th Baron of Reading (cr 1933), and a Baronet (cr 1916).

# MITCHELL

The surname Mitchell comes from the Hebrew Michael through the French form Michel. It was a common baptismal name in several countries, and its introduction to Scotland was probably due to French influence. King Malcolm IV confirmed to the hospital of St. Andrews, one carucate in Kedlock, Fife, granted to it by Simon, son of Michael. Michael (*Flandrensis*) was clerk to King William and sheriff of Edinburgh between 1198 and 1214. An early appearance as a surname occurs in the indenture of the treaty drawn up at Berwick, 3 October, 1357, for the release of David II, where Thomam Mitchell is mentioned. Robert Michael de Hyrmanston was a charter witness in 1438. Richard Michel was admitted burgess of Aberdeen in 1475, and in 1489 John Michell had a remission for his part in holding Dunbarton Castle against the king.

Mitchells appear as landowners in Ayrshire, where the surname is still common, and in various locations all the way to the Shetland Isles. The Mitchells of Bandeth, in Stirlingshire, traced their ancestry to James Mitchell, who had the lands confirmed to him in 1578. John Mitchell, Vth of Bandeath, became archdean of Tingwall, Shetland, in 1629, and his descendant, John Mitchell of Westshore, was cr. a baronet in 1724. The title became extinct about 1783. Thomas Mitchell, Provost of Aberdeen, 1668-1700, and 1702-04, who purchased Thainston, Kintore, from the Forbes family in 1717, was second son of Thomas Mitchell of Tilliegreig, a baillie of Aberdeen in 1666. His descendant, John-Forbes Mitchell, 1843-1882, left a widow, Jane Maria Rawson, in possession of the estate in 1925. The Mitchells of Carwood, Biggar, produced James Denniston Mitchell, 1853-1910, one of Lanarkshire's foremost educationalists. Probably the wealthiest landed family became Mitchell-Innes of Stow. William Mitchell, younger son of Alexander Mitchell of Darrahill, Aberdeenshire, inherited in 1839 (after litigation), the estate of his cousin, Jane Innes of Stow. He assumed the name of Mitchell-Innes. William held the lands of Aytoun and Whitehall, Berwickshire, and inherited Parson's Green. He also owned Bangour and Ingliston, where, in 1846, he built the mansion there, since 1958 the property of the Royal Highland & Agricultural Society of Scotland. William Mitchell-Innes of Whitehall, married in 1933, Mary Gibson, daughter of George Robert Fortune, of Rosebank, Colinsburgh, and had a daughter Janet Julia, who married Matthew W.B. White in 1955.

Many individual Mitchells left their mark, none more so than Stephen Mitchell, of the famous Glasgow tobacco firm of Stephen Mitchell & Son, originally of Linlithgow. In 1870 Stephen Mitchell bequeathed £66,998: 10s: 6d to the Town Council of Glasgow, to create a library bearing his name. When they obtained premises at East Ingram Street in 1874, interest had enlarged the sum to £70,000. In 1891 the library moved to Miller Street, where it remained until 1911, when it was transferred to the present location in North Street. The Mitchell Library is, next to the National Library in Edinburgh, the most important repository in Scotland. In recent years it has been enlarged and now has conference facilities.

Sir Thomas Livingston Mitchell, 1792-1855, who had a distinguished military career, emigrated to Australia in 1827, where he became Surveyor-General of NSW, and an explorer. Another knight, Sir Peter Chalmers Mitchell, 1864-1945, from Dunfermline, was the creator of Whipsnade Zoo.

George W. Mitchell has had an outstanding career in television and has been Director of Programmes with Grampian TV since 1989.

# MOLLISON

The surname Mollison is associated mainly with north-east Scotland, and especially with Aberdeen from the 15th century. It is derived from the personal name Malise, recorded in Scotland as early as the reign of David I (1124-53). Malise was a marischal under that king, and is stated by the distinguished medievalist, Geoffrey W.S. Barrow, to have been of Celtic origin. Probably the meaning of the name in Gaelic was *Mael Iosa*, 'shaveling,' or 'tonsored servant of Christ.'

Malisio or Malisius, son of Leod, appears as a witness to a charter of Lundin, in Fife, by Malcolm IV in 1164, to Philip the Chamberlain and his heirs, in fee and heritage. Malise, son of Ferteth, Earl of Strathearn, gave to the Abbey of Arbroath, half a merk annually, from the fishery of Meiklour, in Perthshire, confirmed by William the Lion, about 1199. The name Malise was much favoured by the old earls of Strathearn, and by the Stewarts who succeeded them. It passed also to the Grahams of Menteith, through Euphemia, Countess Palatine of Strathearn.

Malisone or Malyceson appears as a surname, in 1391, when Malcolm, so named, witnessed an agreement between the Bishop of Aberdeen and the Laird of Forbes, regarding the land of Lurgyndespok. Robert Malisei was a juror in an inquest over a third part of Ledyntusche and Rothmais, in 1413. Thomas Malisone was admitted a burgess of Aberdeen in 1445, and William Malitesone appears as a witness in 1469. John Malison witnessed a charter by William Futhus to the chaplains of the choir, of two annual rents, in 1500. In the early part of the 16th century, John Malison, a priest, appears as master of a music school at Cantore (Kintore). Patrick Malyson was admitted burgess of Aberdeen, 1551/52. He was a goldsmith, and died about 1590, leaving a son Thomas.

Alexander Malison, related to Provost Alexander Reid, had a son Gilbert, who became an influential burgess of the town, and was the ancestor of numerous Mollisons who were involved in municipal affairs. His eldest son John was killed at the Battle of Pinkie in 1547, and a younger son, Thomas, became clerk to the Town Council. He was chosen in 1602 to represent the burgh in purchasing a discharge from the king, of their taking part in his proposed Lowland colonisation of Lewis. The douce folk of Aberdeen wanted no part in this hazardous enterprise. Gilbert (1613-89), son of Thomas, became an officer of militia and was a commissioner to the Convention of Royal Burghs in 1673 and 1676. His daughter Christian married the Quaker apologist, Robert Barclay (1648-90) of Urie. Gilbert's son Gilbert (1659-1730), went to London, where he became a draper-freeman and Quaker correspondent. Another son, John emigrated to Piscataway, New Jersey. Other members of the family remained in Aberdeen.

In the present century, Glasgow-born Jim Mollison (1905-59), distinguished himself as an aviator, breaking many records, including Australia-England, 1931; first solo westward flight, North Atlantic, 1932; first solo westward flight, South Atlantic, 1933. With his first wife, the famous aviator, Amy Johnson (d. 1941), he undertook the first UK-USA flight in 1933, and also with her made a record-breaking flight (22 hours), England-India. A film, based on some of their flights, called *They Flew Alone*, was made with Anna Neagle and Robert Newton starring. Mollison published *Death Cometh Soon or Late* (1932), in which his portrait appears, and *Playboy of the Air* (1937). He received many awards overseas, and in 1946 was made MBE.

Dr Denis Mollison has been Professor of Applied Probability at Heriot Watt University since 1986.

# MONTGOMERIE EARLS

According to Dr Black, the surname Montgomerie or Montgomery is derived from the old castle of Saint Foy de Montgomery, in the diocese of Lisieux, in Normandy. The first of this name to settle in Scotland was Robert Mundergumbrie, who had a grant of the manor of Eglisham, in Renfrewshire, in the reign of David I. Mrs Platts makes him the second son of William, Count of Ponthieu, and great-grandson of Roger de Mundegumbrie who acted as William the Conqueror's liasion office with the Flemish wing of his army in 1066. His sister-in-law, Ada de Warenne, married in 1139, Prince Henry of Scotland, and he may have come north in her retinue. On his blue shield he displayed a gold fleur-de-lis to denote his Ponthieu connection.

Information about the early lairds is scant, but Sir John Montgomerie, who signed the 'Ragman Roll' in 1296, was probably IVth of Eaglesham. John Montgomerie, the next on record, had sons Alexander and Alan, and Marjorie, his daughter, appears with another Marjorie (?younger) in 1363, conveying the lands of Cassillis to John Kennedy. Alexander's son, John VIIth of Eaglesham, distinguished himself at Otterburn in 1388, when he fought hand to hand with Sir Henry Percy, called 'Hotspur,' heir to the Earl of Northumberland, and made him captive. He profited from an enormous ransom, and had a pension from Robert III as a retaining fee. John married Elizabeth, heiress of Sir Hugh Eglinton of that Ilk, and it was probably through this union that he obtained the lands of Eglinton and Ardrossan. He then quartered the Eglinton arms with his own.

Alexander, grandson of John, was cr. a Lord of Parliament in 1445, and was frequently an envoy to England. Hugh, son of his eldest son Alexander, was the

2nd Lord, and his second son, George, was ancestor of the Montgomeries of Skelmorlie. Hugh was cr. Earl of Eglinton, 1506-7. From him descended the later earls, and the Montgomeries of Lainshaw. Hugh, 3rd Earl, was one of those who escorted Queen Mary from France to Scotland in 1561, and he remained loyal to her throughout her troubled reign. His elder son, Hugh, succeeded him and his elder daughter, married Robert, son of George, Lord Seton, who became Earl of Winton. Their third son, Alexander, succeeded his cousin Hugh as 6th Earl of Eglinton. After some problems regarding recognition, he became a firm favourite of King James, whom he entertained at his house in Glasgow in 1617. Another link with the Setons was created in 1662, when Mary, daughter of the 7th Earl of Eglinton, married George, 4th Earl of Winton.

Hugh, 12th Earl of Eglinton was cr. a peer of the UK in 1806 as Baron Ardrossan of Ardrossan. He had previously rebuilt the castle of Eglinton and improved his lands. His grandon, Archibald William, became 13th Earl, and is remembered as the projector of the Eglinton Tournament, in 1839, intended to honour the ancient code of chivalry. It was attended by Lady Seymour, appearing as the 'Queen of Beauty,' but heavy rain marred the event. The 5th Earl of Winton, George Seton, an attainted Jacobite, died unmarried in 1749, and in 1840, Archibald William Montgomerie had himself served heir male general and heir male of provision to him, but did not establish his right to the peerage dignities. However, in 1859 he was cr. Earl of Winton. Archibald George Montgomerie, the 18th Earl of Eglinton, is also Lord Montgomerie, Lord Seton and Tranent, Earl of Winton and Baron Ardrossan of Ardrossan, and Hereditary Sheriff of Renfrewshire.

# MONTGOMERIE OFFSHOOTS

Branches of the Eglinton family are found spelling their surname Montgomerie and Montgomery. The Montgomerys of Stanhope descend from the Giffen cadets. Troilus, son of Adam Montgomery, of this line, held the lands of Magbiehill, in Ayrshire. From him descended William Montgomery, who in 1712, purchased the estate of Coldcoat, in Peeblesshire, which he renamed Magbiehill. His son William, 1682-1768, an advocate, had two sons. The elder was William, cr. a baronet in 1774, but the title expired with the death of his son Sir George, unmarried, in 1831. The younger son of the advocate, James 1721-1803, was Chief Baron of the Exchequer in Scotland, and was cr. a baronet in 1801. He purchased Lot 34 in Prince Edward Island, Canada, in 1770, and sponsored emigration to Stanhope, Covehead and Brackley Point. His second son, Sir James, was an eminent lawyer, and the family has given the country local and national politicians, soldiers and clergyman. The 8th Bt., Sir Basil, died without issue in 1964, and was succeeded by the son of his brother Henry, Sir David Montgomery, 9th Bt., who was a Tayside Region councillor, 1974-79, and Vice-President of COSLA.

George, second son of the 1st Lord Montgomerie, was progenitor of the family of Skelmorlie. Sir Robert, VIIth of Skelmorlie, was cr. a baronet of NS in 1628. The direct male line ended in 1735, and Lilias, heiress of the 5th Bt., carried the estates to her husband, Alexander Montgomerie of Coilsfield, descended from Col. James, fourth son of the 6th Earl of Eglinton. Their eldest son, Hugh, inherited the earldom of Eglinton in 1796, and in 1806 was cr. Baron Ardrossan of Ardrossan. Alexander, his brother, was ancestor of the Montgomeries of Annick Lodge, Ayrshire.

The Montgomerys of Lainshaw descended from Sir Neill, 3rd son of the 1st Earl of Eglinton. He married Margaret Mure, and their elder son John died without male issue. The younger son, Neil, married Jean, heiress of Lord Lyle, and their son, Neil, assumed the title of Lord Lyle, but was refused the vote in the election of representative peers in 1721 and 1722. By his wife Barbara Kennedy, he had a daughter Jean, who married David Laing, who assumed the name Montgomery. Their daughter and ultimate heiress Elizabeth, married Capt. Alexander Montgomerie Cunningham, Corsehill. He also assumed the title of Lord Lyle and was refused the vote in the election of peers in 1784. Lainshaw was sold to the Cuninghams of Bridgehouse.

Branches settled in Ireland. The family of Montgomery of Grey Abbey, Co. Down, descended from Sir Hugh Montgomery of Braidstane, descended from Robert, second son of Alexander, Master of Montgomery, and grandson of the 1st Lord Montgomery. Hugh, elder son of Adam, Vth of Braidstane, was raised to the peerage of Ireland in 1622 as Viscount Montgomery of Ardes. His grandson, Hugh, 3rd Viscount, was cr. Earl of Mount Alexander in 1661, but the honours expired with Thomas, 7th Earl, in 1758. Robert, younger son of Adam of Braidstane, went to Ireland early in the 17th century with his cousin Hugh, and continued the Braidstane line, now represented by William Howard Clive Montgomery of Grey Abbey.

Another Montgomery family settled near Dunkineely, Co. Donegal, in 1628, and prospered. From them descended the famous Field-Marshall of World War II, Sir Bernard Law Montgomery, 1887-1976, KG, cr. Viscount Montgomery of Alamein, in 1946

Glasgow-born Colin Montgomerie is currently Scotland's top golfer. For the past two seasons he has led the European Order of Merit.

# MORRISON

Morrisons in various parts of the country do not descend from a common ancestor. The usual interpretation of the name is 'son of Maurice,' a common name in medieval times. The Maurice or Mourice, who is the eponymous ancestor of the Morrisons of Lewis – the *Clann MhicGillemhoire* – was a natural son of Olaf the Black, King of Man and the Isles from about 1226. His mother appears to have been Lauon, daughter of a Kintyre chief, and his wife was the daughter of the chief of the Gows. Mourice was a natural brother of Leod, progenitor of the MacLeods of Lewis and Harris.

The heirs of Mourice became hereditary brieves or justices of Lewis. Hutcheon (Gaelic *Uisdean*), brieve of Lewis, was summoned to Inverness with Rory MacLeod in 1551, for harbouring rebels. The brieves were experts in Gaelic law, and before the fall of the Lordship of the Isles in 1493, there was probably a right of appeal to the Council of the Isles. John Morrison, brieve of Lewis, was a supporter of Torquil Cononach during the troubles caused by the Fife Adventurers in the time of King James VI. Another Hutcheon appears as brieve in 1616. Those later brieves were MacDonalds by blood, as the Morrison heiress about 1346 married Cain MacDonald of Ardnamurchan. The only Hebridean Morrisons who recorded arms were those of Ruchdi, who traced their ancestry to the Morrisons of the Dun of Pabbay, descended from the brieves. William S. Morrison, Speaker in the House of Commons, 1951-59, was a younger son of this family, and became Viscount Dunrossil. His elder brother John was granted arms in 1959 as chief of the Morrisons. A Lewis man, Alexander, son of Alexander Morrison of Habost, Ness, graduated at Aberdeen in 1908, and had a distinguished teaching career in South Africa.

In Aberdeenshire, a notable family descended from Alexander Morison, who obtained the lands of Bognie in 1635. His son George married Christian, Viscountess Frendraught, and he purchased the wadset of Frendraught. In 1673 he had a grant of arms: Azure, three saracen's heads conjoined on one neck Argent. The arms are similar to those recorded, 1672-78, for Alexander Morison, son of Alexander Morison of Prestongrange, a Lord of Session, whose kinsman, Henry Morison, W.S., also registered arms. Theodore Morison, son of George, attended Aberdeen Grammar School, and excelled at archery, for which he provided a medal bearing his father's arms. From his second son, James, of Strawberry Vale, Finchley, Middlesex, descended the later lairds of Bognie and Frendraught.

The Hon. Lord Morison (Alastair Malcolm Morison), a Senator of the College of Justice since 1985, comes from a family who have been prominent in legal circles. His father was Sir Ronald Peter Morison (1900-76), Q.C., admitted Advocate at the Scottish Bar in 1923, and to the English Bar in 1940. He was son of Rt. Hon. Thomas B. Morison (1868-1945), P.C., who was admitted Advocate in 1891, and to the English Bar in 1899. He became a K.C. in 1906; was Solicitor-General for Scotland, 1913-20, and Lord Advocate, 1920-22. In 1922 he became a Senator of the College of Justice, and retired in 1937. He was son of Peter Morrison, S.S.C.

Morrison is a prolific surname around Durness, in Sutherland, and according to tradition the ancestors came from Lewis. Their tartan is that of their Mackay neighbours, with a red line added.

# MUNRO

Modern clan historians, while agreeing that the Munros were of Celtic origin and that the name is territorial, do not favour the old derivation: "Man from Ro," meaning one from the foot of the River Roe, Derry, Ireland. Moreover, the tradition that Donald, from whom their territory of Ferindonald (roughly equivalent to the Ross parishes of Alness and Kiltearn) is supposed to have been named, came to Scotland with some forces to assist Malcolm II, 1004-34, against the Danes, and was rewarded with some lands to the east of Dingwall, no longer has credibility. In Gaelic the Munros form *Clann Rothaich*, and their origin has been described as one of the great problems of clan history.

At first the Munros were vassals of the Lords of the Isles and Earls of Ross, and were becoming established as a clan in the reign of Alexander III, 1249-86. George Munro witnessed a charter of lands in Badenoch in 1338. In 1364, Robert Munro was granted a charter by William, Earl of Ross, "of the haill clavoch of lands of easter Foules and the fortar of Strathskea, with the milne, fishings and other pertinents." He married Jane Ross, a niece of Queen Euphame, consort of Robert II. Robert Munro was killed in 1369 in a scuffle in defence of his superior. After this time, the Munros appear in numerous documents. Hugh Munro had grants of land from his dearest cousin, Euphame, Countess of Ross, in 1394, and these were confirmed to his son George, in 1426. In 1453, John Munro had sasine of Easter and Wester Foulis, as heir to his father George. Hugh, a younger son of George, was ancestor of the Munros of Coul. A relative, Fr. Thomas Munro, sub-dean of Ross, acted at times as secretary to the Lord of the Isles.

In the time of Mary, Queen of Scots, Robert More Munro of Foulis was sincerely attached to her cause, as a reward for which he had a tack of the Crown customs of the town and shire of Inverness. His grandson, Robert, was in favour with James VI. A later laird, Robert, was a poor economist and greatly encumbered the estate, but his brother Sir Hector, who succeeded him, did much to restore the family fortunes. He fought in the German Wars, and on his return was cr. a baronet of Nova Scotia, 1634. The 2nd Bt. died at the age of sixteen, and the honours passed to his kinsman, Robert Munro of Obsdale. Sir Harry Munro, 6th Bt., commanded the Black Watch at Fontenoy in 1745. He was killed at Falkirk in 1746. The Munros supported the government throughout the Jacobite Risings. Their old castle at Foulis was rebuilt in 1750 by the 7th Bt., Sir Harry Munro, MP. The late baron and chief of the clan, Capt. Patrick G Munro, assumed in 1937 the surname and arms of Munro of Foulis. He was the son of Eva Marion, daughter of Sir Hector Munro, 11th Bt. (d 1935), who married in 1904, Lt. Col. Cecil Orby Gasgoigne, Seaforth Highlanders. She assumed the surname Munro of Foulis in 1935 and relinquished it in 1938.

Four sons of Robert Munro, who died in 1633, descended from the chiefly line, fought against Cromwell. One of them, William, with some clansmen, was captured at Worcester in 1651, and transported to New England, where his family flourished. A descendant, Ebenezer Munro, 1752-1825, claimed to have fired the first shot in the American War of Independence. From another prisoner, Andrew Munroe, taken at Preston in 1648, descended James Monroe, 1758-1831, 5th President of the United States, remembered for his dual principle of American foreign policy enunciated in the Monroe Doctrine.

# MURE/MOOR

Since Muir, and variants such as Mure, Moor(e) and More, all stem from people who lived on or beside a moor or heath, it is not surprising that the surname is prolific in lowland Scotland, especially in the west because of several landowning families. The earliest reference appears during the reign of Alexander II, 1214-49, when David de More, of the house of Polkelly, Ayrshire, witnessed a charter. He may have been the father of Reginald of Craig (of Rowallan) and others who swore fealty to Edward I in 1296. Gilchrist More, another signatory, was ejected from Rowallan, in Ayrshire by Sir Walter Cumyn, and ordered to keep to his castle of Polkelly. He eventually married Isobel, daughter of Sir Walter Cumyn, and secured his lands of Rowallan and some others in Roxburghshire. The remote ancestry of those landed men is obscure, but they may have come from Kent, the original home of the ancestors of the Earls of Drogheda, in Ireland.

Archibald Mure of Rowallan, who was slain at Berwick in 1297, left a son William, his heir, and another, possibly Reginald, ancestor of the Mures of Caldwell. An important member of the family was Sir Adam of Rowallan, who married his distant relative, Janet, heiress of Polkelly, and had two sons, Sir Adam and Andrew, and a daughter Elizabeth, who married in 1348, Robert, Steward of Scotland, afterwards King Robert II. The parties were in the fourth degree of consanguinity, and although a dispensation was obtained arguments regarding the legitimacy of their son Robert III, were once commonplace. Sir William Mure of Rowallan, 1594-1657, was a notable poet and he translated Boyd of Trochrig's Latin poem, 'Hecatombe Christiana.' His main work was his *True Crucifix for Catholics*, published in 1629. Sir William became a Covenanter. He was twice married and had seven sons and eight daughters. His heir, William, was also a Covenanter, and the youngest son, Patrick, was cr. a baronet of Nova Scotia in 1662. The title did not long survive. The last lineal descendant was William Mure, died 1700.

Sir Reginald Mure of Caldwell, by his marriage to Sybilla, daughter of Sir John Graham of Dalkeith and Abercorn, obtained extensive lands. Sir Adam, a later laird, who died about 1513, was the father of John, who married Lady Margaret Stewart, grand-aunt of Lord Darnley, second husband of Mary, Queen of Scots. They had two sons, John, of Caldwell, and William of Glanderstoun. In 1666, Sir Robert Mure of Caldwell raised a troop of horses for the Covenanters, and was forfeited. His estates were restored to his daughter Barbara, who married John Fairlie, without issue. Caldwell was then inherited by William Mure, IVth of Glanderstoun, who in turn was succeeded by a nephew of the same name, eldest son of James Mure of Rhoddens, in Ireland. The Mures of Caldwell have distinguished themselves in many fields, including the military, literature, the law, and politics.

Sir John Moore, 1761-1809, son of Dr John Moore, a Glasgow physician and miscellaneous writer, was a celebrated military commander, and fell at Corunna in 1809. Thomas Muir, 1765-98, of Hunterston, a 'political martyr' of 1793, was transported to Australia, but escaped and died in France. John Muir, 1838-1914, a native of Dunbar, emigrated to America in 1849, settling in California. He was an explorer, naturalist, and pioneer conservationist, largely reponsible for the creation of Yosemite National Park. Lesmahagow-born Alexander Muir, 1830-1906, went to Ontario, Canada in 1833, and wrote the words and music of 'The Maple Leaf Forever."

# MURRAY OR MORAY: ANCIENT

The great families of Moray of Bothwell, whose castle is an impressive ruin, and Murray of Tullibardine, from whom came the Earls and Dukes of Atholl, descended from William of Petty, son of William of Moravia, son of Freskin the Fleming. He died before 1226, when his second son, Sir Walter, made an agreement with Andrew, Bishop of Moray, his cousin, regarding lands and tiends granted to that church by his father. Sir Walter's grandson also Sir Walter, inherited estates in Moray, and perhaps through his wife, a daughter of David Olifard (Oliphant), obtained Bothwell, in Lanarkshire, and lands in Berwickshire. His sons, William and Andrew, who were staunch supporters of Sir William Wallace and King Robert I, succeeded in turn to the estates. Andrew's son, Sir John, Lord of Bothwell, was a hostage for King David II, and died in an English prison before 1351. Having no issue he was succeeded by his brother, Sir Thomas, who was the last of the Bothwell line of whom anything is known. His widow, Joanna, heiress of Sir Maurice Moray of Drumsargard, Strathearn, married about 1362, Sir Archibald Douglas, 'The Grim,' afterwards Lord of Galloway.

The Tullibardine, Perthshire, line favoured the spelling Murray. They descended from Sir Malcolm Murray, grandson of William of Petty, and held the lands of Llanbryde and others in Moray, and probably some farms in Roxburghshire. His son, Sir William obtained the lands of Tullibardine, east and west, half through his marriage to Ada, daughter of Sir Malise, steward of Strathearn, about 1284. For Sir David Murray, VIIth of Tullibardine, the lands were erected into a feudal barony in 1443. His son William was scutifer or esquire to King James III, and sat frequently in Parliament. In the time of his son Sir William, there was a bitter feud with the Drummonds, who set fire to the church of Monzievaird. They made peace before 1500. Sir William, XIth of Tullibardine, was Comptroller of Scotland, and had a hand in the escape of Queen Mary from Lochleven Castle in 1568. Sir John, his son, was cr. Earl of Tullibardine in 1606. By his wife, Catherine Drummond, he had five sons: William, 2nd Earl; Capt. John who died before 1607; Sir Patrick of Redcastle, who became 3rd Earl; Sir Mungo of Drumcairn, who became 2nd Viscount Stormont; and Robert, alive in 1618. The 2nd Earl resigned Tullibardine in the hands of his brother Sir Patrick seemingly on the promise of the king to make his issue by Lady Dorothy Stewart, Earls of Atholl. The Tullibardine line was continued by Sir Patrick, who had a charter of the earldom in 1628. James, his son, Earl of Tullibardine, died in 1670, without issue, and his titles and estates passed to his kinsman, John Murray, 2nd Earl of Atholl.

The Earls of Dunmore descend from John, 1st Marquess of Atholl. Cadets of the Tullibardine family include the Earls of Dysart (1643), and those of Mansfield (1776), also the baronets of Ochtertyre (NS 1673). Other associated families include the Murrays of Glendoick, Ayton, Pitcaithly, Dollary, Lintrose, Arbenie, Pitcullen and Woodend, Strowan and Tippermore. Important families in the south include the Murrays of Cockpool, who came to be Earls of Annandale (1624), and their cadets, Touchadam and Polmaise, in Stirlingshire, and Falahill, Mid Lothian, from whom came the baronets (NS, 1628) of Blackbarony, in Peeblesshire, and their cadets, not least Dunerne, also baronets (NS, 1630). The Morays of Abercairny, who kept the old spelling, claimed descent from the Drumsargart line of the Morays of Bothwell.

# MURRAY OF ATHOLL

John, son and heir of William, 2nd Earl of Tullibardine, was cr. Earl of Atholl in 1629. His sons John and Mungo were Royalists. John succeeded to the titles and estates of Tullibardine on the death of his kinsman, James Murray, in 1760. In 1676, he was cr. Marquess of Atholl and Earl of Tullibardine. His son John was cr. Duke of Atholl and Marquess of Tullibardine in 1703. John, his eldest son, was killed at Malplaquet in 1709, and William, the second son, along with his younger brothers Charles and George, played important parts in the Jacobite Risings. William, styled Marquis of Tullibardine, fought at Sheriffmuir and was attainted of high treason. His brother Charles commanded a regiment of the Atholl Brigade, and was taken prisoner. He was sentenced to death, but reprieved, and died in 1720. William and George escaped to the Continent. George was pardoned in 1724, but in 1745 his Jacobite sympathies were as strong as ever, and he joined the army of Prince Charles. William returned from France with the Prince, landing at Borrodale, and he raised the standard at Glenfinnon. He and the Prince took up quarters at Blair Castle. William took possession of the family estates and assumed the title of Duke of Atholl. His brother, Lord George, commanded the left wing of the army at Prestonpans and the right wing at Culloden. It has been remarked that if the Prince had slept during the campaign and left full command to Lord George Murray, he would have found the crown of Great Britain on his head when he awoke. William sought refuge in Dumbartonshire, but was betrayed by a Buchanan of Drumakil, and died in an English prison. Lord George escaped to Holland, and died in 1760, leaving issue. His eldest son, John of Strowan, succeeded as 3rd Duke of Atholl, on the death of his uncle, James, 2nd Duke.

John, 3rd Duke, 1729-74, regained the honours by petition. He became a representative peer, and in 1767 was cr. a Knight of the Thistle. In 1753, he married his cousin, Charlotte, daughter of the 2nd Duke, on whose death she succeeded to the Barony of Strange in the peerage of England, and to the sovereignty of the Isle of Man. The latter was sold to the crown, reserving patronages, and with a reddendo of two falcons to the kings and queens of England on the days of their respective coronations. Their eldest son, John, raised a regiment in 1777, called the 77th or Atholl Highlanders, which saw service in Ireland and was disbanded in 1783. The title 'the Atholl Highlanders' has since the disbandment been the name of the Duke of Atholl's regiment of Highlanders in Blair Atholl. It is the only 'private' army in Great Britain. The 4th Duke, John, was cr. Baron Murray of Stanley and Earl of Strange (UK, 1786).

The 7th Duke, John James, served in the Scots Guards before 1865. He succeeded to the Barony of Percy in right of his grand-mother, Lady Glenlyon, on the death of his uncle, Algernon, Duke of Northumberland, in 1865, becoming senior co-heir of John, 14th Earl of Oxford, who died in 1526. He was already co-heir to Henry 18th Earl, who died in 1525, and as such he claimed but unsuccessfully, to be entitled to execute the office of Great Chamberlain at the King's coronation. Their son John George, 1871-1942, was chairman of the committee that planned the Scottish National War Memorial. He was succeeded as 9th Duke by his brother, James Thomas, who died unmarried in 1957, when his kinsman, George Ian Murray, descended from the 3rd Duke, succeeded as 10th Duke. He is chief of the surname. The family home of Blair Castle, rebuilt after the '45, contains priceless heirlooms.

# NICOLSON/MacNICOL

There are Nicolsons (with variant spellings) scattered all over Britain and the only certainty about their origins is that they did not all descend from a common ancestor. In Scotland, Highland and Lowland Nicolsons carry the heads of hawks on their armorial bearings, but it is highly improbable that even those families had a common origin. The baronets of Kensington, Luddenham and Winterbourne, in England, do not have those charges on their armorial bearings. It is probable their surnames mean 'son of Nicolas.'

It is reasonably certain that the Nicolsons of Wester Ross and the Hebrides came originally from Norway. Some authorities think those who bore the name Nicolson came first, and that the meaning of the name is 'nic' Olsen, derived from a female ancestor. Later, a wave of 'mac' Nicols arrived. Their chief is said to have died about 1340, leaving no sons, and both groups then merged. Certainly there is ample evidence to show that the surnames became interchangeable, but probably the Nicolsons of Scorrybreac, in Skye, were originally MacNicols. The Nicholsons obtained land in Lewis through marriage with a MacLeod heiress, but they may have previously been in Assynt and Coigach. Angus Nicolson, tacksman of Kirivig, was the ancestor of Alexander Morison Nicolson, a shipbuilder in Shanghai, who founded the Nicolson Institute in Stornoway. When the Nicolsons settled in Skye is uncertain, but in 1507 Mulconil MacNicoll appears in Trotternish. The eponymous ancestor was Greagall, whose descendants are given as Nicail, Neailbh, Aigi (Hugh), Nicail, John and Ewan. The list is probably mythical before John, who appears to have been the ancestor of the Nicolsons who came to be recognised as the chiefs of *Clann Mhic Neacail Scorrabreac*, now Clan MacNicol. This line continues in the person of Ian Nicholson, a sheep farmer in New South Wales. There are branches in the U.S.A., Canada and Australia. Hammond Burke Nicholson, jr., of Atlanta, Georgia, USA, a company director, obtained in 1988, a grant of arms for his ancestor, Duncan Nicholson, a Scot who emigrated to North Carolina before 1809, and he and other members of the family have matriculated arms. He is now Baron Balvenie, Banffshire, having purchased the ruined castle there.

Nicolsons who were under the impression that Nicolson of Scorrybreac was chief of all the Nicolsons in Scotland, and not simply of *Clan Mhic Neacail Scorrabreac*, were troubled in 1983, when Sir David Arthur Henry Arthur Nicolson of Carnock, petitioned the Lord Lyon for recognition as chief of the surname, or 'Nicolson of that Ilk.' The petition was granted, and rightly so, as he could prove his connection with the Nicolsons of Lasswade, who were styled "of that Ilk." Those Lowland Nicolsons formed a prominent legal family. James Nicolson, a writer (solicitor) in Edinburgh, who died in 1580, was the progenitor of the Nicolsons of Lasswade, Carnock and Cockburnspath. His son John was admitted an Advocate in 1586, and became Commissary of Edinburgh. John Nicolson, his elder son, became a Baronet of Nova Scotia in 1629. The collaterel line of Carnock, were raised to the same order in 1636. The male line of the Lasswade baronets failed in 1952. Arthur Nicolson, 11th Baronet of Carnock, a distinguished diplomat, had been created Baron Carnock in 1916, and it was his grandson, the 3rd baron, who was recognised as Nicolson "of that Ilk."

The MacNicols of Argyll are said to have descended from Nicol MacPhee, a native of Lochaber. Some Nicolsons shortened their name to Nicol.

# OGILVY

The Ogilvys descend from Gilliebride (Normanised Gilbert), Earl of Angus, who witnessed charters between 1150 and 1187. Gilbert himself was probably a descendant of the ancient mormaers of the district. From his third son, Gilbert, who received lands in Angus about 1177, descended the Ogilvys of that Ilk, Airlie and cadets, and Inverquharity. In the branches of Findlater, Boyne, Banff and Inchmartine, they spread themselves over large areas of Aberdeenshire and Banffshire. Among the lands granted to Gilbert were those of Ogilvy, deriving from *Ocel Fa*, meaning 'high plain.'

Patrick de Ogilvy signed the 'Ragman Roll' in 1296, and from him descended a line of Ogilvys of that Ilk, which expired when the branch of Auchterhouse became the stem family. Their founder was Sir Partick Ogilvy of Wester Powrie, ancestor of Sir Walter Ogilvy of Auchterhouse, who had two sons, Alexander, his heir, and Sir Walter of Lintrathen, progenitor of the house of Airlie. Sir John, 2nd of Lintrathen, received a charter of Airlie in 1491, and his son Sir James was cr. Lord Ogilvy of Airlie in 1491. James, the 8th Earl, was cr. Earl of Airlie in 1639, and although not the heir male, was acknowledged as chief of the surname.

The Ogilvys had a deadly feud with the Lindsays, ostensibly because Sir Alexander Ogilvy of Inverquharity displaced the Master of Crawford as justiciar of the Regality of Montrose. The quarrel resulted in a clan battle at Montrose in 1646, where the Ogilvies suffered heavy losses. They also had a feud with the Campbells of Argyll, who razed 'The Bonny Hoose o' Airlie.' During the troubles of the Stewart monarchs, the Ogilvys remained loyal, and several representatives were Jacobites. For their part in the risings of 1715 and 1745, they were attainted. In 1778, a pardon was granted to Lord Ogilvy because of his youth at the time of the '45, and in 1826 the Earldom of Airlie was restored to David Ogilvy as 4th Earl. His son David married Henrietta, daughter of Edward, 2nd Lord Stanley, and had a son David, 6th Earl, and several daughters, the third of whom, Henrietta Blanche, married in 1878, Sir Henry Montague Hozier of Stonehouse. They were the parents of Clementine Ogilvy Hozier, who married in 1928, Sir Winston S. Churchill, Great Britain's famous Prime Minister during World War II. Another notable marriage took place in 1963, when Angus, second son of Sir David Ogilvy, 12th Earl of Airlie, married HRH Princess Alexandra of Kent. His brother David George, is the 13th Earl.

The Ogilvys of Deskford and Findlater derive from Sir Walter Ogilvy of Deskford, younger son of Sir Walter of Lintrathen. James, 2nd Lord Ogilvie of Deskford, was cr. Earl of Findlater in 1638, and in 1701, James. 4th Earl, who supported the Act of Union in 1707 and repented it by 1713, was cr. Earl of Seafield. James, 7th Earl of Findlater, died without issue in 1811, and the title expired, but other dignities devolved on his cousin, Lady Margaret, daughter of the 5th Earl of Findlater and 2nd of Seafield, who had married (as his second wife) Sir Ludovic Grant, Bt. Their grandson, Sir James Grant, became 5th Earl of Seafield. Here it is worth noting that the Earls of Findlater were acknowledged as chiefs in the north-east, but in 1641, the Earl of Findlater arranged that the succession should pass through his daughter to Ogilvy of Inchmartine. This was an older line and the Earl of Airlie, fearing this family would claim precedence, obtained a royal mandate confirming him as chief.

The Inverquharity branch of the family possess a baronetcy (NS, 1626). The 14th and present holder is Francis Gilbert Ogilvie, surveyor and farmer.

# OLIPHANT

The first Oliphant to come to Scotland belonged to a family seated in Northamptonshire, and deriving their name from Lilleford, a crossing on the River Nene, often given as Holyford, because the Abbot of Peterborough had a manor on one side. David Olifard, godson and namesake of David I, King of Scots, 1124-53, was serving in King Stephen's army at the rout of Winchester in 1141, and saved the monarch from being taken prisoner. Soon afterwards he appears in Scotland and was rewarded with lands, as well as being made Justiciar (probably of Lothian). David Olifard was probably second son of William, son of Roger Olifard, who witnessed a charter of Simon de Senlis about 1107. The landowner was the wealthy Countess Judith, widow of Waltheof of Northumbria, and daughter of Adele, sister of William the Conqueror, by her second husband, Lambert, Count of Lens, in Flanders. Maud or Matilda, daughter of Waltheof and Judith, and widow of Simon de Senlis, married David I, King of Scots. David Olifard was of Flemish extraction, and his armorial device, three red crescents on a silver shield, suggests descent from the family of Lens and some link with the Setons.

Some Olifard lines remained in England, although for a time the manor of Lilleford was possessed by the Scottish family. David Olifard had several sons, and his heir, Walter, Justiciar of Lothian, held lands in East Lothian and Berwickshire. By his marriage to Christian, daughter of Ferteth, Earl of Strathearn, he obtained lands at Dupplin, in Strathearn. There appears to have been two lines stemming from them, one descending from Walter the younger, who died in 1242, and another coming from a son David, whose son William, was ancestor of the Lords of Oliphant. During the War of Independence there were two Sir William Oliphants, cousins, who fought bravely.

From one of these, came Walter Oliphant, who married Elizabeth, daughter of King Robert I. From them descended Laurence Oliphant cr. Lord Oliphant in 1463. His grandson Colin was killed at Flodden, 1513, and his great-grandson, Laurence, 3rd Lord, was taken prisoner at Solway Moss in 1542, and ransomed. The 4th Lord, also Laurence, was present at Bothwell's marriage to Mary, Queen of Scots. The 5th Lord, another Laurence, encumbered all the estates, except for Gask, which had passed to a cadet, descended from the 2nd Lord. He attempted to transmit his title to his only daughter, Anna, but failed, and Charles I bestowed it on his cousin Patrick, nearest male heir. The 9th Lord, William, was a Jacobite, involved in the campaigns of 1688 and 1715. He died without surviving male issue, and the title passed to Francis, younger son of the 6th Lord. He died without issue in 1748, and the title became dormant, although claimed by various Oliphants.

The Oliphants of Gask, Perthshire, were also a Jacobite family. Laurence Oliphant of Gask, married in 1748, Amelia Anne, second daughter of William 2nd Lord Nairne. Their house was looted by Cumberland's troops. Caroline, their grand-daughter, married her second cousin, William, grandson of John, 3rd Lord Nairne, forfeited for his part in the '45. William was restored to the title as 4th Lord Nairne. Lady Nairne, 1766-1845, was a noted songwriter. Among her lasting songs are *Caller Herrin'* and *The Auld House*, but she is best remembered for *Will ye no' come back again*, which reminds us of the family's Jacobite sympathies. Another interesting branch of the Oliphants is that of Condie, Perthshire, descended from the 3rd Lord Oliphant through the Newton line. This family is represented by Lt. Cdr. Ralph Henry Hood Laurence Oliphant, who served with distinction in World War II.

# PATERSON

A prolific surname in Scotland, Paterson (sometimes spelt with double 'tt') simply means 'Patrick's son.' As Patrick is often synonymous with Peter, the name is occasionally rendered Peterson. Patison is another variant. At one period there was a group of Patersons on the north side of Loch Fyne, known as *Clann Pheadirean*. Patrick being a favourite name in the Middle Ages, appears all over Scotland (Gaelic *Padruig*), and there is no question of a common ancestor. Nor can any credence be given to the tradition of Scandinavian origin. Among early references to the name are William Patrison and John Patonson, 'gentillmen', witnesses at Aberdeen in 1446, and in 1494, Donald Patryson was admitted burgess there. Robert Patryson was captain of a Dundee ship in 1544. In 1557, Fyndlay Patersoun had a lease of the lands of Owar Elrik from the Abbey of Cupar, and George Peterson was a monk in the monastery of Culross in 1569.

The fine old fortalice of Castle Huntly, in Longforgan parish, Perthshire, belonged to a Paterson family from 1777 to 1948. It was probably built in the latter part of the 15th century by Andrew, 2nd Lord Gray. In 1615 it passed to the Lyons, Earls of Kinghorn. George Paterson, who purchased the castle, married Ann, daughter of the 11th Lord Gray, and he made additions to the building and renovated the interior. A later George Paterson, who married another Paterson, Janet, daughter of James of Longbedholm, Dumfriesshire, left two sons, George Frederick and Charles James, successively owners of Castle Huntly. A kinsman, Col. Adrian G. Paterson, purchased the property from the executors of Charles James Paterson, and it was sold by his widow in 1948.

A Jacobite family once owned the estate of Bannockburn. Hugh, son of John Paterson, was admitted

Writer to the Signet in 1661, and was cr. a baronet (NS) in 1686. He was succeeded by his son, Sir Hugh, whose younger daughter, Katherine, married John Walkinshaw, IIIrd of Barrowfield, and had ten daughters, the youngest of whom, Clementine, 1720-1802, met Prince Charles Edward Stuart in January, 1746, probably at Bannockburn House. She later joined him in France and became his mistress. Clementine bore him a daughter, Charlotte, 1753-89, legitimated by him in 1784, and who was known as Duchess of Albany. Sir Hugh Paterson, 3rd Bt., was involved in the '15 Rebellion, and was forfeited. The title became extinct on his death, 1777.

In 1688, the estate of Granton, near Edinburgh, came into the possession of Sir William Paterson, Bt. (NS. 1687), son of John, Bishop of Ross, and brother of John Paterson, the last Archbishop of Glasgow. He was for a time Regent of Philosophy in the University of Edinburgh. His son, Sir John, sold the estate in 1708, and purchased that of Eccles, in Berwickshire. Among Paterson property owners in the south-west was the family of Balgray, Dumfriesshire. Robert Jardine Paterson, 1878-1942, of Balgray, served in the Coldstream Guards in World War I. His son, Capt. David Paterson of Balgray, served with the Gurkha Rifles in World War II. A Dumfriesshire man who achieved lasting fame was William Paterson, 1658-1719, a farmer's son. He became a financier, and in 1691 submitted to the London merchants his scheme for forming the Bank of England. Dissatisfied with lack of encouragement for other projects, he withdrew and devised his grand scheme for colonisation by Scotland of the Isthmus of Panama. It ended in disaster through poor supplies, the unhealthy climate, and internal dissention.

# RAMSAY

The first of this surname recorded in Scotland was Simon de Ramsay, who took his name from Ramsey, in Huntingdonshire, where he had an estate which was ravaged in 1140 by Geoffrey de Mandeville. He was probably of Flemish extraction and related – perhaps a son – to Walter de Lindsay, by his Seton wife. Simon was given an estate in Lothian, under the protection of the Setons. He appears as a witness to charters between 1153 and 1198. Simon was the ancestor of Sir Alexander Ramsay of Dalhousie and Sir William Ramsay of Inverleith. Sir Alexander was Warden of the Middle Marches about 1342, and died about 1335, when he was succeeded by Sir William.

The Ramsays firmly established themselves at Dalhousie, and in 1617, Sir George Ramsay was created a Lord of Parliament by the title of Lord Ramsay of Melrose, but had the title changed to Dalhousie. His eldest son, William was created 1st Earl of Dalhousie and Lord Ramsay of Kerington in 1633. He led a regiment of the Covenanting army at Marston Moor and Philiphaugh. William, the 8th Earl, succeeded to the estates of his maternal uncle, William, Earl of Panmure. He married Elizabeth, niece of James Glen, Governor of South Carolina, whose estates and wealth came to him. The Earl was succeeded by his eldest son, George, while his second son, William, became Lord Panmure, assuming the name and arms of Maule. George, 9th Earl of Dalhousie was Lt. Governor of Nova Scotia, 1816, and Governor of Canada, 1819-28. He was created Baron Dalhousie in 1815. His third son, James 10th Earl, was Governor-General of India, 1847-56, and was created Marquess of Dalhousie in 1849. He died in 1860, when the marquessate and barony (U.K.) became extinct. The Scottish honours devolved on his cousin, Fox Maule, a noted politician. The Maule title became extinct when he died in 1874, and he was succeeded by his cousin George, 12th Earl of Dalhousie. Simon Ramsay, the 16th and present Earl, lives at Brechin Castle, in Angus. The Dalhousie Muniments are in the Scottish Record Office.

By the middle of the 13th century, the Ramsays appear as landowners in Angus and in the following century were divided into several branches. From the Ramsays of Carnock, in Fife, descended Sir John Ramsay, Lord of Bothwell, who died in 1513, leaving a son William of Balmain, lineal ancestor of Sir Alexander Burnett Ramsay (1758-1810) of Balnain, Bt. (U.K., 1806), father of Dean Ramsay, author of *Reminiscenses of Scottish Life and Character* (1857).

Allan Ramsay (1684-1758), a native of Leadhills and a wigmaker in Edinburgh, became a successful poet. He produced a collection of Scottish songs titled *Tea Table Miscellany*, but is best remembered for *The Gentle Shepherd*. His son Allan (1713-84), studied art at London and Rome, and on his return commenced a series of fine portraits, including that of John, 2nd Duke of Argyll. In 1761 he was appointed portrait painter to King George III. Sir Andrew Crombie Ramsay (1814- 68), educated at Glasgow, was appointed to the Geological Survey of Britain, and became Director-General, as well as President of the Geological Society. William Ramsay (1806-65), a classical scholar, became Professor of Mathematics at Glasgow in 1833, and Sir William Ramsay (1852- 1916), F.R.S., K.C.B. (1902) educated at Glasgow and Tubingen, distinguished himself as an organic chemist. He discovered several new gases and was a Nobel prizeman in 1904. Sir William was the author of several text-books of chemistry.

Maj. Gen. Charles Alexander Ramsay, C.B., O.B.E., who had a distinguished military career, is chief executive of Caledonian Eagle (GB) and Caledonian Eagle (Carribean).

# REID

Reid, Read or Reed is a surname, originally indicating red hair or ruddy complexion. In Latin charters it is often rendered *Rufus*, and in Gaelic, *Ruadh*. Writers of books about tartans tell us the Reids were a sept of Clann Donnachaidh, and this is occasionally correct. The surname is widespread and borne by many families who do not have an ancestor in common. Ade Rufus witnessed a resignation of the lands of Ingilbriston in 1204, and William Rufus was a juror on an inquest on the lands of Padevinan (Houston) in 1259. Gilbert 'le Rede' of Coul died in prison in 1296. 'Red' is found as a surname in Aberdeen in 1317, and is one of the oldest in Kildrummy parish. John Reed was collector of the tithes in the deaneries of Stormonth and Atholl in 1362. John Reed had a charter of lands in Pelanyflatt, in the Park of Cardross, Dumbartonshire, in 1362. In 1367, Simon Reed, Constable of Edinburgh Castle, had a charter of the lands of Lochendorbe, in Inverness-shire. William, son of John Rede, had confirmation of lands in Kyle in 1375. William Rede held Wester Foddels, Aberdeenshire, in wadset from his cousin, Alexander de Moravia, in 1389. In 1494, when Archbishop Blackadder summoned 30 members of genteel Ayrshire families to be interrogated for heretical opinions, including the denial of papal indulgencies and adoration of images, Adam Reid of Barskimming, bold spokesman for the 'Lollards of Kyle,' showed "little respect for proud prelates."

Down through the centuries Reids have distinguished themselves in various walks of life. John, 1655-56–1723, son of John Reid, gardener to Lord Seton at Niddry Castle, Winchburgh, published his celebrated book, *The Scots Gard'ner*, in 1683, when he emigrated to East New Jersey with his Quaker wife, Margaret Miller. He became Surveyor General and owner of a large estate called

Hortensia. Peter Reid, 1777-1838, physician, was son of David Reid, a West India merchant, and Elizabeth Boswell, descended from the Balmuto family. Born at Dubbyside, near Leven, Fife, he distinguished himself as editor of Dr Cullen's *First Lines of the Practice of Physics*, and other medical tracts. A successful teacher of chemistry, Dr David Boswell Reid, 1805-63, was son of Dr Peter Reid, Edinburgh, and Christian, eldest daugher of the historian, Hugo Arnot. He devised a method of ventilating public buildings, and went to America in 1863, to employ his system in military hospitals. Unfortunately he died at Washington, DC. Dr John Reid, 1809-49, a native of Bathgate, became Professor of Anatomy and Medicine in the University of St. Andrews in 1841, and published a volume of essays.

General John Reid, 1721-1807, composer of the air, 'The Garb of Old Gaul,' left money to establish a chair of music at the University of Edinburgh. He was in fact a Robertson, whose ancestors had held the estate of Strathloch, in Strathardle, for eleven generations. The progenitor of this family was Patrick Robertson of Lude, who bore the cognomen of 'Red,' second son of Duncan de Atholia. Dr James Reid, 1849-1923, Physician in Ordinary to Queen Victoria, 1889; to Edward VII, 1899-1910, and to George V, was cr. 1st Baronet of Ellon, Aberdeenshire, in 1897. His grandson, Sir Alexander, is the present Bt. The Baron Reid, 1890-1975, had a distinguished legal career. He was MP for Stirling & Falkirk Burghs, 1931-35, and for Hillhead, Glasgow, 1937-48. He was Solicitor-General in 1936, and Lord Advocate in 1941. In 1948 he was cr. a Life Peer as Baron Reid of Drem, in East Lothian. Hugh Reid, 1860-1935, Lord Dean of Guild of Glasgow, was cr. 1st Bt. of Springburn in 1922. The 3rd Bt. is Sir Hugh, travel consultant who served in the RAF 1952-6, and in Egypt and Cyprus, with the RAF (V.R.T.), 1963-75.

# ROBERTSON

It had been said that the Robertsons are the oldest documented clan in Scottish history. They descend from the Celtic Earls of Atholl, who were of the royal line of the kings of Dalriada, themselves probably descended from Niall of the Nine hostages, who ruled Ireland about the time the Romans left Britain. Conan, second son of Henry, 3rd Earl of Atholl, inherited extensive lands in Atholl, including Glenorchie. His descendant, Duncan de Atholia (1275-1355), was the first chief of *Clan Donnachaidh*. At first the chiefs were called Atholl or Duncanson, but when surnames began to emerge, adopted Robertson from Robert *Riach*, 4th chief. Some others called themselves Duncanson or MacConochie, Macinroy or MacLagan, Stark or Collier, and Reid.

Robert received a charter in 1451, erecting his lands into the Barony of Struan. His brother Patrick obtained Lude, and his descendants formed the oldest cadet branch. Patrick's youngest son married a kinswoman, Matilda Robertson, and was progenitor of the celebrated barons Reid of Straloch, from whom descended the Durdin-Robertsons of Huntington Castle, in County Carlow, Ireland. Other cadets were Inches, Kindeace, Killichangy, Calvine, Auchleeks, Ladykirk, Faskally, Drumachuine, Woodsheal, Inverack and Trinafour. The Auchleeks line is now represented by Robert Alexander Dundas, great-grandson of Ralph Dundas, WS, who married in 1869, Emily Bridget, daughter of Robert Robertson, 10th Laird. In olden times the Robertsons of Struan had castles in Rannoch and at Inverack.

The Robertsons chiefs were famous for their loyalty to the Stewart kings. Donald, Tutor of Struan during the minority of the 12th chief, raised a regiment for Charles I in 1644. Alexander, the 17th chief, a noted poet, first joined Viscount Dundee in support of James VII in 1688, and had his estates forfeited. He was pardoned in 1703, but was 'out' in the '15 and '45 Jacobite Risings and again forfeited. His sister Margaret recovered the estates, which passed to Duncan, 14th chief, son of Alexander Robertson of Drumachuine. He was succeeded by his son Alexander. Capt. Alasdair Stewart Robertson, 20th chief, styled "Struan Robertson," broke the entail of the barony, and sold the mansion of Rannoch Barracks to his sister Jean Rosine, who sold the remaining parts of the estate. On her death the representation passed to Robert Joseph Stewart Robertson, 21st chief, descended from Alexander, 16th chief. The family reside in Jamaica. His brother, George Duncan Robertson, 22nd chief, who was in the Colonial Civil Service in Kingston, was the father of Langton George Duncan Haldane Robertson of Struan, who matriculated arms in 1954. His son Alexander Gilbert Haldane Robertson is the present chief.

A Clan Donnachaidh Society was formed in 1893, and in 1969, a Clan Museum was opened at Bruar Falls, between Blair Atholl and Struan. Biographical dictionaries show Robertsons as statesmen, astronomers, writers, mathematicians, actors, inventors, lawyers, politicians and clergymen. The historian, Rev. William Robertson (1721-93), was descended from the clan chiefs, through the Robertsons of Gladney. In modern times, Lord Robertson (Ian Macdonald Robertson), now retired, was a Senator of the College of Justice from 1966 to 1987. Sir Lewis Robertson, born in Dundee, is a distinguished administrator and historian, and George Robertson, Labour MP for Hamilton, born in Islay, is Opposition Spokesman of Scottish Affairs.

# ROSE

The Rose family has held the lands of Kilravock, Nairn, for nearly eight centuries. They may have come to Scotland in the reign of William I, 1165-1214, with the Bissets, Anglo-Norman family, who founded the Benedictine priory of Beauly in 1232. The name is obviously derived from 'ros,' a promontory, but the headland must have been in their place of origin: possibly the Cotentin peninsula of Normandy. The bougets which appear on their arms may point to a more remote ancestor who fought in the crusades and carried their water in leathern buckets or carriers.

Hugh Rose, who witnessed the charter to the priory of Beauly, held the lands of Geddes, and it was his son Hugh, who obtained Kilravock through his marriage with Mary, daughter of Sir Andrew de Bosco and his lady, Elizabeth, co-heiress of Sir John Bisset of Lovat. It was confirmed by King John Baliol, about 1295. Hugh died about 1306. His son William, IInd of Kilravock, probably fought at Bannockburn and was knighted by Sir Robert Bruce. The next three lairds were all called Hugh, a favourite family name. The second of them married Janet Chisholm and by her acquired some other lands in Strathnairn. In 1390, in the time of his son, the Vth laird, the family muniments, kept at Elgin Cathedral, were destroyed when Alexander Stewart, the 'Wolf of Badenoch,' burned the building. John, VIth of Kilravock, resigned his lands (reserving the liferent) in the hands of his superior, John, Lord of the Isles and Earl of Ross, and his son Hugh received a new charter in 1440. He married Isobel Cheyne and had four sons: Lachlan, a cleric; Hugh, his heir; Alexander of Dunearn, from whom descended several provosts of Nairn; and William, progenitor of some families in Mar.

The VIIth baron, Hugh, built Kilravock Castle about

1460, and additions were later made, particularly in 1553 by 'the Black Baron,' Hugh, who was taken prisoner at Pinkie in 1547 by the English. He was ransomed and married More, daughter of Malcolm, Captain of Clan Chattan. Hugh welcomed Queen Mary at Kilravock in 1562. William, his successor, was a peaceable man, but the clan, having many branches including Holme and Belivat, were not always on good terms with their neighbours, and William, as chief, and his son Hugh, were imprisoned at Edinburgh for a period by the Privy Council, and fined. Hugh, XII the baron, supported the Covenant, as did his son Hugh, who commanded his fighting men at Auldrearn in 1645. He raised a regiment in support of King Charles I, which resulted in burdening his estate. When he died in 1649, his son Hugh was a minor, and the tutor was William Rose of Clava.

Hugh Rose, XVIth baron, was an advocate, and one of his daughters was the mother of Henry Mackenzie, 1745-1831, author of *The Man of Feeling*. Hugh, XVIIth of Kilravock, was sheriff-depute of Ross and Cromarty. His eldest son, Hugh, was succeeded by his sister, Elizabeth, who married his kinsman, Hugh Rose of Brea, and their grandson, Hugh XXIst laird, died in 1747, and was succeeded by his brother, John Baillie Rose. James, XXIIIrd of Kilravock, his half-brother, succeeded. His eldest son Hugh commanded the 1st Battalion of the Black Watch in the South African War, and at Kilravock in 1922, entertained Queen Mary. He married Ruth Guillemard, a French lady, and had two daughters, Elizabeth and Madeleine, who married Hugh Baird and emigrated to Australia. Elizabeth succeeded in 1946 as XXVth of Kilravock, and in 1967 opened the ancient castle as a Christian Guest House.

# ROSS

Hugh, a younger son of Hugh, 4th Earl of Ross, of the O' Beolin line, was the progenitor of the Rosses of Balnagowan, who were recognised as chiefs of *Clann Rois*. From his father he received the lands of Rarichies, and his brother William, the 5th Earl, gave him the lands of Balnagowan, which became the designation of his heirs. The family probably came of the same stock as the O'Beolin abbots of Drumcliff, in Ireland, whose ancestor was Cairbre, a son of King Niall of the Nine Hostages.

The headland (*ros* in Gaelic) jutting into the North Sea between the firths of Cromarty and Dornoch, gave its name to the earldom, to a county and a clan. Under the Celtic mormaers, Ross formed part of the province of Moray, but the feudalising sons of David I. (1124-53) separated Ross to form an earldom held in 1168 by Malcolm MacHeth. Farquhar (*Fearchar Mac an t-Sagairt*, 'son of the priest'), who held lands in Wester Ross, was the first of the O'Beolin line. He had brought numerous warriors to the assistance of King Alexander II, against rival claimants to the throne, for which he was knighted about 1216. A decade later he was entrusted with the Earldom of Ross.

When the 5th Earl died in 1372, Hugh Ross of Rarichies continued the old line of the family. The honours passed to Euphemia, the Earl's daughter and heiress, who married Sir Walter Leslie. Their line ended with an heiress, who resigned in 1415, and probably entered a nunnery. By 1587, the surname Ross was one of the most numerous in the county. From about the end of the 15th century to the middle of the 16th, there was bitter warfare between the Rosses and the MacKays of Strathnaver. In a conflict at Alt a' Charrais, in Strathcarron, in 1486, Alexander Ross of Balnagowan was slain, and his followers defeated. During the time of

Alexander Ross, IXth of Balnagowan, a turbulent chief, the clan embraced the Reformation.

The last laird, David (1644-1711), was plagued with litigation about the succession, and about 1694, a new intriguant appeared in the person of William, Lord Ross, of the Halkhead family, who claimed descent from the Balnagowan line, but who in fact belonged to a Lowland family which derived its name from the Norman *de Roos*. However, through various shady financial transactions, he obtained Balnagowan Castle and extensive lands. The Pitcalnie line succeeded to the representation of the family, and the present chief is David Campbell, son of Sheriff Charles Campbell Ross of Shandwick. He succeeded his aged kinswoman, Miss Rosa W. Ross of that Ilk in 1968. David is a grandson of Sir Ronald Ross (1857-1931), K.C.B., F.R.S., whose work in tropical medicine gained him a Nobel prize in 1902.

In modern times William Ross (1911-88), M.P. (Lab) for Kilmarnock, Ayr and Bute, figured prominently in politics, and was Secretary of State for Scotland, 1964-70, and 1974-76. Today, the Rt. Hon. Lord Ross (Donald MacArthur Ross), son of a Dundee solicitor, is a distinguished Senator of the College of Justice (since 1977), and Lord Justice-Clerk since 1985. He was educated at Dundee High School and the University of Edinburgh, where he graduated M.A. in 1947, and LL.B. (with distinction) in 1951. After National Service with the Black Watch, and Territorial Service, he passed Advocate in 1952. He was Vice-Dean of the Faculty, 1967-73, and Dean, 1973-76, during which period he was Sheriff Principal of Ayr and Bute.

# SCOTT

According to an old tradition the first Scotts on the borders of Scotland and England were of the race of the Scots of Galloway, who were of Celtic origin. Every Scott family does not however, have a common ancestor. The earliest on record is Uchtred *filius* Scot, who witnessed the foundation charter of Selkirk about 1120. The name suggests he belonged south of the border. John le Scot, who was Archdeacon of St. Andrews and became Bishop of Dunkeld late in the 12th century, is believed to have come from Podoth, in the earldom of Chester. His father was a Scot and his mother was related to some other churchman associated with Dunkeld and St. Andrews. In the same manner, John, Earl of Chester, who died in 1237, appears as 'Johannes Scotus' in England, his father, Earl David of Huntingdon (grandson of David I, King of Scots), having married the heiress of the Earl of Chester.

Even in the 13th century, Scotts were widespread. Michael Scott the Wizard, who died about 1235, was probably born in the Tweed Valley. Ade le Scot was a burgess of Berwick (then in Scotland) in 1263. Among those who rendered homage to Edward I. in 1296 were Alisaundre Scot of Perthayk, John le Scot, burgess of Haddington, Wautier le Scot of Peeblesshire, and Richard le Scot of Murthoxton, now Murdostoun, in Lanarkshire. The latter had also Rankilburn in Selkirkshire, and may have acquired Murdieston through marriage. He is said to have had a son Michael, father of Robert, who died before 1390, and was the progenitor of the Scotts of Buccleuch, whose cadets spread out between Ettrickdale and Liddesdale. Robert's son Walter had a charter from Robert II of the superiority of Kirkurd, in Peeblesshire. In the last quarter of the 13th century, Scotts appear in Fife. Michael

Lescot of Fife agreed to serve Edward I overseas in 1297. He may have been of the Scotts of Balweary, the first of whom married the heiress of that estate before 1280. William Scott of Balweary is recorded in 1395.

From the Scotts of Rankilburn and Murdostoun came Sir Walter Scott, who inherited half of Branxholm, near Hawick, and excambed Murdostoun in 1446 for the other half. From a cleuch in the glen of Rankilburn the family took the designation of Buccleuch. David Scott had a charter by James III, erecting the lands of Branxholm and others into a barony. His descendant, Sir Walter of Buccleuch, survived the Battle of Flodden, where he lost many followers. A later Sir Walter, 1565-1646, was cr. a Lord of Parliament in 1606 by the title of Lord Scott of Buccleuch, and his son of the same name was cr. Earl in 1619. Frances, the 2nd Earl, was succeeded in turn by his daughters, Mary, and Anna, whose husband, James, Duke of Monmouth, was executed in 1685 and had his titles forfeited, except the honour of Duke of Buccleuch (cr. 1663), which passed to their grandson, Francis. Henry, 3rd Duke of Buccleuch, became also Duke of Queensberry under the limitation to the heirs male of Lady Jane Douglas. The titles and estates have descended to Walter Montague-Douglas-Scott, 9th Duke of Buccleuch and 11th of Queensberry, who lives with his Countess Jane, at Drumlanrig.

The Polwarth line of the Scotts, has produced many eminent men, not least the 10th Lord, Henry Hepburne-Scott, who was Minister of State for Scotland, 1972-74. The Harden branch of the Scotts gave us Sir Walter Scott, 1771-1832, who qualified as an advocate, but became a popular poet, then Europe's greatest novelist. He became 1st Baronet of Abbotsford in 1820. A definitive 'Edinburgh' edition of his novels is now being published by Edinburgh University Press.

# SETON

The surname of Seton appears in Scotland about 1146, when Alexander Seton witnessed a grant by David I. of lands in Roxburghshire and Berwickshire to Walter Ryedale. The family appear to have originated in Flanders, and probably descended from the Counts of Boulogne. There were possibly links with Normandy, and according to George F. Black, the surname derives from Sai, near Exmes.

Phillip de Seton, probably son of Alexander, had a grant of the lands of Setune, Winton and Winchelburgh (Winchburgh), about 1182, confirming a grant to his father. These lands were again confirmed to Philip's son, Alexander, about 1195, when the service was one knight. An important member of the family was Christopher de Seton, who fought under Wallace and Bruce, whose sister he married. He was knighted by Bruce for rescuing him at the Rout of Methven in 1306. It seems that the reins of Bruces's horse were cut, and that Sir Phillip de Moubray seized these and was making off with the king when Seton intervened, "and to Philip sic rout he raucht, that thocht he wes of mekill maucht." The story is told in *Barbour's Bruce*.

The family were prominent in Scottish history during the 14th and 15th centuries. In 1451, Sir George Seton appears as Lord Seton. While the Lords Seton had an imposing residence at Seton, in East Lothian, they built Niddry Castle, at Winchburgh, shortly before 1500, doubtless to execute their functions as baillies of the ecclesiastical regality of Kirkliston, and as superiors of Dundas. Mary, a daughter of the 4th Lord, was the most pious and devoted of the maids of honour of Mary, Queen of Scots, and the only one to go into captivity with her. The 5th Lord was one of those who waited on the shores of Loch Leven in May, 1568, when the Queen escaped from imprisonment there. She was escorted to Niddry, where she rested before proceeding to Hamilton. It was one of the brightest incidents in her tragic career. Robert, the 6th Lord, was created Earl of Winton in 1600. The 4th Earl sold the Barony of Niddry and the lands of Winchburgh to John Hope of Hopetoun in 1678, progenitor of the Earls of Hopetoun, who later built Hopetoun House, in Abercorn Parish.

The Setons paid dearly for their attachment to the House of Stewart. Alexander, a son of the 5th Lord Seton, was created Earl of Dunfermline in 1405, but his grand-son James, the 3rd Earl, was forfeited in 1690 for Jacobite sympathies. Alexander Seton, a younger son of the 4th Lord Seton, was created Viscount Kingston in 1651, immediately after the coronation of Charles II. The title was terminated through the involvement of James, 3rd Viscount, in the Jacobite Rising of 1715. The 5th Earl of Winton was also implicated, and suffered forfeitures and attainder.

The Gordon family of Huntly became merged with that of Seton, through the marriage of Elizabeth Gordon and Alexander, son of Lord Seton, in 1408. She succeeded her brother, John of Strathbogie, a few months earlier. Sir Alexander, their son, was created Earl of Huntly about 1454, and changed his name to Gordon. The 6th Earl was created Marquis in 1599. The Setons of Abercorn descend from a son of the 1st Earl of Huntly, through the Setons of Touch, and gave rise to a baronetcy (N.S.) conferred on Sir William Seton in 1633. The 13th Baronet is Sir Iain Bruce Seton, who resides at Bridgetown, Western Australia.

James R. Seaton, who retired in 1983, was Principal Keeper of Printed Books in the National Library. He joined the staff in 1947, after service in the Royal Artillery, and was appointed Principal Keeper in 1966. His service earned him the O.B.E. in 1979.

# SINCLAIR LORDSHIP

The surname St. Clair or Sinclair is derived from Saint-Clair-sur-Elle, in the Contentin peninsula of Normandy. The progenitor appears to have been Walderne, Count de Sancto Claro, who came to England with the Conquerer. His son by his wife Margaret, daughter of Richard, Duke of Normandy, was William de Sancto Claro, who came to Scotland. Sir Henry St. Clair, a vassal of Richard de Morville, in 1162, who obtained the lands of Herdmanston and Carfrae, must have been of the same stock, but the exact relationship is not clear. He was granted the lands of Herdmanstoun and Carfrae. Alan de St. Clair of this family, had a charter of lands in Lauderdale. William de Sancto Claro was knighted and had a grant of the barony of Rosslyn (Roslin). His son, Sir Henry, witnessed charters and died before 1270. He was probably the father of Sir William de St. Clair, Sheriff of Edinburghshire in 1263. This man was high in favour with King Alexander III, and was one of the magnates who, in 1285, negotiated the king's marriage with Yolanda, daughter of the Count of Dreux. The king gave him the lands of Inverleith, Edinburgh. Sir William signed the 'Ragman Roll' in 1296. He left three sons, Sir Henry, his heir; William, Bishop of Dunkeld, 1312-37; and Gregory, ancestor of the Sinclairs of Longformacus.

At the time of the submissions to Edward I, Sir Henry Sinclair was on the English side, but afterwards supported Robert the Bruce, who gave him lands at Pentland. He became chief butler to the royal family. His son, Sir William, died in Spain with Sir James Douglas, in 1330. The young heir, Sir William, by his marriage with Isabel, co-heiress of Malise, Earl of Strathearn, greatly added to the family influence. Their son, Henry, obtained through his mother the earldom of Orkney. He was a notable seaman and while conquering the Faroes in 1391, enlisted the aid of a shipwrecked Venetian mariner, Nicola Zeno. They crossed to Greenland, and are thought to have reached America. His grandson, William, 3rd Earl of Orkney, surrendered the earldom to the crown, and was created Earl of Caithness in 1445. He it was who built the stately chapel of Rosslyn, famous in the world of freemasonry, with which the family have always played a prominent part. He became a Lord of Parliament about 1449. By his first wife he had a son, William, 2nd Lord Sinclair, and by his second, Sir Oliver of Rosslyn, ancestor of William, who sold his estate in 1736, and whose line failed in 1778; and; among others, William, 2nd Earl of Caithness.

After the death of Henry, 10th Lord Sinclair, in 1723, a complicated situation arose. His son John, who died without issue in 1750, had been attainted for his part in the '15 Rising. He or his brother, Gen. James, purchased Rosslyn in 1736. The latter died without issue in 1762, and his sister, Grizel, and her heirs by John Paterson of Prestonhall became the heirs of line. A younger sister, Catherine, had married Sir John Erskine of Alva, Bt., and their son Col. James, succeeded his uncle, Alexander Wedderburn, as 2nd Earl of Rosslyn, and assumed the additional surname of St. Clair. Charles St. Clair of Herdmanston inherited a claim to the attainted Sinclair peerage by a patent of 1677, granted to the 10th Lord, and became *de jure* 12th Lord Sinclair, without descent from the original lords. His grandson, Charles, was recognised as 13th Lord in 1782. The present Lord Sinclair is Charles Murray Kennedy St. Clair, residing in St. John's Town of Dalry, Kirkcudbrightshire. The Rosslyn peerage has descended to Sir Peter St. Clair-Erskine, Baron Loughborough (1780) and 10th Bt. (NS, 1666).

# SINCLAIR EARLDOM

William Sinclair, 1st Earl of Caithness, cr. 1455, was Lord High Chancellor of Scotland, and by his second wife Marjory, daughter of Alexander Sutherland of Dunbeath, had issue, including William, 2nd Earl, who obtained a new charter of the earldom in 1476. He was slain at Flodden in 1513, leaving by his wife Mary Keith, two sons, John, 3rd Earl, and Alexander. George, the 4th Earl, resigned the earldom in favour of his son John, Master of Caithness. His second son was William of Mey, who left two natural sons, Patrick and John, from whom descended the Sinclairs of Ulbster. The Master of Caithness died before his father, leaving by Jean Hepburn his wife, three sons: George, 5th Earl; James of Murchil, ancestor of the 8th Earl; and Sir John of Greenland, ancestor of the 10th Earl.

George, 6th Earl, son of John, succeeded his great-grandfather, and died in 1676, bankrupt and childless, with his lands mortgaged to John Campbell of Glenurchy, later Earl of Breadalbane. The heir was George, son of Francis Sinclair of Keiss, and he seized some of the lands. This led to John Campbell marching an armed force to Caithness where he defeated George's little army at Old Marlack. However, George was eventually recognised as 7th Earl by Parliament. The lands were purchased in 1719 by the Sinclairs of Ulbster and those of Dunbeath. The 7th Earl died unmarried and the dignity devolved on John Sinclair, grandson of John of Murchil. He was father of Alexander, 9th Earl, and of John of Murchil, an advocate who was raised to the bench in 1733 as Lord Murkle. Alexander held the title for sixty years, and died in 1765, without male issue.

William Sinclair, on whom the title devolved, was descended from Sir John Sinclair of Greenland. His eldest son, John, 11th Earl, soldiered in the American

Revolutionary War, and was wounded. When he died unmarried in 1789, the title went to a distant relative, Sir James Sinclair of Mey, who was the 8th baronet of his line (cr. NS, 1636). His grandson, James, was cr, Baron Barrogill (UK) in 1866, but that title expired when his son, George, 15th Earl of Caithness died without issue in 1889. The Scottish title then passed to his kinsman, James, descended from the Mey line. He was a chartered accountant in Aberdeen, and father of John, 17th Earl, and of Norman, 19th Earl, who had a distinguished military career. Malcolm, 20th Earl, who succeeded his father in 1965, has held a number of Government posts.

Patrick, second son of William Sinclair of Mey, obtained the estate of Ulbster in 1596, from his cousin, the 5th Earl. He was twice married and had sons, Patrick of Ulbster, and John of Brims. Patrick was succeeded by his son, Patrick, whose son, John of Ulbster, married Janet, daughter of William Sinclair of Ratter. His cousin, John of Brims succeeded as heir of entail. From him descended Sir John Sinclair, 1754-1835, voluminous writer and editor of the first *Statistical Account of Scotland*, who was cr. a baronet in 1786. His large family included George, 2nd Bt.; Alexandera family historian; and Catherine, a noted authoress, to whom a memorial was erected in Edinburgh. The 4th Bt., Archibald, was Leader of the Liberal Party, 1935-45, and held important Government posts. He was cr. Viscount Thurso in 1952, and was succeeded in 1970 by his son, Robin, 2nd Viscount and 5th Bt. His sister Elizabeth, 1921-1994, who married Major Patrick Lyle, founded Butterstone House Preparatory School for girls in 1947.

Alexander Sinclair, O.B.E., is president of the Golf Foundation. A former Scottish golf internationalist, he was the recipient of the Frank Moran Award in 1979 for his services to the sport.

# STEWART

The Stewarts derive their name from the office of High Steward of Scotland, bestowed on their ancestor, Walter Fitz Alan, by King David I. (1124-53). Alan Fitz Flaald, the father, came from Brittany and was sheriff of Shropshire, at the commencement of the 12th century, and his father succeeded his brother Alan as Steward of Dol. Alan Fitz Flaald married Avelina de Hesdin, daughter of the Count of Dol and Dinan. The family had links with Flanders, and were related to William de Graham, who also came to Scotland. Walter was a younger son and came to Scotland from England on the return of David I, from whom he received grants of land, particularly in what became Renfrewshire. He founded the Abbey of Paisley about 1136, and died in 1177, leaving by his wife Eschina de Molle, a son Alan.

Alan Fitz Walter became hereditary High Steward, and was the father of Walter, who was the first to take the surname Stewart. Besides being the ancestors of the Stewart kings, the family branched out and held at one time or another, numerous titles. The first four dukes and the first ever marquess to be created, were all Stewarts. Others held the earldoms of Angus, Atholl, Arran, Bothwell, Buchan, Bute, Caithness, Carrick, Fife, Galloway, Mar, March, Menteith, Moray, Orkney, Strathearn and Traquair. Walter, the 6th High Steward, was the progenitor of the Stewart kings, having married as his first wife, Marjory Bruce, sister of Robert the Bruce. Their son Robert, succeeded David II as King of Scots, in 1371. On the death of King James V, the direct male line of the royal Stewarts ended, but was continued through Queen Mary's marriage with Lord Darnley, descended from Sir Alan Stewart of Bonkyl, a younger brother of James, 5th High Steward. Their son, James VI. was both heir male and heir of line of the

House of Stewart, but it was as heir of line that he represented the Stewarts descending through Marjory Bruce, and the long lines of the old Scottish and Pictish kings. On the death of Bonnie Prince Charlie and his brother Benedict, the male line of the royal Stewarts or Stuarts ended. Today, H.R.H. Prince Charles is High Steward of Scotland because he is the female-line descendant of Walter Fitz Alan. The chiefship of the Stewart clan passed to the Earls of Galloway, through descent from the second son of Sir Alan Stewart of Bonkyl, and the Stewarts of Garlies.

The present Earl of Moray, Douglas John Moray Stuart, descends from James, natural son of King James V, by Lady Margaret Erskine, daughter of John, Earl of Mar. In 1580, James Stuart, Master of Doune, became the 2nd Earl of Moray in right of his wife, daughter of another James Stuart, Regent of Scotland and natural brother of Mary, Queen of Scots. He was the 'Bonnie Earl of Moray,' of the old ballad which laments his death at the hands of the Gordons. The present home of the family is Darnaway Castle, Forres. Another important branch of the Stewarts is represented by Sir John Colum Crichton-Stuart, 7th Marquess of Bute, Keeper of Rothesay Castle, who descends from Sir John Stewart, a natural son of King Robert II. The Stewarts of Appin spring from an allegedly natural son of John Stewart of Lorne (d.1463), descended from Sir John Stewart of Bonkyl.

It is interesting to note that the Stewart 'chequy,' which first appears on the seal of Alan, High Steward of Scotland (1177-1204), is said to represent the chessboards anciently used to calculate accounts; only one function of the ancient office.

# STIRLING: ORIGINS AND HERALDRY

The surname Stirling derives from the town of that name. It seems likely that those styled in early records, 'de Striueling,' were important people in a key town of Scotland, but not necessarily related. 'Petro clerico de Striueling,' son of Walter, was a chamber official under Malcolm IV, and William I, witnessing charters, 1153-77. Richard of Stirling was a chaplain of Malcolm IV, and held the benefice of Forteviot about 1175. This was to be attached to the Abbey of Cambuskenneth on his decease. John of Stirling witnessed charters, 1204-10. Gilbert of Stirling, whom Keith describes as a man well-born, was clerk to William I and Alexander II, and was Bishop of Dunkeld, 1228- 39. He may have been a brother of Thomas of Stirling, also a clerk and archdeacon of Glasgow. Robert of Stirling was a deacon of Dunkeld in 1263. Five men styled 'of Stirling' signed the 'Ragman Roll' 1292-97, among them, 'Mestre Henry de Strivelyn'of Stirlingshire. A family of Stirlings settled in the north at an early period, and one of those, 'Johannes de Striviling de Moravia,' also swore fealty. His seal displayed six stars.

The heraldry of the Stirlings has been subject to much confusion. Those – and this means most – whose arms show buckles, usually on a bend, were of Flemish extraction, probably descended from the Malets, who ruled the lordship of Voormezele, near Ypres, and held estates adjoining Dixmude. Buckles go back to the time of Charlemagne and the dawn of heraldry. The seal of William of Stirling, in 1296, shows, on a chief three buckles. The shield, suspended from a tree, is flanked by two small lions rampant. Sir John of Stirling (of East Swinburne, Northumberland), Sheriff of the Lothians and Warden of Edinburgh Castle, around 1335, bore semee of crosses three covered cups, and for crest on a helmet front face with coronet, a covered cup between two bull horns. The seal of William Stirling of Cadder, chief of the surname, about 1492, is couche, on a bend engrailed three buckles, and for crest on a helmet with mantling and coronet, a swan head, neck and wings. The legend is *S' villelmi striuelin de cadder*. There was some uncertainty when *Lyon Register* commenced in 1672, and the blazon for Cadder was entered as Argent, on a bend Azure (or rather Sable), three buckles Or. There is added a note to the effect that in old books the bend is found ingrailed. In 1621, when John Stirling of Keir was knighted, his arms were blazoned Argent, on a bend engrailed Sable, three buckles Or.

It seems clear that the progenitor of the Stirlings of Cadder, in Lanarkshire, was Thoraldus, 'vicecomes (i.e., 'my minister') de Strivelyn,' on record in 1147. William, his son, was living 1165-1214, and his son, Alexander, died about 1244. All were sheriffs of Stirlingshire. John, IVth of Cadder, had three sons. The eldest was Sir Alexander of Cadder, and the youngest, Sir William, was probably ancestor of the Stirlings of Keir. Sir Alexander's son, Sir John, was killed at Halidon Hill in 1333, and his son, Sir John, died about 1408. Sir William of Cadder, the next on record, also owned Redgorton. He died about 1434, having had issue two sons, Sir William, IXth of Cadder, and Gilbert of Craigbernard, ancestor of the Stirlings of Glorat. Sir William Xth of Cadder, held also Lettyr. He died about 1505. His son William left an heiress, Janet, who married Sir James Stirling of Keir. This was an unhappy union, probably forced, and she formed an attachment to Thomas Bishop, an adventurer, and was divorced. Cadder remained with her husband, but she retained Ochiltree, in Linlithgowshire.

# STIRLING: THE
# LEADING FAMILIES

An influential family for over 500 years, the Stirlings of Keir have produced many fine soldiers. William Joseph Stirling, 17th of Keir, was Hon. Lt. Col. of the Scots Guards and fought in World War II. His father, Archibald of Keir and Cadder, was a much decorated soldier, having served in the Nile Expedition of 1899, the So. African War as a Brig. General, and in Gallipoli and Egypt in World War I. The progenitor of this family was Lucas de Striveling, who died before 1462. He appears to have been descended from John Stirling, Vth of Cadder. William Stirling, IIIrd of Keir, in Perthshire, espoused the cause of the nobles headed by Prince James, opposed to King James III, and was knighted by James IV. The VIth laird, Archibald Stirling, had with other issue, James, his heir; Archibald, ancestor of the Stirlings of Kippendavie, and John, progenitor of the Stirlings of Garden. George, son of James, followed his grandfather, but died without surviving issue and was succeeded by his cousin, Sir Archibald of Garden, a Royalist who became a Lord of Session in 1661. His grandson, James, took part in the Jacobite Rising of 1715, and was forfeited. Friends purchased the estates for his sons, John, Archibald and William, who all followed one another as lairds. William, 1725-93, left a son and heir, Archibald, and another son, William, who married Jean Stewart of Castlemilk, 1781, and succeeded to that estate. Their descendants are the Stirling-Stewarts. William Stewart, 1818-78, of Keir and Cadder, succeeded his maternal uncle, Sir John Maxwell of Pollock, as 9th Bt., and assumed the surname Maxwell in addition to Stirling. By his wife Ann, he had a son John, who continued the Pollok line, and another son, Archibald, who succeeded to Keir and Cadder. He was the soldier associated with the Scots Guards and Lovat Scouts, and in fact married Margaret, daughter of the 10th Lord Lovat.

The Stirlings of Glorat, near Milton of Campsie, descended from Gilbert of Craigbernard, son of Sir William Stirling, XIth of Cadder. His grandson, Sir John, left two sons, George, of Craigbernard, whose line expired in 1805, and William of Glorat. His descendant, George Stirling was cr. a baronet of NS, 1666. The title came down to Sir George Murray Home Stirling, 1869-1949, 9th Bt. His son Charles was lost at sea, 1938 and his younger son, Capt. George, died of wounds received at Tobruk in 1941. The title is now dormant.

Another branch held the estate of Muiravonside, in Stirlingshire. This family descended from the Stirlings of Auld Keir and Lettyr. Of this family came Andrew Stirling of Drumpelier, recognised as heir male of the Cadder line by Lyon Court in 1818, and allowed supporters to his arms. He married in 1778, Anne, daughter of Sir Walter Stirling of Faskine, RN. They had two sons, John, his heir, and Charles of Muiravonside, who married in 1827, Charlotte, daughter of Vice-Adm. Charles Stirling. Their eldest son, Andrew, IInd of Muiravonside, sold the estate to his cousin, Thomas Mayne Stirling, who married his cousin Anna, daughter of Charles, 1st of Muiravonside. Their eldest son Thomas Willing Stirling, was the father of Arthur C. Stirling, VIth laird. The family came to be represented by his cousin, Sir Charles Norman Stirling, 1901-86, a diplomat. Muiravonside House suffered a fire and became ruinous. The old house was the first stop on her way to St Kilda, of Lady Grange, kidnapped for political reasons. A prisoner for over 20 years, she died on Skye in 1745.

The Stirlings of Ardoch, Strathallan, baronets of NS (1666) descended from the Keir line, are represented by the Drummond-Morays of Abercairney.

# SUTHERLAND

Historians and genealogists are agreed that those who took the surname of Sutherland – from *Sudrland*, the country south of Caithness, were descended from Freskin the Fleming, whose family probably intermarried with the old royal house of Moray. Freskin had several sons, the eldest of whom, Hugh, died before 1226, and was succeeded by his eldest son, William, cr. Earl of Sutherland about 1235. William, 2nd Earl, succeeded his father about 1248. In 1283-84, he attended the Parliament at Scone which accepted the infant Margaret of Norway as Queen of Scots, failing direct issue of Alexander III. He signed the homage roll in 1296, and seems to have died in allegiance to Edward I about 1307.

William was succeeded in turn by his sons William and Kenneth. The latter, who was killed at Halidon Hill in 1333, left two sons, William, his heir, and Nicolas, who had a charter of land in Torboll, in 1360, by his brother. He was ancestor of the Lords Duffus. William, 5th Earl, married about 1345, Margaret, daughter of King Robert I. and Elizabeth de Burgh. They had a charter of the earldom in free regality, the same year, augmentedby further grants of land in Aberdeenshire and Kincardineshire. They had a son John, party to a treaty made at Berwick in 1360. By a second wife, Joanna Menteith, three times widowed, he had two sons, Robert, who became 6th Earl, and Kenneth, ancestor of the Sutherlands of Forse.

Dunrobin, which simply means 'Robins's Castle,' was named after the 6th Earl, and it has ever since remained the main residence of the chiefly line. Robert married about 1389, Margaret Stewart, daughter of the 'Wolf of Badenoch,' King Robert III's fierce brother. King James IV gave the Gordons power to quell disorders in the north, and John, 8th Earl of Sutherland was served with a brieve of idiotry in 1494. His son, the 9th Earl was also weak-minded, and placed under the care of his sister, Elizabeth, who married Huntly's brother Adam and they became Earl and Countess of Sutherland. Their grandson, John, 10th Earl, was forfeited after the Battle of Corrichie in 1562, but rehabilitated in 1565.

In 1598, John, 13th Earl, caused the first coal pit to be sunk at Brora, where he also installed salt pans. Soon afterwards the earldom was erected into a regality. He had feuds with Lord Reay and the Mackays, and in 1651, outfitted a contingent of his clan, who marched with Charles II to Worcester. In the time of John, 16th Earl, a wolf was killed within twelve miles of Dunrobin. It was he who resumed the old surname of Sutherland instead of Gordon. William, 17th Earl, was succeeded in 1766 by his infant daughter, Elizabeth, who after a celebrated litigation became Countess of Sutherland. She married George Leveson-Gower, Marquess of Stafford, cr. Duke of Sutherland (UK) in 1833. The Duke and Duchess were responsible for improvements to their estates, which, however well-intentioned, led to the notorious clearances and depopulation. After the succession of the Countess, the male resentation fell to Sutherland of Forse, and John of Forse received the arms, appropriately differenced. His son George unsuccessfully claimed the earldom in 1771, and arms granted to the daughters of John Sutherland of Forse, who died in 1909, were later negatived. On the death of the 5th Duke in 1962, that UK dignity passed to the Egerton Earls of Ellesmere, whilst the earldom and chiefship passed to his niece, the present Countess of Sutherland. Her son and heir is Lord Strathnaver.

# THOMSON

"**W**e're all Jock Tamson's bairns" is a common saying when people are 'all in the same boat,' or position, and points to the fact that Thomsons are numerous. Thomson simply means 'son of Thom.' As a forename Thomas goes back to biblical times. The usual abbreviation is Tom or Thom, hence the surnames Thomas, Thomson, Thompson and Tomlinson. The surname is not recorded in Britain until after the Norman Conquest, and there must be Thomsons of differing origins. 'Mc kChuim Tomson, Baron of Pharnua,' was associated with the Bisset family in Lovat early in the 13th century. John Thomson, 'a man of low birth but approved valour,' led the men of Carrick in Edward Bruce's war in Ireland in 1318. David Thomson was a student at St. Andrews in 1408. Bessie, daughter of William Leslie, IVth of Balquhan (who died in 1467) and Euphame Lindsay, married Duncan Davidson, alias Thomson in Auchinlampers. Henry Thomson of Keillor was Lord Lyon King of Arms, 1496-1512, and Peter Thomson, Islay Herald in 1547, was admitted burgess and guild-brother of Edinburgh in 1558-59.

Thomsons of Argyll and Perthshire are really MacTavishes. The surname in those districts is an Anglicized form of the Gaelic *MacThomais*, 'son of Thomas,' or *MacThomaidh*, 'son of Tommie.' The name was given as MaKcome or MacComie in some areas. It was common on Deeside. Alexander Thomeson in Strathdee is recorded in 1527. Christie Thomson appears in Hoy, Orkney, in 1502. The form Tomison is common in South Ronaldsay. There have been a number of small landowners surnamed Thomson. The Thomsons of Banchory, Deeside, descended from Andrew in Cammachmore and Elizabeth Muir, married in 1746. Their descendant, Andrew Thomson, 1772-1806, was

Professor of Mathematics in Marischal College, Aberdeen. The Thomsons of Charleston held estates in Fife for several generations. Grizel, heiress of John Thomson of Charleston, married in 1774, Col. John Anstruther (of the Balcaskie family), and their descendants became known as Anstruther-Thomsons. An estate at Duddingston, Edinburgh, was possessed for about six generations by a family of Thomsons. Thomas, son of Alexander Thomson and Margaret Preston, was cr. a baronet (NS) in 1634. His son Sir Patrick, sold Duddingston in 1668 and died about 1674.

Thomsons have left their mark in various fields. James Thomson, the poet of 'The Seasons,' one of the classics of English literature, was a native of Oxnam, Roxburghshire. In association with David Mallet, he composed 'The Masque of Alfred,' in which his national song, *Rule Brittania*, first appeared. George Thomson, 1757-1851, editor of a 5-volume collection of songs, was a friend of the poet Burns. Thomas Thomson, 1768-1852, an eminent record scholar, graduated at the University of Glasgow in 1789, and was admitted an advocate in 1793. He became a competent record scholar, and was Deputy Clerk Register for Scotland, 1806-39. His youngest brother, Rev. John Thomson, 1778-1840, became minister of Duddingston, Edinburgh, and was a very fine landscape painter. Thomas Thomson, 1773-1852, from Whittinghame, East Lothian, was an eminent chemist. Alexander 'Greek' Thomson, 1817-75 from Balfron, was the architect of many fine buildings in Glasgow. William Thomson, Baron Kelvin, 1824-1907, scientist and inventor, was born in Belfast, but in 1832 the family moved to Glasgow, where he was educated. Baron Thomson of Fleet, the newspaper magnate, descends from Archibald Thomson, a stonemason who emigrated from Bonese, Westerkirk, Dumfriesshire to Scarborough Township, Ontario, Canada, about 1802.

# WEMYSS

Although the accredited ancestor of the Earls of Wemyss and their numerous cadets was Michael of Wemyss and Methil, in Fife, who died about 1202, there is strong circumstantial evidence that the family descended from the ancient Earls of Fife (Clan MacDuff), whose progenitor was Eathelred or Aedh, lay Abbot of Dunkeld and 1st Earl, who was a son of Malcolm III and Queen Margaret. The succeeding earls were men of substance, with lands on both sides of the Firth of Forth, but their line ended with an heiress, Isabella, Countess in her own right. Michael of Wemyss and Methil was probably descended from Hugh, second son of Gillemichael, 3rd Earl.

Michael was succeeded by his son John, who flourished in the reign of Alexander II, and died about 1263. His descendants took the surname of Wemyss, a corruption of Uamh, meaning a cave. Below the ruins known as MacDuffs Castle, on the Fife coast, are caves containing Pictish drawings, and these gave rise to the place-name of Wemyss. A later Wemyss, Sir David, was one of the ambassadors sent to Norway to escort Margaret, 'The Maid of Norway,' to Scotland in 1290. He was also a signatory of the Declaration of Arbroath, 1320. The family obtained further estates in Fife, and in the time of Sir David Wemyss, who was killed at Flodden in 1513, these were erected into the Barony of Wemyss. His grandson, Sir John, fought under Arran at Pinkie in 1547, and at Langside in 1568 for Queen of Scots.

Sir John Wemyss of Wemyss, in 1625, was cr. a baronet of Nova Scotia, and in 1628, by which time Nova Scotia had been ceded to the French, he was cr. Lord Wemyss of Wemyss. In 1633 he was cr, Earl of Wemyss. He extended his estates by the purchase of East Wemyss, Lochead and Grange of Elcho, and was owner of a coal pit and saltworks. His son David, 2nd Earl, entertained King Charles II to dinner at Wemyss Castle in 1650 and again in 1651. The sons of this earl all died young and he was succeeded by his daughter Margaret, who married in 1672, a distant kinsman, Sir James Wemyss of Burntisland, who was raised to the peerage of Lord Burntisland. He died in 1682, and the only surviving son, David, succeeded as 4th Earl of Wemyss. Both he and his son James, were leading officers in the Royal Company of Archers, the latter winning the silver bowl for shooting in 1720. David, eldest son of the 4th Earl, soldiered for the Young Pretender in 1745, and was forfeited. His brother Francis *de jure* 5th Earl, succeeded to the estates of Col. Charteris of Amisfield, which included lands in England, and assumed the surname Charteris in addition to Wemyss. His grandson, Francis Wemyss Charteris was cr. a peer by the title of Earl of Wemyss. His grandson, Francis Wemyss Charteris was cr. a peer by the title of Baron Wemyss of Wemyss, and in 1826 was restored to the title of Earl of Wemyss. Another descendant of the 5th Earl, Michael John, as inheritor of the ancestral estates of Wemyss, was recognised officially as chief of the Clan MacDuff and had the arms of Wemyss confirmed to him in 1910. The present representative is Lady Jean, widow of the chief, Capt. David Wemyss.

Francis Wemyss Charteris, 8th Earl of Wemyss, inherited the Earldom of March and lands and Lordship of Neidpath, in 1810, on the death of William, 4th Duke of Queensbery. He also laid claim to the title of Earl of March, but this was not recognised at the time. The present 12th Earl of Wemyss and 8th of March, Francis David Charteris, has been Lord Clerk Register of Scotland and Keeper of the Signet since 1974.

# WHITE/WHYTE

The surname White or Whyte is found all over Britain. It appears in Old English charters as a personal name, in the form of *hwit*, 'white,' and as a byname. As a surname the name appears before 925. Uuiaett Wwite witnessed King Eadgar's charter of Coldingham, between 1097 and 1107. In Latin documents the name is rendered as *Albus*. Adam Albus appears as a charter witness between 1180 and 1214. John Albus was steward to Matilda, Countess of Angus, about 1242. Adam Albus held lands in Kincardineshire during the reign of Robert II (1371-90). The surname was common in Fife, Angus and Aberdeenshire in the 15th century. Several Quhytes were admitted as burgesses of Aberdeen during that age, and Andrew Qwhit was a citizen of Brechin in 1472.

According to Sir Robert Douglas, the Whytts of Bennochy were of French extraction, descended from the Les Blancs, whose armorial bearings are similar. Matthew Whytt of Maw, in Fife, alive about 1490, was ancestor of John Whytt, who held Maw and Lumbenny by charters dated 1451. His son Robert, a merchant and first Provost of Kirkcaldy, purchased Bennochy and part of Abbotshall. His son John married Jean, daughter of Thomas Melville of Murdocarney, and they were the parents of Robert, an advocate who died in 1714, leaving a son George, who was succeeded in 1728 by his brother Robert Whytt (1715-66), who was physician to George I, and was knighted. He was Professor of Medicine in the University of Edinburgh. Sir Robert had a large family by his second wife, Louisa Balfour (Pilrig), and was succeeded by his sons, Robert, died 1776, and John Whyte-Melville (1755-1813), who held also the estate of Strathkinness. His second son, John, who served in the 9th Lancers, was the last Whyte of

Bennochy, as his son George John Whyte-Melville, the novelist, died in his lifetime, without male issue.

The Whites who owned Kellerstain, in Mid Lothian, were supposed to be of the same stock. They descended from John White of Millthird, Clackmannan, whose grandson, John, married Elizabeth Logan. One of their daughters married Henry, son of the eminent painter, Sir Henry Raeburn, and their eldest son, William Logan White (1793-1877), an advocate, purchased Kellerstain in 1823. On the death of his son James Maitland White in 1914, the property passed to two nephews.

Whytes were prolific around Rutherglen and Carmunnock. Walter Whyte, born about 1667, was a baillie of Rutherglen, and married late in life, Elizabeth, daughter of Provost John Spence. His eldest surviving son, George, became proprietor of Bankhead, and registered arms in 1786. Walter (1780-1847), his son, matriculated at the University of Glasgow in 1794, and besides Bankhead, owned lands at Whitburn, Kenmuir and Shettleston. His only son Walter, was served heir to him and to his aunts, Jane Whyte or Reddoch, and Elizabeth Whyte, in 1865. James Whyte, a member of the Faculty of Procurators of Glasgow in 1835, was probably of the same stock. He became a chemical manufacturer, and was the father of John Campbell Whyte, raised to the peerage as Baron Overton in 1893.

Most of the Whytes once numerous in Cowal were in fact Macgillebháins, 'sons of the fair gillie,' whose name was Englished in the 17th century when parish schools were widely established in Argyll. The 'fair gillie' is said to have been Duncan *Ban*, son of John MacLeod, of the Raasay family.

# WISHART

The writer of the inscription on the tomb of George Wishart, 1599-1671, Bishop of Edinburgh, thought the surname meant 'wise-heart.' Although not strictly correct, the meaning was not far wrong. The name is recorded in England as Wischard (Latinised *Wischardus*) in 1170, and appears in similar forms in Scotland in the 13th century: Wiscard, Wischard and Wyschard, and is from Old Norman French, *Guischard*, meaning 'prudent, or sagacious.' The Wischards probably came from Normandy. They appear as landholders in Kincardineshire, and while some later held land elsewhere, the family is better known for having produced clergymen down through the centuries, including George Wishart, ?1513-46, an early martyr for the Reformation of religion in Scotland. William Wischard was Chancellor Scotland in 1256 and became Bishop of St. Andrews in 1272. He was son of John Wiscard, Sheriff of the Mearns in 1230, ancestor of the Wisharts of Pitarrow. Another William Wischard was a canon of Dunkeld in 1288, and was probably a brother of Mary, spouse of William Oliphant of Aberdalgie. Robert Wishcard (Latinised *Guiscardus*) was nephew of Bishop William Wischard, and became Bishop of Glasgow in 1272. John Wischard del Meirnes; Gilbert Wichard, Forfarshire; John Wischard, 'Kincardineshire in Mearns'; and Master John Wischard, chevalier, all appear on the Ragman Roll in 1296.

Sir John Wishart of Pitarrow went on a mission to France in 1434. His second son, David, was vicar of Brechin about 1453, and his grandson, Sir John Wishart of Pitarrow was forfeited in 1499. Sir James Wishart of Pitarrow and Carnbeg, was joint-King's Advocate (with James Henderson of Fordell) in 1513, and appears to have been Advocate and Justice-Clerk after Henderson was killed at Flodden. By his first wife, Janet Lindsay, he had sons John and James, successively lairds of Pitarrow and Carnbeg, and by his second wife, Elizabeth Learmont, he was the father of George Wishart, the martyr burned at St. Andrews. Sir John Wishart, who succeeded to the estates in 1607, sold Pitarrow to his brother, Capt. John Wishart, who sold the estate to Lord Carnegie, and died in Ireland, without issue. His brother, Rev. William Wishart, a graduate of Aberdeen, came to represent the family. He was minister at Fettercairn and later at South Leith. His son John, a royalist soldier, was killed at Edgefield in 1642, when the representation passed to his cousin, Rev. William Wishart, 1621-92, minister at Kinneil, West Lothian. He married Christian Burne and from them descended many distinguished Wisharts.

Lt. Col. George Wishart of Cliftonhall, in the Mid Lothian part of Kirkliston parish, eldest son of Rev. William Wishart, was cr. a baronet in 1706. The third son, Rev. William Wishart, 1660-1729, was Principal of the University of Edinburgh, and had two sons in the ministry. Rev. William, the elder, also became Principal of the University. From him descended the Wisharts of Foxhall, Kirkliston. Rev. George Wishart, brother of the second Principal Wishart, was minister of the West Kirk, Edinburgh. He married Ann, daughter of John Campbell of Orchard, 1682-1768, and had a son George, 1748-60, and five daughters, only two of whom were married. Janet, the eldest, married Maj. Gen. John Beckwith, and had issue. Jane, the youngest, married in 1865 Baron Christian Heinrich von Westphalen. Their son, Ludwig von Westphalen, married Caroline Huebel, with issue a daughter, Johanna Julie Jenny von Westphalen, who married in 1843, Dr Karl Marx, 1818-83, the political reformer, and left issue.

# SHORT NOTICES

**ARMSTRONG**   This Border surname comes from a personal attribute, 'strength of arm.' The earliest reference to it occurs in 1235, when Adam Armstrong was pardoned at Carlisle for causing a death. The name became more prolific in the 14th century. Gilbert Armstrong was a steward in the Royal Household and ambassador to England in 1363. The Armstrongs occupied Mangerton in Liddesdale and later spread into the 'debateable lands' along the English border. Many of them marched into Border legend. Armstrong of Gilnockie, a freebooter, was executed in 1529. James VI had a jester named Archie Armstrong, and 'Kinmont Willie' Armstrong, aided by Scott of Buccleuch, escaped from Carlisle Prison. The noted coloured musician, Louis 'Satchmo' Armstrong, and the astronaut, Neil Armstrong – who made the first moonwalk – gave the name prominence in America. Michael Armstrong is proprietor of the popular *Family Tree Magazine*.

**BARCLAY**   People of this surname – derived from Berkley, in Somerset – came north in the 12th century, and in 1165, Walter de Berchelai held the office of Chamberlain of Scotland. Sir John de Barclay of Gartly signed the bond of submission to Edward I of England in 1296. His male line failed in 1465, but a sister of Walter of Gartly married the laird of Towie-Barclay, in Aberdeenshire, and carried the chiefship to the House of Towie. A descendant, Sir Patrick Barclay, rebuilt their castle about 1598. The representation passed to Rev. John Barclay, 1705-81, minister of Delting. On the failure of his line the representation passed to the descendants of his brother James, and in 1901, Charles Alexander Barclay was awarded the chiefly arms. The most important cadets are the Russian family of Barclay de Towie, and the Barclays of Mather and Urie. Robert Barclay, 1648-90, of Urie was the Quaker author of *An Apology for the True Christian Divinity.*

**CARNEGIE** Undoubtedly the best-known bearer of this surname was Dunfermline born Andrew Carnegie, 1835-1919, who emigrated to America in 1848, settling at Allegheny, later at Pittsburgh. He acquired interests in oil and steel and became a multi-millionaire and philanthropist. His benefactions include libraries in North America and Britain, 'hero' funds, and the Palace of Peace at The Hague. The surname derives from the lands of Carnegie, in Angus, which came into possession of a family styled de Balinhard, who adopted the surname Carnegie. From them descends the present chief of the surname, David Charles, 12th Earl of Southesk, whose home is Kinnaird Castle, Brechin.

**COLQUHOUN** Umfridus de Kilpatrick had a grant of the lands of Colquhoun (probably derived from *Cuil cumhann* = 'narrow corner'), in Dumbartonshire, before 1241. The first to bear the name was Robert de Culchon, on record in 1259. The lands of Luss, on the western shores of Loch Lomond, came into the family through marriage with an heiress, the 'Fair Maid of Luss'. Sir John Colquhoun of Luss was Governor of Dunbarton Castle in the reign of James II (1437-60), and in 1583, Sir Humphrey Colquhoun of Luss was made hereditary coroner of Dumbartonshire. In 1625, Sir John Colquhoun was cr. a baronet of NS. The 5th Bt., Sir Humphrey, left a daughter Anne, who married in 1702, Sir James Grant of Pluscardine. Their eldest son, James, inherited the Grant estates, and the Luss estate went to the second son, James, who carried on the Colquhoun line and was cr. 1st Baronet of Luss. The 8th bt. is Sir Ivar Ian Colquhoun, clan chief, residing at Rossdhu, Luss. A number of Colquhouns achieved fame in Sweden.

Walter Colquhoun, a 16th century cannon-founder, has descendants existing under names such as Cahum and Ghan. Henry Cahun was physician to the Swedish Navy in 1781. In Gaelic the Colquhouns are known as *Mac a Chounich.*

**CUNNINGHAM** As a surname, Cunningham is derived from the Ayrshire district of that name. It is now widespread. The *eponymous* is believed to have been Wernebald, a vassal of Hugh de Morville, who came to Scotland early in the 12th century, and he obtained Cunningham from his superior. His son Robert gave the church of Kilmaurs to the monks of Kelso. In 1462, Sir Alexander Cunningham, Lord Kilmaurs, was cr. Earl of Glencairn. The 5th Earl was a promoter of the Reformation in 1560. John, 15th Earl, died without issue in 1796, since when the title has been dormant. He was a friend of the national bard, who named a son James Glencairn Burns. The chiefship may lie with descendants of Andrew Cunningham of Corsehill, which family possess a baronetcy (1672). Important families include the Cunynghame baronets (1702) of Milncraig and the Fairlie-Cunningham baronets (1630) of Robertland.

**DALZELL** This is another territorial name, derived from the old barony of Dalzell, in Lanarkshire, and is found in a variety of spellings. Hugh de Dalzell, was sheriff of Lanark in 1288, and Sir William Dalzell was progenitor of the family styled 'of that Ilk' from 1446. A later laird was loyal to Mary Queen of Scots., and his son, Sir Robert, was cr. Earl of Carnwath in 1649. The title became dormant on the death of the 16th Earl, Sir Arthur Edward Dalzell, 1851-1941. The Binns family descend from the Lanarkshire Dalzells, but favour the spelling Dalyell. General 'Tam' Dalyell, 1615-85, was a General in the Russian army, and as a Royalist fought against the Convenanters on his return. He has marched ferociously

280

into legend. His son Thomas was cr. a baronet in 1685. The present representative – who does not use the title – is Tam Dalyell, the well-known MP for Linlithgow. Andrew Dalzell, 1742-1806, son of a Kirkliston carpenter, became Professor of Greek in the University of Edinburgh in 1779.

**DUNBAR**  The first to use the name Dunbar were descendants of Gospatrick, Earl of Northumberland, 1067-72, and took their name from the lands, meaning 'Fort on the point'. His third son, also Gospatrick, on record in 1119, was known as Earl or Lord Dunbar. The last Earl was George, forfeited in 1434. William Dunbar, 1460-1520, was a distinguished poet, and Gavin Dunbar was Bishop of Aberdeen in the reign of James IV, 1488-1513. An eminent Greek scholar, George Dunbar, was born at Coldingham in 1774, and succeeded Professor Dalzell as Professor at Edinburgh. There are a number of titled families, including Dunbar of Durn, Dunbar of Hempriggs and Dunbar of Mochrum. A former jockey, who once worked in the rag trade in New York, was declared heir to the Mochrum baronetcy (NS, 1675) in 1984. He is Sir Jean Ivor Dunbar, 13th Bt., also recognised as clan chief.

**DUNDAS**  The antiquity of the Dundas family is unquestionable. The lands, near Queensferry, meant 'South Fort', Gaelic *dun deas*. They were owned by the family of Gospatrick, ancestor of the Earl of March, and his lands of Inverkeithing lie due north of Dundas. The lands were granted by Waldeve, son of Gospatrick, to Helias, son of Huchtred, before 1145. They took their names from the estate, sold in 1874 to James Russell, a rich commoner, who re-sold, in 1899, to Stewart Clark, of the famous Paisley threadmaking firm. It was justly remarked that any Prime Minister could raise a man to the peerage, but it took seven centuries to make a

Dundas of Dundas. There is still a Dundas of that Ilk in the person of David Duncan Dundas, residing at Bergvliet, Cape Town, in South Africa. James Dundas, first of the distinguished branch of Arniston, was a son of Sir George Dundas of Dundas, who died in 1589. From him descended the families of Beechwood and Dunira, and the Viscounts Melville. Henry Dundas, 1742-1811, 1st Viscount, was a distinguished statesman.

**DUNSMORE** The name appears in various forms – Dunsmure, Dunsmuir, &c. – and comes from the lands of Dundemore, near Lindores, in Fife. The meaning is obscure. The old family of Dunsmore supported Wallace and Bruce during the War of Independence, but ended in an heir female about 1330. There are several other places called Dunmore, and the Earldom of Dunmore, in the forest of Atholl, was bestowed in 1686 on Lord Charles Murray, a son of the Earl of Atholl. The name became prolific in the west. One James Dunmore took the hated 'Test' at Paisley in Covenanting times, and Robert Dunmore was a merchant-burgess of Glasgow in 1793. A Dunsmuir family worked in coal mines around Glasgow in the 18th century. Some members migrated into Ayrshire. Robert Dunsmuir, 1825-88, from Hurlford, went to British Columbia in 1851, as a coal consultant. His son James, 1851-1920, was Premier of the Province, 1900-1902. Others went to Ulster and the USA.

**DURIE** There was an old family, Durie of Durie, in Scoonie parish, Fife, and most people who bear the surname probably had some link with the family or with the estate. The lands passed by marriage to a Kemp family, from whose posterity these were purchased in 1614 by the eminent lawyer, Sir Alexander Gibson. On being appointed a Lord of Session in 1621, he assumed the judicial title of Lord Durie. Although the Duries lost the estate there is still a Durie styled 'of Durie,' in the person of Lt. Col. Raymond V. Dewar Durie. who has had a military career with the Argyll & Sutherland Highlanders, and claims descent from George Durie, the last Abbot of Dunfermline. The earliest references to the name appear between 1258 and 1271, when Duncan de Durry witnessed charters. John Durie, a monk of Dunfermline, was imprisoned for heresy, but escaped and became minister at Colinton in 1569. Another John Durie, from Edinburgh, published a pioneer work on librarianship at London in 1650.

**FARMER** The earliest known reference to the surname Farmer appears in Latin form in 1262, when Richard Fermarius was a juror at Peebles. The name is now fairly widespread, but for long was more strongly represented in East Fife. It originally meant a farmer of the revenue, rather than an agriculturist, but many came to be tillers of the soil. Alan Fermour witnessed a document at St. Andrews in 1391, and James Fermour attended the University there in 1424. A notable farming family descended from Thomas Farmer in Over Carnbee, who married Elizabeth Imrie in 1813. Their eldest son William, farmed at Drumrack, Crail. Three other sons emigrated to New Zealand, and one of these, James, made a fortune there and returned to Scotland in the 1880s and purchased the farm of Brownhills, near St. Andrews. Another branch settled in Edinburgh.

**FENTON** While the earliest known person of this surname was John de Fenton, Sheriff of Forfar in 1261, the name derives from an old barony near North Berwick, East Lothian, and anciently there was a family so named in possession of the rich lands. Sir William de Fentone married before 1270, Cecilia, daughter of Sir John Bisset of Lovat, and received the estate of Beaufort and some lands in Ireland. This same man swore fealty to Edward I in 1291 and did homage in 1296. Alexander de Fentoun gave a donation to Dryburgh about 1330, and in 1362, William de Fenton gave lands at Lynros to the chapel of Baikie, in Airlie parish. The Angus Fentons ended with co-heiresses about the middle of the 15th century. One married a Halket and the other a Lyndsay. The family name is preserved in Fenton Hill, near Lindertis. There was a Fenton family in The Aird, Inverness-shire, 1253-1422. William de Fentoun, Lord of that Ilk, acquired lands in Clydesdale in 1413. Alexander Fenton, a native of Shotts and a graduate of Aberdeen, was a director of the Museums of Scotland from 1978 to 1985.

**GOURLAY** Ingelramus de Gourlay came to Scotland with Prince William in 1174, and received lands in Clydesdale and Lothian. The name may derive from a lost place-name. His son Hugh possessed lands in Fife, and around 1190 witnessed a charter to Arbroath Abbey. Hugh and William Gurle attended a conference at Roxburgh in 1254, and in 1293 William, son of William Gurley made a gift to Newbattle Abbey. Adam de Gurle of Roxburghshire rendered homage in 1296, and Sir Patrick Gourlay, a clergyman, witnessed charters before 1320. The old family of Gourlay of Kincraig, in Fife, held the lands for about 600 years. The estate descended to heirs female, Gertrude Gourlay, who died in 1908, and her sister Susan, who live in Bath. Robert Fleming Gourlay, 1778-1863, emigrated from Ceres, in Fife, to Upper Canada about 1815. He was a pioneer, but also a controversial journalist and published at London in 1817, a *Statistical Account of Canada*.

**GUNN** The Gunns were a warlike clan in Caithness and Sutherland, deriving their name from the Norse *gunnr*, meaning 'war.' The first of the name associated with Caithness was Olaf, a 12th-century chief. For generations the Gunns had a feud with the Keiths. When Helen, the lovely daughter of Lachlan Keith of Braemor, was to marry her cousin, Alexander, Keith of Ackergill had her abducted and she became his victim. The girl ended her misery by jumping from the tower of Ackergill. A clan battle resulted, but it was indecisive. Eventually, George Gunn, a 15th century chief, agreed to meet the Keiths with 12 horsemen a side, but the Keith chief came with two men on each horse, and inflicted heavy casualties. Later, a kinsman of the Gunns, William McKames, killed Keith of Ackergill, his son and several others at Drummoy. In modern times, James A. Gunn, 1882-1958, distinguished himself as Professor of Pharmacology at Oxford, and Neil Gunn, 1891-1973, enriched Scottish literature with *The Silver Darlings* and other novels.

HALDANE   The surname Haldane is held to derive from *Healf-dene*, meaning 'Half-Dane.' The name was associated with the Hocingas and Secgans, who took part in the campaign against Finn in the lay of *Beowulf*, and it later became an Old English personal name. Halden *filius* Eadulf was a witness at Earl David's inquest into the church of Glasgow about 1124. A younger son of a Halden family in the Borders became possessed of the estate of Gleneagles in Perthshire by marrying an heiress. Aylmer de Haldane de Gleneagles swore fealty in 1296. The family held the estate until Robert Haldane, who purchased the estate from his brother Patrick in 1760, made an entail by which the 3rd Earl of Camperdown came into possession in 1766. James Chinnery-Haldane, 1868-1941, became the owner in 1918, in terms of the entail. His son Alexander Chinnery-Haldane, 1907-84, waged war on anyone who associated the estate with the famous golf course. A kinsman was the distinguished physiologist, John Scott Haldane, 1860-1936.

HUNTER   The surname is derived from the chase, and as the name is widespread, there is no reason to think there was a common ancestor. Instances of the name appear as early as 1124. The Hunters of Hunterston, Ayrshire, thought to be of Norman origin, appear to be the oldest family. Precedence was disputed by the Hunters of Polmood, in Tweedsmuir, but significantly the Ayrshire family were styled 'of that Ilk.' Robert Hunter of Hunterston subscribed the bond in defence of the reformed religion in 1562. In 1585, Michael Hunter of Polmood was outlawed for a raid on Belstone Tower. An heiress of the Ayrshire family married her cousin, Robert Caldwell, who assumed the surname of Hunter. The present chief is Neil A. Hunter, residing in Andorra, in the Pyrenees. The brothers William, 1718-83, and John Hunter, 1728-93, distinguished themselves in the medical profession, and the 'collections' of the former are found in Glasgow's Hunterian Museum.

**ISBISTER** The Orkney place-name of Isbister comes from the lost place-name of Isbister, in the parish of Harray, and also from Isbister in Birsay parish. There are places so named in South Ronaldsay, and at Northmavine and Whalsay, in Shetland, and the name probably means 'river mouth farm.' Robert Ysbuster appears at Harray in 1557, and again in 1565 as Robert Ysbister 'of that Ilk.' Malcolm Ysebuster was a baillie of Harray in 1607. He may be the same as Malcolm Isbuster, of Harray parish, who died in February, 1613, leaving ten children. At least seventeen men of this surname were employed in Canada by the Hudson's Bay Company between 1709 and 1860. One of those, Thomas Isbister, began as a labourer in 1812 and rose to having charge of a trading post at Nelson River. He was killed by a bull in 1836. His eldest son, Alexander K. Isbister, graduated at the University of Edinburgh in 1858, and became a schoolmaster with the company.

**KINNIBURGH** No less than 343 spellings of this name have been found. It is derived from Conisborough, in Yorkshire. Members of the family came to Scotland before 1164, when Galfridus de Coningesburg witnessed a confirmation charter by Malcolm IV to the Abbey of Scone. William de Cunnigeburc of Staplegorton granted a chapel there to the monks of Kelso in 1153. Sir William de Conyngesburgh of Lanarkshire, Duncan de Conyngesburgh in Dumfriesshire, and Gilbert de Conyburke in Ayrshire, all signed the Ragman Roll in 1296. William of Cuniburgh is recorded in connection with Bute in 1468, and William Cunyburgh was heir to certain lands there in 1554. John Cunninburc was a baillie of Kirkintilloch in 1563. Kinniburghs appear in Edinburgh after 1769. Robert Kinniburgh, 1780-1851, from Kirkintilloch, taught at an institution for the deaf and dumb in Edinburgh, later merged with Donaldson's School.

**LAW** The meaning is usually 'hill' or 'summit.' In some cases the surname is a diminutive of Lawrence, and in others appears to be a variant of Low, on record in 1331. Those considerations account for the fact that the surname is of comparatively late origin. Robert de Law had a safe conduct through England on his return from Spain in 1428, and James of Law was an accuser at a court at Prestwick in 1331. Rev. James Law, minister at Kirkliston, 1585-1610, was rebuked for playing football on the Lord's Day, but became titular Bishop of Orkney in 1605, and in 1615, Archbishop of Glasgow. John Law of Lauriston, Cramond, 1671-1729, a financier and speculator became Comptroller-General for France. A grand-nephew, Gen. James A.B. Law, 1768-1828, was a favourite aide-de-camp of Napoleon I, and was cr. Compte de Lauriston. The British Prime Minister, 1922-23, Andrew Bonar Law, was born in New Brunswick, but brought up by his mother's relations in Glasgow.

**LOGAN** There are several places named Logan in Scotland, but Dr G.F. Black was of the opinion that the surname comes from Logan, in Ayrshire. The derivation is probably from the Gaelic *lagan*, meaning 'little hollow.' The Logan Water in Ayrshire prompted Burns to write *Logan Braes* in 1793. Robert Logan appears as a witness in Roxburghshire in 1204, and in 1226, Adam de Logan witnessed a charter of land in Gowrie. Wautier Logan in Lanarkshire and others of the surname signed the Ragman Roll in 1296. John de Logan held the lands of Grugar, in Ayrshire, in 1304. A charter of John Logan to William Douglas of Kingscavil, of lands at West Linton, was inspected in 1340. Logans held lands in Forfarshire for generations. The bones of Robert Logan of Restalrig, Edinburgh, who died in 1606, were exhumed in 1609 and exhibited in court, when sentence of forfeiture was pronounced against him, thus depriving his family of Fast Castle and other lands. Logie and Loggie are probably variants of Logan.

**LUMSDEN** The surname Lumsden or Lumsdaine derives from a place-name in Coldingham parish, Berwickshire. The earliest reference to the name is around 1170, when Gillem and Cren de Lumisden witnessed a charter by Waldeve of Dunbar. Adam and Roger de Lummesdene rendered homage in 1296. A branch of the family settled in Fife before 1350, and obtained lands in Aberdeenshire. John Lumsden of Ardhuncar owned the lands of Towie-Clatt, and died before 1740. A son of the same name was killed at Culloden in 1746. The Clova line ended with an heiress, Catherine, who married in 1754, John Leith. From them descended the Leith-Lumsdens. In 1985, Patrick Gillem Sandys Lumsden, then of Innergellie, was recognised by the Lord Lyon as chief of the name and arms.

**MACAULAY** Curiously, there were two MacAulay clans, one at Ardincaple, in Dumbartonshire, and the other in Lewis and Harris. The Ardincaple family may have derived the name from *Amhalgadh*, meaning in Irish Gaelic, 'Aulay.' Sir Aulay MacAulay of Ardincaple, a vassal of the Earl of Lennox, appears in a roll of landlords and baillies in 1587. The MacAulay lands passed to the Duke of Argyll in 1767. The MacAulays in the Western Isles derived the name from *MacAmhlaidh*, a Gaelic form of the Norse *Olafr*, and are said to have been originally at Lochbroom. The Hebridean family may all have come from a common ancestor, the earliest known being Donald *Cam*, grandfather of Rev. Aulay MacAulay of Harris, from whom sprang a talented family, many of whom were clergymen. His son Rev. John, 1720-89, minister successively at South Uist, Lismore and Appin, Glenaray, and Cardross, had by his second wife, Isobel MacNeill, a large family, of whom Lt. Gen. Colin, 1760-1836, fought at Seringapatam. Another son, Zachary, FRS, Governor of Sierra Leone, was the father of Thomas Babington MacAulay, 1800-59, the eminent Anglo-Scottish historian, cr. Baron MacAulay in 1857.

**MacCALLUM** It is generally agreed that the original homeland of the MacCallums was the district of Lorn, in Argyll. Their early history is not well documented, but the main line of the family came to be represented by Donald McGillespie vich O Challum, who had a charter of Poltalloch, in Kilmartin parish, from Duncan Campbell of Duntrune in 1562. Archibald MacCallum, 8th laird, died without male issue in 1758, and was succeeded by his brother Alexander of Glennan, who, for aesthetic reasons, preferred Malcolm as a surname. It is usually thought of as the English equivalent of Calum or Callum, but in fact derives from the Gaelic Maolcolum, or 'devotee of St. Columba.' John Wingfield

Malcolm, 15th laird was cr. Baron of Poltalloch in 1896. The present clan chief is Robin Neill Lochnell Malcolm, residing at Duntrune Castle, Lochgilphead.

**MACEWEN**   The MacEwens (MacEwans, MacEuens, MacEwings, &c) have a long history and were associated with the district of Cowal, in Argyll. They were recognised in Gaelic as *Clann Eoghain na h-Oitrich* – the MacEwens of Otter. MacEwens appear in different parts of the country from about 1219, and the earliest chief flourished in the latter part of that century. He was succeeded by Severn of Otter, and the chief about 1315 was Gillespie, ancestor of Swene, last of the Otter family, who had a re-grant of the lands in 1432, with remainder to Archibald Campbell, Earl of Argyll. When the lands passed to the Campbells the MacEwens became a scattered clan. Some took new names, such as MacLaren and MacDougal. There was a family of MacDougals *alias* MacEwens, who were seannachies to the Campbells but it is thought they were originally MacDougals. The McEwens of Marchmont, Berwickshire, descend from James McEwen of Bardrochit, in Ayrshire, who died in 1737, and they possess a baronetcy (UK, 1953). The 5th and present baronet is Sir John Roderick Hugh McEwen.

**MACINNES**   The MacInnes's – *Clann Aonghais* – are of Celtic origin, and were early inhabitants of Ardnamurchan and Morvern, who suffered when King Alexander II, 1214-49, conquered Argyll. The last chief is said to have been murdered at Ardtornish in 1390, and part of the clan became identified with the Campbells of Craignish. Some others went to Skye, and became hereditary bowmen to the Mackinnon chiefs. Descendants of the murdered chief probably recovered Kinlochaline Castle, at least as Constables. A MacInnes may have been its Governor in 1645, on behalf of the

Tutor of Kintail, when it was under seige by 'Young Colkitto.' At a later period the Kinlochaline branch were under the patronage of the Campbells of Argyll, and supported the Covenanting and Hanovarian interests. Some followed Stewart of Appin in the '45 Jacobite Rising, and four were killed and two wounded. The Rt. Rev. Duncan MacInnes, who died in 1970, matriculated arms when elected Bishop of Moray, Ross and Caithness, in 1953.

**MACINTYRE** The *Clann-an-t-Saor*, 'Children of the Carpenter,' were located in Glen Noe, near Bonawe, in Argyll, but tradition brings them from the Hebrides in a galley, with a white cow, in the latter part of the 15th century. Curiously, the tenure under which they held Glen Noe from the Campbells of Glenorchy was an annual payment of a snowball and a white calf. This agreement continued until early in the 18th century when the Glen Noe tenant arranged for the payment to be commuted into money, which then became rent. When they could no longer afford to pay increases, the MacIntyres lost their glen. Donald, eldest son of James MacIntyre of Glen Noe, and his sisters Ann and Catherine, emigrated to New York State before 1784. He left descendants in Fulton Co. The clan produced some famous pipers. Alastair MacIntyre, a BBC broadcaster, chieftain of the *Camus-na-h' Eircadh* branch, matriculated arms at the Lyon Office in 1955.

**MACKINLAY** The name is synonymous with Finlayson, 'son of Finlay,' and the first of the name is said to have been Finlay, a son of Buchanan of Drumakil. There can be no doubt they originated in the district of Lennox, and in Gaelic orthography the name is *MacFionnlaigh*. Although distinctly Scottish it was taken to Ulster by Presbyterian settlers. A variant is McGinley. William McKinley, 1843-1901, 25th President of the USA, was descended from Stephen McKinley, 1730-1819, an Ulster-Scot. Some MacKinlay families migrated into Glenorchy and Glen Lyon. Sir John Finlosoun *alias* McAlan McKewella (the attempt of a non-Gaelic scribe to write MacFinnlaigh) was vicar of Kilmorich in 1511. In 1574, Sir Andrew Finlayson was chaplain of an altar in St. Machar's Cathedral, Aberdeen. Donald McKindlay appears at Innerchocheill, Perthshire, in 1696. Peter McKinlay was a clock and watchmaker in Edinburgh around 1840. Col. Hamish Grant MacKinlay, from Tillicoultry, is Deputy-Governor (Security) of the Tower of London.

MACQUEEN The surname comes from *MacSuibne*, or 'son of Suibne,' a personal name meaning 'good going,' and is of ancient Celtic origin. Hector MacSouhyn attended an inquest at Dunbarton in 1271. Duncan McQuene was a burgess of Perth in 1613. The 'hanging judge,' Robert MacQueen, 1722-99, was born at Lanark and died in Edinburgh. It is generally agreed that the Skye MacQueens are of Norse origin, from the personal name *Sveinn*. They produced numerous clergymen, who ministered at Uig, Durinish, Snizort, Kilmuir-in-Trotternish and other Hebridean parishes. Rev. Adam MacQueen, son of Murdo in Uig, Skye, emigrated to Ontario, Canada in 1849. It was probably a branch of the Skye MacQueens who migrated into Moidart, and early in the 15th century attached themselves to Clan Chattan and rose to the status of a minor clan. Professor John MacQueen was Director of the School of Scottish Studies, at Edinburgh, 1969-88.

MAXWELL The surname is of territorial origin, derived from lands on the Tweed, near Kelso Bridge. The lands (now Springwood) were granted to Maccus, son of Undewyn, a Saxon lord, and from an attached fishery (OE, *wael*, a pool, or whirlpool) became known as

Maccusweil. Maccus witnessed a charter of David I about 1149, and in 1159, it is recorded that Herberti Macchuswel had donated the church of Macchuswel to the Abbey of Kelso. Sir John de Maccuswel was Sheriff of Roxburgh and Teviotdale early in the 12th century, and became Chamberlain of Scotland. His son Aymer obtained through marriage lands in Renfrewshire and Lanarkshire, and from him descended numerous families in the west and south-west. The eldest son, Herbert, rendered homage in 1296. His castle of Caerlaverock was captured by the English but restored to his son Sir John. A descendant, Herbert, was cr. Lord Maxwell before 1445. Robert, 10th Lord, was cr. Earl of Nithsdale before 1581. The 5th Earl was forfeited in 1716 for his part in the '15 Rising. Families possessed of baronetcies are the Stirling-Maxwells of Pollok (dormant), the Heron-Maxwells of Springkell, and the Maxwells of Monreith, from whom descended the novelist Gavin Maxwell, 1914-69.

MERCER This is an occupational surname, deriving from a draper or dealer in fine cloths (French *mercier*), and is probably of Norman origin. The name appears in Scotland around the year 1200, when William le Mercer witnessed charters in favour of the Abbey of Kelso. Aleumnus Mercer was party with others to a bond given by Alexander II to Henry III in 1214, to keep the peace. He had a grant of Tillicoultry from Walter, son of Alan. Duncan Mersar appears in Aberdeen, 1272-81. Two old families were the Mercers of Aldie, near Fossoway, and of Innerpeffry, in Strathearn. Several Mercers were clergymen in Aberdeenshire. Hugh Mercer, 1725-77, born in Pitsligo manse, became a Brig. General in the American Revolutionary War.

MOWAT Of Norman-French origin, the earliest Mowats took their name from *Mont Hault*, Latinised *Monte Alto*.

They settled in North Wales, where Montealt, reduced to Mold, is a form of their name, which appears in Scotland during the reign of David I. The family rose to power and position in their new home. In the reign of William the Lion they obtained lands in Angus, and spread out from there, all the way to the Orkneys. William de Montealto witnessed an inspection of the marches of Arbroath Abbey in 1219. Sir Bernard de Monte Alto and other knights, accompanied Princess Margaret to Norway, and on his return voyage was drowned. In 1296, Willielmus de Monte Alto signed the Ragman Roll. Axel Mowat, 1593-1661, a scion of the Mowats of Balquholly, Aberdeenshire, became an Admiral of the Norwegian-Danish Fleet. Another branch of this family, through the Dumbreck line, obtained Ingliston (site of the Highland Show since 1959) around 1664, when Sir George Mowat, knight, was cr. a Baronet. The title descended to his grandson, Sir Alexander, but became extinct. Several Orkney Mowats, variously recorded as Moat and Mouat, served in the Canadian fur trade.

NAPIER   This old surname is occupational: coming from 'naperer,' a person in a great household charged with keeping and handling table linen, perhaps also with making it. The first recorded in Scotland was John Naper, who obtained about 1290, some land in the Lennox. He signed the Ragman Roll in 1296 as John le Naper. One Alexander Naper was a peace commissioner in 1451, and his son Sir Alexander of Merchiston was several times Provost of Edinburgh between 1453 and 1472. His descendant, John, 1550-1617, 6th of Merchiston, was the celebrated inventor of logarithms. Sir Archibald, his eldest son, was cr. 1st Lord Napier in 1627. The 9th Lord was cr. Baron Ettrick in 1872. The honours are today held by Sir Frances Nigel Napier. The Napiers, Barons Magdala, descend from Sir Robert Napier, 1810-90.

**NIMMO** This name, the origin of which is obscure, was thought to be Huguenot, but occurs in Scotland long before the Massacre of St. Bartholomew in 1572. The earliest notice found is that of Johannes Newmoch, juror on an assize at Liston (now Kirkliston), in West Lothian, 1459. Other forms of the name are Nemo, Nemmo, Nemmock, Nimoke and Nymmo. Alexander Nemok was a witness in Glasgow in 1587. Rev. John Nimmill, son of William in Dalkeith, was minister of Corstorphine, 1589-90. Alexander Nemo was retoured heir of John Nemo de Mydilmount in Kylestewart in 1616. James Nimmo, the Covenanter from Bridgehouse, Torphichen, fought at Bothwell Brig in 1679. The name was prolific in west Lothian, with farming families at Philpstoun, Craigton and Duntarvie, spanning a period of three centuries. James Nimmo, Receiver-General of Excise in Scotland, died about 1759. Kirkcaldy-born Alexander Nimmo 1783-1832, son of a watchmaker, was involved in building harbours, bridges and railways, in many parts of Great Britain.

**PRIMROSE** Primrose appears as a place-name in 1150, when it occurs in a charter of the Abbey of Dunfermline, and the meaning may have been 'tree of the moor,' derived from the British *prenn*, 'tree,' and *rhos*, 'moor.' It is highly probable that the surname comes from the Fife place-name. John Prymros, mason in Edinburgh, was one of those who contracted in 1387, for building chapels at St. Giles parish church, Edinburgh. Archibald Prymrose was a friar at Culross in 1569, and from him descended Sir Archibald Primrose of Carrington, clerk to the Privy Council in 1641, from whom came the Earls of Rosebery. His son Archibald, by a second marriage, was cr. Viscount of Rosebery, in 1700, and in 1703, Earl of Rosebery, Viscount of Inverkeithing, Lord Dalmeny and Primrose. The 7th Earl is Sir Neil Archibald Primrose. John Primeroose emigrated to Sweden in the 17th century.

His son Henry was ennobled in 1653, and became governor of Johannsborg.

**PRINGLE** The old form of this surname was Hoppringle, from the lands of that name on the Gala Water, near Stow. The earliest notice found of the name is in a Soutra charter in which Robert de Hoppryngil is witness to a gift to the hospital, confirmed by Alexander III, 1249-93. Thomas de Oppringill or Hopyringhil, occurs in 1368, and Johyn Pryngel appears in Fife in 1406. Robert of Hoppringill witnessed a charter about 1413. The leading family were the Hoppringles of that Ilk, afterwards of Torsonce. Other families of note were at Burnhouse, Hawtree, Glengelt, Rowchester, Lees, Stitchell, and at Whitsome, in Berwickshire. From the Whitsome branch descended the Pringles at Whytebank. The male line of the Torsonce family failed in 1737, but a daugher of John Pringle had married Gilbert Pringle of Stitchell, and carried the estates to that family. Robert Pringle of that family, was cr. a baronet (NS) in 1682/83. John, youngest son of the 2nd Bt. was a distinguished physician. Thomas Pringle, 1789-1831, from Teviotdale, was a pioneer settler in South Africa, but returned to become secretary of the Anti-Slavery Society.

**SKENE** Of territorial origin, this surname derives from the lands of that name, in Aberdeenshire, erected into a barony in 1317. The meaning is not clear, but the family arms bear *sgians* or daggers, perhaps to mark some important event. Johan de Skene of Edneburk and Johan de Skene of Aberdeenshire rendered homage in 1296, and the seals prove they were of the same stock, if not one and the same person. The Skene family possessed the lands for over five hundred years, but the direct line failed in 1827, and the estates devolved on a nephew, James, 4th Earl of Fife. The Skenes of Curriehill descended from James, second son of Alexander Skene of Skene. Sir John Skene of Curriehill, 1549-1611, was an eminent feudal lawyer, and William Forbes Skene, 1809-92, was Historiographer Royal for Scotland.

**TURNBULL** According to tradition the name derives from a man named Rule, who saved the life of Robert the Bruce at Stirling by twisting the head of a bull which attacked the monarch, and he was rewarded with a grant of the lands of Bedrule, in Roxburghshire. The name, however, is probably Old English *Trumbald*, 'strongly bold.' Robert the Bruce did grant some land at what is now Philiphaugh, to 'Willielmo dicti turnebule' in 1315. The family spread out in the Border counties, and some moved to Angus. The main line of the family appears to have been that of Bedrule, and the Minto branch were once powerful. The Turnbulls were among the most turbulent of the Border clans, and the old tale about the bull is recalled in the arms of a number of branches, including one in France. William Paterson Turnbull, 1830-71, the American ornithologist and author, hailed from Gladsmuir, East Lothian. Frederick Turnbull, 1847-1909, born in Glasgow, pioneered turkey-red dyeing in the USA.

**TWEEDIE** For well over 200 years the valleys of the Upper Tweed were inhabited by an unruly family named Tweedie. Tradition says that the first of the name was a water-sprite of the River Tweed, but in fact they derived the name from the lands of Tweedie, at Stonehouse, Lanarkshire. Finlay de Twydyn of Lanarkshire rendered homage in 1296. Roger, son of Finlay of Twydyn, had a charter of the lands of Drumelzier, in Peeblesshire, about 1320, and held the lands until the reign of Charles I, 1600-49. In 1498, John Tweedie and others were fined by the Privy Council for ejecting Oswald Porteous and his spouse from Upper Kingledores. They came into conflict with the powerful

Flemings in 1524, and in 1582 the 'wild bunch' were again in trouble when James Tweedie murdered an old foe, James Geddes, in Edinburgh. After James Tweedie was killed in single combat with a Veitch in 1608, peace came, but the encumbered family estates had to be sold.

**WALLACE** Despite the fact that a Shropshire knight, Sir Richard Walency, attested a charter at Paisley by Walter Fitz Alan, around 1170, it is still generally believed that the Wallaces derive their name from the old British kingdom of Strathclyde, the inhabitants of which were called *Walensis*. The most famous bearer of the name was of course Sir William Wallace, who commenced the War of Independence in earnest by slaying the English governor of Lanark, who had caused the death of his wife. Wallace, after a gruelling campaign, came to a barbarous end at London in 1305, but his aims were later achieved by King Robert the Bruce. Other early Wallaces include Adam Walleis, who witnessed a charter to the monks of Cupar between 1212-49, and John Walens, who attested gifts to the Abbey of Paisley before 1228. Several families of the name owned land in Ayrshire. Rev. Robert Wallace, 1697-1771, minister of Greyfriars, Edinburgh, was an eminent divine and statistical writer, and William Wallace, 1768-1843, from Dysart, Fife, was a distinguished mathematician.

**WYLLIE** The surname Wylie or Wyllie may derive from 'Willie,' a diminutive of William, or from a personal trait, 'wiley,' or shrewd. Donald Wyly, tenant in Thornhill, Dumfriesshire, is on record in 1431, and William Wyly was a witness at Prestwick in 1446. Thomas Wylie, merchant-burgess of Edinburgh, registered arms about 1672. A number of Wylies achieved fame. Sir James Wylie, 1768-1854, educated at Aberdeen, entered Russian service as a regimental surgeon, and became physician to the imperial court, and surgeon-in-ordinary to the Grand Duke Alexander. He was founder of the Medical Academy of St. Petersburg in 1804, and its first president. Norman Russell Wylie, an advocate in 1952, was Solicitor-General in 1964, MP for Pentlands, 1964-74, and Lord Advocate, 1970-74. He became a Senator of the College of Justice in 1974, as Lord Wylie, and retired in 1990.

# FURTHER READING

In his *Memoirs*, Sir Walter Scott wrote: "Every Scottishman has a pedigree. It is a national prerogative, as unalienable as his pride and his poverty." Robert Louis Stevenson had much the same thoughts when he wrote in *Weir of Hermiston*, "That is the mark of the Scot of all classes – that he stands in attitude to the past unthinkable to Englishmen, and remembers and cherishes the memory of his forbears, good and bad." The learned authors of three of the four volumes of 'The Edinburgh History of Scotland' show by the use of drop-line charts how important to the understanding of national history is a clear view of family relationships.

While Scotland did not have a national body interested in such matters until the founding of the Scottish Genealogy Society in 1953, it must be remembered that numerous clan associations existed, the earliest dating from 1725. An age of more leisure, if not affluence, is reflected in the fact that Scotland now has also more than a dozen family history societies, all producing newsletters or magazines. It is therefore essential for those interested in family history to have a broad view of the past, hence the publication of this book, which outlines the history of over one hundred and fifty families. Honours and titles – if we can include chiefships – are more widely spread in Scotland than elsewhere, and some families will find links with landed proprietors; others with the soil they owned. In the vast ocean of printed works it is therefore helpful to know what to read.

The first essential in any genealogical library, and a most important book to consult is Dr George F. Black's monumental *Surnames of Scotland* (New York,1946), reprinted several times and now available in paperback. While much new material has been uncovered since that book was written, notably the acts of our early kings in the 'Regesta Regum Scottorum' series, covering 1124-1424, and Mrs Platt's *Scottish Hazard*, Black's work is still of immense value. Moreover, bibliographers have provided essential finding aids. *Scottish Family History*, by Margaret Stuart, published at Edinburgh in 1930 (reprinted Baltimore, 1978), is still worth consulting. The main guide now to printed family histories is *Scottish Family Histories*, edited by Joan P. S. Ferguson, and published in 1986 by the National Library. A splendid guide to the numerous genealogical publications of John and Bernard Burke (Burke's Peerage Ltd.) is titled *Burke's Family Index*, compiled by Rosemary Pinches and published in 1976. The peerage articles often supplement those in *The Scots Peerage*, in 9 volumes, published, 1904-14, and the *Landed Gentry* entries are very useful.

Clanship and kinship being of paramount importance in Scotland, *Clans, Septs and Regiments of the Scottish Highlands*, (8th edn., 1984), by Frank Adam, revised by Sir Thomas Innes, is well worth consulting. So also *The Highland Clans* (1964), by (the late) Sir Iain Moncreiffe of that Ilk. For the related subject of heraldry, Sir Iain's *Simple Heraldry* (1953 and reprints) is a good introduction. *Scots Heraldry*, by Sir Thomas Innes of Learney, 3rd edn. by Malcolm R. Innes 1978, is the standard work.

People starting out on a search for their ancestors would do well to consult *In Search Of Scottish Ancestry*, 2nd edn., 1983, by (the late) Gerald Hamilton-Edwards. Also of assistance is Kathleen B. Cory's *Tracing Your Scottish Ancestry*, published in 1990.

Serious students would find it worth while to join the Scottish Genealogy Society (library at 15 Victoria Terrace, Edinburgh), and/or one of the local family history societies. These all publish magazines.

# ANCESTRY RESEARCH: GETTING STARTED

Many people at home and overseas, seeking their roots, head for repositories such as New Register House, Edinburgh, without doing any 'homework.' This is often a complete waste of time. The best place to begin is at home, and it is surprising how much information can be gleaned from family sources, which apart from old bibles, may include degrees, diplomas, references, testimonials, school reports, service discharge papers, medals, rings, seals, letters, journals, diaries, executry papers, wartime identity cards (which reveal changes of address), heirlooms, portraits, photograph and postcard albums, passports, bank pass books, insurance papers, property deeds, stock transactions, silverware, proclamations of marriage, baptismal certificates, funeral intimations and obituary notices, telegrams, rent books or leases, newspaper cuttings, scrapbooks and samplers.

In every family there is always one member – perhaps a maiden aunt – who is knowledgeable and has preserved items such as those listed, and who has probably kept in touch with relatives who have emigrated. A personal visit is best, and if there are initial difficulties, the production of family photographs is fairly easy to encourage. You can then seek to identify people and gather details. A good notebook is essential, one which preferably opens right to left, rather than the flip over type. Write clearly and do not attempt to invent a new form of shorthand. Four 'keys' which unlock many doors are NAME, RELATIONSHIP, DATE AND PLACE. Record the information, and add the name of the informant, the place and the date.

When you have digested the information it is worth attempting a drop-line chart, or preserving the information on genealogy charts and family group sheets such as those obtainable from the Scottish Genealogy Society Library at 15 Victoria Terrace, Edinburgh. If you are a 'computer buff,' it is worth investigating what software programmes are available for making family records. There are usually a number advertised in *Family Tree Magazine*. You may now be ready to visit record repositories. Scottish records are mainly centralised in Edinburgh. In New Register House, the Registrar General has charge of the 'Old Parochial Registers of Scotland,' pre-1855 (available on microfilm); the decennial census returns, 1841-91, and the statutory registers of births, deaths and marriages, from 1855. The indices for the latter group are computerised, and the record pages are now on microfiche. Fees are charged for access to the records.

Practice will bring familiarity with old handwriting and, having extracted all the information available at New Register House, you may visit the Historical Room of the Scottish Record Office. Here are preserved the public records of Scotland; a vast array of documents of various kinds. Those usually sought first are testaments. The earliest were recorded in commissariots, and there are printed indices down to 1800 printed in volumes issued by the Scottish Record Society. In the SRO are typed indices which carry us forward to around 1823-30, when the jurisdiction was transferred to the Sheriff Courts. There is a register of confirmations from 1876, and for some areas of the 1830-65 period, a printed *Register of Defuncts*. Before going on to consult other records in this great repository, searchers should consult (better still purchase) a splendid guide compiled by Cecil Sinclair: *Tracing Your Scottish Ancestors in the Scottish Record Office*, published by HM Stationery Office in 1990.

# INDEX

For specific surnames, see articles listed under **Contents**. The following names (kings and queens excepted), appear where indicated.

# INDEX TO SHORT NOTICES